✳

I Am Evelyn Amony

WOMEN IN AFRICA
AND THE DIASPORA

Series Editors

STANLIE JAMES
AILI MARI TRIPP

*

I
Am
Evelyn Amony

Reclaiming My Life
from the Lord's Resistance Army

Evelyn Amony

EDITED WITH AN INTRODUCTION BY
ERIN BAINES

THE UNIVERSITY OF WISCONSIN PRESS

The University of Wisconsin Press
1930 Monroe Street, 3rd Floor
Madison, Wisconsin 53711-2059
uwpress.wisc.edu

3 Henrietta Street, Covent Garden
London WC2E 8LU, United Kingdom
eurospanbookstore.com

Printed in the United States of America

Library of Congress Cataloging-in-Publication Data
Amony, Evelyn, author.
I am Evelyn Amony: reclaiming my life from the Lord's Resistance Army /
Evelyn Amony; edited with an introduction by Erin Baines.
pages   cm — (Women in Africa and the diaspora)
Includes bibliographical references.
ISBN 978-0-299-30494-2 (pbk.: alk. paper)
ISBN 978-0-299-30498-0 (e-book)
1. Amony, Evelyn.   2. Kony, Joseph.
3. Lord's Resistance Army.
4. Human rights workers—Uganda—Biography.
5. Uganda—History—1979- .
I. Baines, Erin K., 1969- editor.   II. Title.
III. Series: Women in Africa and the diaspora.
DT433.287.A46A3   2015
967.6104′4092—dc23
[B]
2015008824

To my mother,

Margaret

My words are scars that remind me of the sharp pain of the moments that my body was broken into, but retain just enough memory, so I don't forget.

Words run through my mind, tumble out of my mouth create whirlwinds of perplexed faces that sit with you around the *wangoo*, waiting for the telling at the fire pit.

You don't have to be shot to know that the force of the bullet will pick you up and throw you away. It will numb you and then waken you to the instant of intense burning arising from the trajectory where metal fragments break into joyous pieces of death swimming about inside your blood stream.

Here, take these words. Catch the whirlwind in your palm. Rest a bit with me. In the afternoon, we can count the lines in the fallen tree trunks scattered about in the landscape.
In the afternoon, we shall sit by the river, looking for river ghosts that dart across the banks.
In the evening, you can sit by me and hold me up as I let the torrents out.

These stories must be told, they must be told, they must be told, they must be told.

They are only scars after all, not like open flesh in the hot sun, not like broken blisters against rubber boots, bone through skin, a persistent and itchy bald spot on the top of your head after the last idea you could use as an *otac* to balance the jerry can on your head disintegrated into nothing.

My words are the skeletal remains of *abii* grass, still standing after the burning, still waving with the afternoon breeze; waiting, waiting for you to touch it so it can crumble into wisps of ash in your palm and take you back with the distinct smell of the smoke from the fires of the last dry season.

Juliane Okot Bitek, "Scars"

Contents

ACKNOWLEDGMENTS

First of all, I would like to thank Erin Baines for taking the time to help me write this book. I also know Erin has spent so much money to ensure that this book comes out, and I know it's not easy for such a book to be written. I know some stories really broke her heart, and maybe she should have not read them, but she did for writing it. I also want to appreciate Ketty Anyeko, because when we just began writing these stories they were just not easy, because she would hear these stories and would begin to cry and leave us to walk around in the compound. I used to think maybe she left to show off. . . . I want to appreciate the strength Erin and Ketty had in their hearts that led to this day for these stories to come out. I know some of these stories are difficult to forget, and I know that Ketty lives now as if she were someone who was just abducted. I also want to appreciate Nancy Apiyo, because she also helped transcribe all I said; she was also the one who would translate all I said into the recorder into English. I also want to appreciate Grace Acan, because even though she also had experienced abduction, she also studied when she returned and was always helpful to me. I also want to appreciate Janet Aber; even though she helped for a short time before she left for school, she really had a heart to help me. These are all the people to help me to write this book. I would also like to thank Boniface Ojok, because he allowed me to work in JRP (Justice and Reconciliation Project), and if I had not been there perhaps this book might have never have been written. I also want to appreciate JRP for the kindheartedness it had and the confidentiality I shared. They knew of the stories about me that might have led some to chase me from the organization, but they did not fear and allowed me to stay there. I think I can end here, but I appreciate all those who helped me. I know I do not have anything to offer them, but it is God who will pay them.

Evelyn Amony

This book is the result of nearly a decade of work, with the assistance of many friends and colleagues along the way. I wish to extend my heartfelt thanks to Evelyn for the remarkable opportunity of working together over these many years and for her laughter, hope, and light in the face of telling difficult stories. In admiration of the remarkable courage and hard work of Ketty Anyeko, Nancy Apiyo, Grace Acan, and Janet Aber that was involved in the process of listening, translating, and documenting—as well as the love and friendship extended to one another throughout. Gratitude to Boniface Ojok, Michael Otim, Lino Owor Ogora, Kasiva Mulli, Sylvia Opina, and Lindsay McClain Opiyo for their support in reading drafts and providing feedback, advice, and moral support. In Canada, the book could not have been completed without endless encouragement, conversations, and exchanges with patient and insightful colleagues, including Pilar Riaño-Alcalá, Chrissie Arnold, Juliane Okot Bitek, Jodie Martinson, Candis Callison, Kim Baines, Beth Stewart, Omer Aijazi, Taylor Owen, and Lara Rosenoff Gauvin. A special thank you is needed for Pilar and Chrissie, who guided and advised me throughout the process. They were unwavering sources of support and always knew when to push me further and when it was time to take a break and go for a walk. Chrissie played an invaluable roll in bringing the book together—from the timeline, maps, and photos to the reviews of rewrites and suggestions on sections, she was always able to stand back and envision the entire book, and she poured her love into it. Thanks to Tanja Bergen, Kiah Van der Loos, Hannah Van Voorthuysen, Letha Victor, Carla Suarez, Julian Hopwood, and Kim Hunter for their support at different points in the making of this book. I am grateful for the continual encouragement of editors at the University of Wisconsin Press, Gwen Walker, Aili Mari Tripp, and Stanlie James, and to Adam Mehring, Carla Marolt, the anonymous reviewers, and to Ron Atkinson and Dyan Mazurana for their insightful suggestions and encouragement. Thanks to the board of the Justice and Reconciliation Project (JRP), the JRP Gender Justice Unit, the Liu Institute for Global Issues, the Social Sciences and Humanities Research Council of Canada, and the University of British Columbia Hampton Fund for making the writing of this book possible. To my partner, Mikis, my children and my family in British Columbia and in Nova Scotia, thank you for supporting us through the long stretches in Uganda and Canada that this project took to complete.

ERIN BAINES

WRITING *I AM EVELYN AMONY*

In this first-person narrative account of life during and after her abduction by the Lord's Resistance Army (LRA), Evelyn contributes to the making of an historical archive in her country and attends to truths about women and war as only a firsthand witness can. Born in a small village in Atiak subcounty in northern Uganda, Evelyn was abducted by the LRA in August 1994, just a few months shy of her twelfth birthday. Evelyn would go on to spend more than ten years in the rebel group, where she was trained as a fighter and acted as the military escort to its leader, Joseph Kony. At the age of fourteen, she would become Kony's wife and, later, the mother of three of his children. Evelyn was captured by the Ugandan military in 2005 and was taken to a rehabilitation center in Gulu, Uganda, where she was reunited with her family. Between 2006 and 2008 she acted as a peace envoy in negotiations between the LRA and the government of Uganda. Today she works at the Justice and Reconciliation Project (JRP), where she conducts community outreach and acts as a peer-support person for other women affected by the war. She is the chairperson of the Women's Advocacy Network, founded to support other war-affected women (see the Epilogue). In the following interview recorded and transcribed in Gulu, Uganda, in July 2013, Evelyn reflects on the process of writing this book and considers its importance.

An Interview with the Author

ERIN BAINES: Why is it important to write this book?

EVELYN AMONY: I want my family to know what I went through, but I cannot just tell them, for they would just begin to weep. If there is a book, they will get to know what I cannot tell them. I also want people in Uganda to know what I went through. Sometimes people say that I did not want to come back home from the LRA, but if they are to read these stories they will know the tough condition I was in, that it was impossible to escape.

   I think it is important for people to know that there are certain misconceptions about the war. For instance, people in Uganda think Kony exchanges children for guns, but that is not true. In addition, if you are abducted, men don't sleep with you just anyhow; it was not like that. It is important for people to know that. It is important that they know how we lived amongst ourselves, how the elder women mistreated the younger girls. How the older men abused young girls fit to be their grandchild.

ERIN: Is there a misconception in Uganda that you wanted to be there in the LRA?

EVELYN: Yes. It is important for people to know it was difficult to escape; if you were caught trying to escape, you were beaten or killed. The LRA threatened to retaliate against your entire hill [family], to revenge against your escape. I didn't want to escape for the sake of the safety of my entire family; I would rather stay in the LRA than see them all killed. People thought we didn't want to return. Some parents ask their children why they didn't return sooner, why they didn't escape as other children did.

ERIN: Why do people have that perception?

EVELYN: People see things differently. If four of you were abducted at the same time and three escaped but you remained behind, they will accuse you of being stupid, of not figuring out how to escape. That perception was so common in Uganda; people thought that you should be able to escape from the LRA and that if you stayed for long in the LRA, it was because you wanted to. In the past, if you escaped it was risky; the government soldiers could easily kill you or take you directly to the military barracks and keep you there.

ERIN: Why do you want your children to read this?

EVELYN: My children can now read. Some of these things I also cannot tell them verbally. It is easier for my children to read and learn about how I was abducted and all that I went through, how I conceived and gave birth to my daughters. They can then ask me for clarifications. If I were to narrate this verbally to my daughters, it would be too heartbreaking. These are difficult stories.

It also helps to clarify any questions my children have in their minds about their father. In the past, they used to ask me why other children had fathers who drove them to school, while I just walked them each day. If they read this book, they will also learn to accept why their father is not here. They sometimes ask for help with their homework and ask me in English for help. But I cannot read or write with confidence, and they do not understand why. I would be heartbroken to tell them why I cannot read or write well. There are things that you cannot tell a child.

ERIN: Do you think it will be difficult for your children to learn their father is Joseph Kony?

EVELYN: The younger children will find it difficult, but the elder child knows who her father is. In the community, people talk. Like when we first returned and my eldest daughter was still young, people would point at her and say she looks just like Kony. She would cry and feel badly, because she knew that he was blamed for this war. She would hear on the radio the crimes he has committed, that he killed, cut people's lips, and then when she heard how she looks like him, it made her cry. Imagine how it feels to be in my child's shoes?

ERIN: What about people in Uganda, why would you want them to read your stories?

EVELYN: As I mentioned earlier on, people just talk but do not understand the circumstances we were in; it is important for them to know how it was we lived. The truth has to be brought out that both sides committed atrocities in this war. The government did certain things, and the LRA did certain things. The future is unpredictable; it is unknown. Suppose the government changes; no one will know what happened during Museveni's government, but if it is written down, it stays forever.

ERIN: Are you fearful of what might happen to you after they read this?

EVELYN: Yes, I have some fear. The government might not want the truth to be told. Sometimes when the truth is told and when you are willing to tell it, they will want to bring your mind down—but you never know, perhaps by the time the book comes out the government will have changed. What makes me feel reassured is that I eyewitnessed these events. These are things I went through. They happened to me; they are not something someone else told me. Even if the government or a soldier calls to ask me why I told these stories, I can still feel confident that these stories are true, because they happened to me.

ERIN: Where do you find the courage?

EVELYN: It came on its own from my heart. I just felt it was important to narrate these things. I experienced such terrible things, but I am not the only one to have had this experience. I also found courage from listening to other women who narrate their stories. I thought that I too could tell my story.

Six Days in Garamba

Evelyn and I met in July 2006. We were part of the same peace convoy leaving Western Equatoria in South Sudan to participate in a series of confidence-building meetings between the LRA and members of civil society.[1] The meetings kicked off the start of the Juba peace talks between the rebels and the government of Uganda following twenty years of conflict in northern and, later, eastern Uganda. Because of my previous work with Acholi religious and cultural leaders from the region where the war had been concentrated, I had been invited to the meetings to act as a documentarian of the proceedings.

I first went to northern Uganda in May 2003, to attend a conference on peace in Gulu on behalf of the director of the Liu Institute for Global Issues, former foreign minister to Canada Lloyd Axworthy; later that year, I became part of an international human rights team disseminating a report on the scale and impact of the war on children.[2] I returned to act as the lead researcher for Mindset Media in the creation of the documentary *Uganda Rising* and to support the advocacy efforts of local civil society members.[3] In 2005, in response to increasing interest in local mechanisms for justice, Michael Otim, director of the Gulu District NGO Forum, and I cofounded a community-based documentation and advocacy project, the Justice and Reconciliation Project (JRP), which was registered as an NGO in 2009.

As we waited for the meetings to begin in the Sudanese People's Liberation Army's (SPLA) military detachment in Nabanga, South Sudan, Evelyn and I passed the time by making small talk. We bathed her daughter, Cynthia, dressed her, and combed her hair. We walked through the small detach together, in no particular hurry because there was nowhere to go. We met with the religious and peace leader Archbishop Odama and laughed at the long and muddy journey we'd taken so far, wondering what was next. We ate groundnuts, watermelon, and mangos. At some point, Evelyn and I realized we had already met in Gulu town the previous year, and we mapped out the six degrees of separation between us.[4]

The group of young LRA soldiers arrived suddenly. They told Evelyn to collect her things and board the vehicle that would transport her to a path leading to the LRA's base in Garamba National Park, just across the border in the Democratic Republic of Congo. "I will be back," Evelyn had whispered before she left, and then she was gone. I spent a few more days waiting with the civil society delegates and the media for Kony to confirm the meeting. Civil society delegates, media, and SPLA soldiers were edgy and irritated by the uncertainty of it all. Tensions within the military detach rose when families of young girls recently abducted from the area arrived and demanded to see their children. At that point, the peace mediator and vice president of South Sudan, Riek Machar, arrived and sat and cooled them down. And so we went back to waiting for Kony.

On the fourth morning, a woman from the UN Children's Agency asked if I wanted to accompany her to meet a group of women and children in the LRA, guided by LRA officer Sunday Otto, who was eager to prove that, contrary to popular perceptions, women and children were in the rebel group willingly. "We will go home when there is peace," said one woman in English, unconvincingly. The commanders made the women and children sing and clap. Other LRA commanders arrived, including Oryem Buk, and he wrote down our names and ordered another song, but the women and children didn't have it in them, and an already weak chorus faded to nothing. The UN security personnel accompanying us told us it was time to leave, immediately. A mother of one of the disappeared children had slipped into the UN group and demanded to see her child. The commanders accused the UN of trickery. We hurried back to the SPLA detach.

The next day we met several LRA commanders, including General Vincent Otti, second in command and an indicted war criminal (now deceased); General Okoto Odhiambo, an army commander who was also under indictment (now deceased); and Brigade Commander Ocan Bunia (now deceased). The terms of the meeting with Kony the following day were set. The group of civil society members I had traveled with returned with the LRA to their base camp in Garamba to spend the night, and I returned to the SPLA detach alone. When they arrived in the morning, we traveled together to meet Kony in the LRA "Parliament," a makeshift shelter built inside Garamba. We sat as the high command assembled, with Kony in the middle and several of his wives and children, including Evelyn and her daughter, seated on the ground by his side. Following a speech by delegates, Kony rose to speak. He looked weak. He kept dotting his face with a blue handkerchief. "Malaria," he told us. He spoke at length on the reasons for the war and all the wrongs committed, and then, abruptly, we were dismissed.

As we prepared to return to the SPLA detach, Evelyn appeared. "Come, meet my family," she said, signaling me away from the others. I shook hands with them and offered to take a photo of Evelyn posing with two of her cousins. Like Evelyn, they had been abducted as children from their village, and now, more than a decade later, they served as Kony's military escorts. Evelyn had been nearly twelve years old when she was abducted from Parabongo village, in Atiak. At the time we met in Garamba, she was twenty-three years old, the mother of three children with Kony, and a peace delegate.

After I took her photo, Evelyn disappeared, and although we exchanged messages through mutual friends, I would not speak to her again directly for nearly two years. I returned to Canada to start a new position as an assistant professor at the University of British Columbia, while Evelyn continued to participate in the talks until 2008, when we would meet again. It was these six days, spent together and apart, that led to the eventual writing of this book.

Editing *I Am Evelyn Amony*

As I sifted through my notes from the talks, I critically questioned my own role in the production of meta-narratives on the war through the reports and policy briefs I would write. I knew little of the LRA beyond popular narratives that described its murderous agenda, and my own impetus to act had been my knowledge of the plight of the tens of thousands of children the LRA had abducted and forced into its ranks. Who were the people who had been affected by this war but effectively silenced—the women and children assembled by the LRA for us to "see" but not listen to, the parents who had come to demand their children and who were told to go away?[5] Who was Evelyn? Who was she in the LRA and, now, in the peace talks?

A number of careful studies challenge the single narrative of either "women" or "children" in wartime that positions them as victims without agency. These studies highlight the diverse roles women and children play in rebel armies,[6] such as fighters, medical workers, sources of intelligence, and/or porters.[7] Yet we know little about how persons within such groups perceive, experience, and bear witness to war over time. We know even less from the perspective of women.[8] A distinct disjuncture between those who respond to crisis and those who have lived through it warps what is written and known, and I was aware I was a part of this problematic reproduction of knowledge.[9]

In January 2007, I returned to Gulu town and met with Michael Otim and the core JRP team: Boniface Ojok, Lino Owor Ogora, and Ketty Anyeko. We discussed the possibility of a research project on young mothers and women who had returned from LRA captivity. We had collaborated on an earlier project on the subject, including a survey of women who had returned with children, in order to put forth policy recommendations (which Evelyn had been involved in).[10] JRP agreed to partner in the project, and so I returned to Canada and put together a research proposal for the Hampton Fund at the University of British Columbia. The intention of the proposed project was to better understand the experiences of women forced into motherhood and the challenges of life after their return. I did not meet Evelyn during this period, as she was involved in the talks, but I did communicate with her via other peace delegates during the talks.

With the success of the grant, in 2008, I returned to Uganda to further design and implement the project. I seconded Ketty Anyeko to the project, and asked Evelyn and two other woman, Grace Acan and Janet Aber, if they would consider becoming collaborators, joining the research team as their schedules allowed to help facilitate the documentation of the project. Grace, Janet, and I had met in 2004, after their own escape from the LRA. Grace assisted JRP in various community-based projects as she completed high school and university. Today Grace is a project officer in community mobilization, and Janet is a nurse. Evelyn, Grace and Janet agreed to collaborate in the project.

In Vancouver, in early 2009, Ketty Anyeko and I developed an initial research design, planning to work with a small group of women to document their life stories. Ketty returned to Uganda, and she and Evelyn began to work with seven women to pilot the project. I joined the team in Uganda in the summer of 2009; we reviewed the materials documented and met the women involved to assess which methods they preferred and to determine how, and if, we should continue with the project. During this period, we also began to work with Nancy Apiyo, a young student who helped translate our discussions from Luo to English and back and who worked well with the women involved. Shortly thereafter, when we decided to move forward with the project, Nancy joined the team full time.

Following the pilot project, we focused our methods on a storytelling format and expanded the group to include just over thirty women. We followed what was then a draft of the resource "Remembering and Narrating Conflict," which details methods employed in other countries to remember and narrate difficult stories.[11] We called the project "Ododo Wa," or "Our Stories," and women who participated agreed to tell their stories to each other and to participate in the project for academic publication and teaching. As part of the agreement to participate, each participant was later given her own personal story in the form of a book at the end of the project. We met the participants periodically over a period of three years to record life stories using various methods (memory quilts, photos, drama, body maps) and held "storytelling sessions" on special topics, such as "children" and "justice."

In the initial stages of the project, I encouraged Evelyn to take home one of the digital recorders and to keep an oral diary of her day-to-day life. We discussed the fact that what she recorded about her day could lend insight into the process of reintegration and would be of interest to students.[12] In the months that followed, Evelyn recorded hundreds of stories in Luo, interspersing her recollections of her daily life (caring for the kids, going to the market, and so on) with memories of life in the LRA. The stories detailed profound insights into the heart of the LRA high command and the fraught, intimate relationships of those within it. Evelyn's narrative is one that "insists on itself,"[13] exposing the fissures, disjunctures, and false truths in dominant narratives of the war by revealing the lives that exist within history and claiming the right to retell it. It is clear that what she had written could and should become her own book.

Knowing the level of stigma and resentment faced by persons who had been in the LRA, Evelyn, Ketty, Nancy, Grace, and I met several times over the next few years to discuss our concerns with proceeding with a publication. We agreed not to rush the process. As time moved on, Evelyn grew more confident. After my own research project had ended, the team had continued to work with war-affected women in storytelling forums. JRP created a Gender Justice Unit, and "Ododo Wa" became one of its central initiatives. Ketty became the team leader of the gender unit and Nancy, a project officer, while Evelyn and Grace became project assistants. Together, they founded the Women's Advocacy Network, which presently consists of more than two hundred women and twelve community-based women's groups across northern Uganda, with Evelyn as the chairperson. Evelyn began doing news interviews and documentaries and speaking out publicly on her experiences in international forums.[14] In 2014 she presented a petition in the Ugandan Parliament requesting reparations for war-affected women. "I have come too far, lived through too much *not* to write this book," Evelyn once said. In 2012 we decided to move ahead with the process of preparing her transcribed stories for publication.

The process of editing the stories took more than a year. Evelyn recorded stories in no particular order, without any reference to specific dates or even necessarily places. After reading through the stories several times, I developed a timeline of Evelyn's life, looking for clues in her stories as to the historical time period within which each took place. Evelyn had a clear memory of the dates her children were born, so I took cues from such things as whether or not she was pregnant, yet married, yet displaced, and so forth and then placed these stories within the chronology of the war. I then divided the narrative into chapters based on major life events, which Evelyn and I reviewed and agreed upon together. In 2012 Ketty and Nancy also reviewed the transcripts of each story with Evelyn to edit or add detail, after which I began to edit the stories for verb tense and sentence structure, while attempting to retain Evelyn's narrative voice. In July 2013 Evelyn, Ketty, and I met each day for nearly two weeks to review the edited chapters once more and to make final decisions about which stories to include in order to ensure that all was captured and edited to her satisfaction. During that period we agreed to keep the names of all senior commanders involved but to use pseudonyms for family members and any other children and adults who appear in the text.

Preparing the manuscript for publication highlighted the complexities of translation.[15] Editing stories and placing them in chronological order is undoubtedly a form of intervention in the text; I did this in consultation with Evelyn, and, although I often suggested the order of stories, she participated in the process and was active in decisions of which stories should remain in the text. Many Acholi words or sayings do not have an English translation or carry with them different meanings depending on the context in which they were said and how they are spoken.[16] Further, the LRA has many terms with meanings that are known only within the group; Ketty, Nancy, and I had to learn this language in the process of translating the stories. In traumatic stories, Evelyn's narrative at times became less comprehensible or sounded detached, and we worked toward a written translation that captures this reaction. Her oral pauses, sighs, and dramatic intonations were difficult to communicate. If storytelling reveals meaning,[17] then we were limited in our ability to fully translate the emotional weight of each story as it was intended while spoken. Yet we wanted the book to be written in English to make it accessible to all Ugandans, where English is the official language and is commonly shared across the linguistically diverse country. These are challenges we were unable to fully resolve but which we wish to bring to the reader's attention.

It is important to recognize this as a book of truths according to Evelyn as she lived them. I did not edit for details that had no supporting evidence, nor did I seek to verify dates or facts. I did edit for verb tense and flow, moving some paragraphs so that they helped guide the reader in the text or adding place or time references to contextualize the speech, but I consciously did this with as light a touch as possible to retain Evelyn's storytelling voice. To focus on the historical accuracy of her account would miss the point of this powerful personal history of the war.[18] The stories within are significant precisely because they relay that which no verifiable historical fact can: the ethical significance of these events. They challenge readers to comprehend that to which they did not bear witness. The stories beg readers to suspend judgment for a time, to think from the perspective of someone who lived through such extreme circumstances of deprivation, fear, and harm, and to try to understand what happened inside the LRA.[19] To borrow from Agamben, the stories within this text speak to the "non-coincidence between facts and truth, between verification and truth."[20]

Notes

1. The confidence-building meetings were held in Garamba between July 26 and August 1, 2006.

2. Human Rights Focus (HURIFO), the Gulu District NGO Forum, the Liu Institute for Global Issues, and Human Rights Watch, *Abducted and Abused: Renewed Conflict in Northern Uganda*, vol. 15, no. 12a (July 2003).

3. For instance, HURIFO, the Concerned Parents Association (CPA), and the Gulu District NGO Forum.

4. Evelyn and I had actually met at the Gulu Support the Children Centre (GUSCO), a rehabilitation center for children who had escaped captivity, several months after she was captured by the Ugandan People's Defense Force (UPDF), in January 2005. I had accompanied two former students, Carla Suarez and Elizabeth St. Jean, who were conducting research on war-affected youth in the region, to the center. Evelyn and I would exchange greetings when we bumped into each other in town; Evelyn had been involved in JRP as a woman leader, providing feedback on our research and policy work on young mothers who had returned from the LRA. She was also well known among the civil society delegates I had accompanied to the peace delegation.

5. As Sylvester asks, what if we began to learn from the lived experiences of those who are affected by a war and those who affect it: what would we relearn? See Christine Sylvester, *War as Experience: Contributions from International Relations and Feminist Analysis* (New York: Routledge, 2013).

6. Jeannie Annan et al., "Women and Girls at War: 'Wives,' Mothers and Fighters in the Lord's Resistance Army," unpublished manuscript (2009); Myriam Denov, *Child Soldiers: Sierra Leone's Revolutionary United Front* (Cambridge: Cambridge University

Press, 2010); Alcinda Honwana, *Child Soldiers in Africa* (Philadelphia: University of Pennsylvania Press, 2011); Ethel Tobach, Susan McKay, and Dyan Mazurana, "'Where Are the Girls?' Girls in Fighting Forces in Northern Uganda, Sierra Leone and Mozambique: Their Lives during and after War," *Peace and Conflict: Journal of Peace Psychology* 10, no. 3 (2004): 305–7; Michael Wessells, *Child Soldiers: From Violence to Protection* (Cambridge, MA: Harvard University Press, 2006).

7. Chris Coulter, *Bush Wives and Girl Soldiers: Women's Lives through War and Peace in Sierra Leone* (Ithaca: Cornell University Press, 2009); Megan Mackenzie, *Female Soldiers in Sierra Leone: Sex, Security, and Post-Conflict Development* (New York: New York University Press, 2012). On studies that examine processes of reintegration of women and girls in northern Uganda, see Grace Akello, "Experiences of Forced Mothers in Northern Uganda: The Legacy of War," *Intervention* 11, no. 2 (2013): 149–56; Jeannie Annan, Chris Blattman, Kristopher Carlson, and Dyan Mazurana, "Civil War, Reintegration, and Gender in Northern Uganda," *Journal of Conflict Resolution* 55, no. 6 (2011): 877–908; Dyan Mazurana et al., "Girls in Fighting Forces and Groups: Their Recruitment, Participation, Demobilization, and Reintegration," *Peace and Conflict: Journal of Peace Psychology* 8, no. 2 (2002): 97–123.

8. Kristopher Carlson and Dyan Mazurana, *Forced Marriage within the Lord's Resistance Army, Uganda* (Somerville, MA: Feinstein International Center, Tufts University, 2008); Erin Baines, "Forced Marriage as a Political Project: Sexual Rules and Relations in the Lord's Resistance Army," *Journal of Peace Research* 51, no. 3 (2014): 405–17; Zoe Marks, "Sexual Violence in Sierra Leone's Civil War: 'Virgination,' Rape, and Marriage," *African Affairs* 113, no. 450 (2014): 67–87; Zoe Marks, "Sexual Violence Inside Rebellion: Policies and Perspectives of the Revolutionary United Front of Sierra Leone," *Civil Wars* 15, no. 3 (2013): 359–79.

9. Liisa Malkki, "Speechless Emissaries: Refugees, Humanitarianism, and Dehistoricization," *Cultural Anthropology* 11, no. 3 (1996): 377–404.

10. Justice and Reconciliation Project and Gulu District NGO Forum, *Young Mothers, Marriage and Reintegration: Considerations for the Juba Peace Talks* (2006).

11. "Remembering and Narrating Conflict: Resources for Doing Historical Memory Work," http://reconstructinghistoricalmemory.com/.

12. We copublished an excerpt in Evelyn Amony and Erin Baines, "Are Human Rights Possible after Conflict? Diary of a Survivor," in *Human Rights: The Hard Questions*, edited by Cindy Holder and David Reidy (Cambridge: Cambridge University Press, 2013), 382.

13. Juliane Okot Bitek, "A Decolonizing Project: History, Memory and the Archives" (Diss., University of British Columbia, 2014).

14. See for example NTV Uganda, "Life Stories—Ex LRA Rebel Wives Part 2," 2012, https://www.youtube.com/watch?v=O5hBsUmy-po; CBC, *The Current*, "To Have and to Hold," 2013, http://www.cbc.ca/thecurrent/episode/2013/01/07/to-have-and-to-hold-evelyn-amonys-story/; Evelyn Amony with Tamara Shaya, "Agents of Change," *Canadian International Council*, November 2012, http://opencanada.org/author/evelynamonyandtamarashaya/; Jodie Martinson, "Stronghearted" (Canada: National Film Board, 2012), https://www.nfb.ca/film/stronghearted.

15. Antjie Krog, Mosisi Mpolweni, and Kopano Ratele, *There Was This Goat: Investigating the Truth Commission Testimony of Notrose Nobomvu Konile* (Durban: University of KwaZulu-Natal Press, 2009).

16. For a more in-depth discussion of the challenges of translation from Luo to English, see Opiyo Oloya, "Becoming a Child Soldier: A Cultural Perspective from Autobiographical Voices" (Diss., York University, 2010).

17. Michael Jackson, *The Politics of Storytelling: Violence, Transgression, and Inter-subjectivity* (Copenhagen: Museum Tusculanum Press, 2002).

18. On this see Dori Laub, "An Event without a Witness: Truth, Testimony and Survival," in *Testimony: Crises of Witnessing in Literature, Psychoanalysis, and History*, edited by Shoshana Felman and Dori Laub (New York: Routledge, 1992), 75-92.

19. This is not to suggest sympathy or forgiveness is required; it is to argue that comprehension is as important to reconciling events as condemnation.

20. Giorgio Agamben, *Remnants of Auschwitz: The Witness and the Archive* (Cambridge: Zone Books, 2002).

Editor's Introduction

"These are difficult stories. Yet they are important for people to know," reflects Evelyn Amony, "so that [the story] does not disappear" and "so that the truth is known." With this, Evelyn not only bears witness to events following her abduction by the LRA but she also begins the hard work of reclaiming life in the face of historical silence and negation.[1] As we learn in her account, life unfolds even in the most dehumanized spaces, and, beyond them, the event is never over but becomes a part of daily life, a person's very sense of who they are.[2] Evelyn recognizes she may never escape her experiences in the LRA, but she refuses to be defined by this identity. With the very act of survival, she reclaimed the right to narrate the story as she remembers it and to define her life as she sees it.[3] Part of this reclamation is to present a story of war from the perspective of those affected by it and to consider its legacies on their present lives. While academics and policymakers might know a great deal about how or why wars begin and end, the subject of how people persevere is seldom attended to or understood.[4] Through stories, we journey into Evelyn's world on her own terms, and the reader is forced to listen differently, to unlearn and think anew.

In this respect, Evelyn asserts herself as a subject of history, not the object of it. Her stories challenge the archetype of "war-affected women," produced and reproduced as a homogenous and overwhelmingly victimized subject of the Western imagination.[5] Today, the act of forcing a woman or girl into marriage in an armed group is recognized as an indictable war crime.[6] Yet Evelyn's life story presents insights into the meaning of this experience for victims in ways the law cannot.[7] The labels "conjugal slave" and "sexual slave," often used in reference to the victims of such crimes, are necessary but overly simplistic.[8] They homogenize pluralistic experiences, reducing them to a singular event: the act of forced marriage.[9] Such terms have been critical to advancing the law and criminalizing the act, yet they fail to capture the complexity of the lived experience,[10] something Evelyn brings us closer to understanding.

When Evelyn was abducted, she told the rebels her name was Betty Ato, and it was by this name that she was called throughout her nearly eleven years in the LRA. This was a simple but common strategy employed by children in northern Uganda to try to hide their identity and protect their relatives. Each time Evelyn recorded a story for this volume, she began with "I am Evelyn Amony." With each short introduction, she reclaims the identity the LRA violently tore from her and the state failed to recognize or protect.

The name Amony translates to "many soldiers," referencing a period of war.[11] Evelyn was born on November 25, 1983, during a period of political crisis in the country, when coups d'état determined who would and would not be president. She was only four years old when war started in northern Uganda and numerous rebel groups formed to fight off the National Resistance Army (NRA), which had assumed state power by force in 1986.[12] Each party pressured the civilian population to support its efforts and to report on the activities of the other.[13] Moreover, each side pressured or forced persons to join its armies, and it was possible for different members of the same Acholi family to become soldiers in opposing armies, each seeking to defeat the other. Social relationships understandably frayed under such conditions, and communities were forced into camps or to sleep in the bush to avoid recruitment or retaliation and to protect those they loved.

Evelyn's childhood memories, recalled in chapter 1, "Childhood," introduce the reader to this very intricacy. In her recollection of atrocities and abuse, the LRA and the Ugandan army both emerge as contradictory actors; in one moment government soldiers induce sheer terror, while in the next they rescue. Rebels, who claimed to fight on the Acholi's behalf, abduct their beloved children. Evelyn's studies were often disrupted by the threat of harm from either rebels or soldiers. If Evelyn's memories of a childhood spent fleeing men with guns appears confusing to the reader, this is precisely the point. It was often difficult for civilians to distinguish a government soldier from a rebel soldier or to be sure of who was an enemy and who was a friend. While Evelyn describes her childhood as one with "very few happy moments," it is also where she locates her most treasured memories. She introduces us to the very persons who were most influential in her upbringing—her parents, her grandparents, and childhood friends—who instilled values of obedience, truthfulness, and hard work. These were the memories and lessons she would cling to during her years in the LRA, ones that kept her afloat as a moral being even in the most debilitating of circumstances that lay ahead.

Evelyn's account both humanizes and troubles expectations of what it means to be a "rebel," a "soldier," a "terrorist," a "child," a "wife," or a "mother." After children were abducted, who did they grow up to become within the rebel group? When a child-soldier died fighting the government, did he die as child or as a rebel? Evelyn's account moves beyond dichotomous distinctions, insisting on a space "in-between" that both disrupts and unpacks simplistic concepts of good and evil.[14]

For instance, Evelyn often reflects on the moral ambiguity that was life in the bush and of persons who repeatedly reappear in her re-storying of this war. Following her abduction, on August 25, 1994, the LRA immediately set about trying to strip Evelyn of her former self. In chapter 2, "*Kurut*" (meaning "new recruit"), the LRA's strategy of instilling fear to generate loyalty among young recruits is tellingly demonstrated. During the first few months after her abduction, Evelyn was forced to work and walk to the point of exhaustion. She listened to the cries of children as they were beaten to death because they were no longer able to work and walk as she did. She had to make the terrible decision of whether to follow unthinkable orders or accept a similar fate. As this brutal initiation continued over time,[15] Evelyn began to depend on the very persons who were the cause of all her pain. Kony would save Evelyn's life on numerous occasions, literally jumping into a river to rescue her from drowning. When she felt like she could no longer continue to walk, it was Kony who encouraged her to keep going, lessened her load, and prevented others from inflicting harm.[16] Within a year, the young Evelyn was willing to risk her own life and to take the life of another to save that of Kony. Yet she did not follow him blindly, nor was her sense of morality completely subordinated to the cruel will of the high command. We learn of the many ways Evelyn and other children resisted their commanders, avoiding or disobeying orders or challenging them when their decisions caused suffering. Each decision, each choice, was weighed against a backdrop of coercion, and Evelyn navigates us through these to explain how it was she survived.

Evelyn began to live in Sudan in late 1994, where she was placed in the home of Kony's first wife, Fatima, to act as her servant and as the caretaker for her children. Eventually they became co-wives and Evelyn, a mother. In chapter 3, "Becoming a Mother," we learn of the power dynamics between women in the LRA and of the complex protocols and duties of a wife and co-wife.[17] Domestic work, such as the preparation of food or bathing water, were sites of dispute and allegation between co-wives, each seeking to secure a position of authority within the polygamous household. These nuances of power and power relations are not insignificant; senior wives held considerable authority, and disobedience could result in great suffering and harm.

In chapter 4, "Leaving Sudan," and chapter 5, "Home," Evelyn takes us through life on the front lines of Operation Iron Fist from the perspective of a mother. She and her children moved in the groups of high commanders and were therefore the target of constant pursuit by the Ugandan People's Defense Force (UPDF). Evelyn does not leave us with an uncomplicated or sympathetic picture of either the Ugandan army or the rebels; both "did their part in this war."[18] She recalls the suffering of civilians at the hands of extraordinarily cruel rebel commanders and also recalls how no one mourned such commanders when they met their own deaths. Some UPDF soldiers unleashed their anger on the women and children they captured, shooting them even if they surrendered. But these chapters also humanize soldiers on both sides. She describes those who perished as persons who had once been loved and who are missed by someone, somewhere. Ugandan military soldiers died from exhaustion, seated at a tree, their nametags revealing that they, too, were Acholi, like the majority of the LRA. One is left to wonder who will bury them. The LRA appeared "pale and thin," women miscarried, and children, hit by bombs, had nothing remaining but pieces of clothing, their shoes. Young soldiers attempted escape, more willing to die trying than to live under the conditions of war as an LRA soldier.[19]

By 2006, the rebels entered into the Juba peace talks (2006–8) between the LRA and the Ugandan government. In early 2005, Ugandan soldiers had captured Evelyn during a military operation. She and her remaining children were transported to a child rehabilitation center in Gulu, Uganda, where she was reunited with her family and settled into a training program for kids until 2006, when she became involved in the peace talks. She tells an extraordinary story of how she became involved in the talks in chapter 6, "Peace Talks." As with her insights into war, Evelyn presents glimpses into the behind-the-scenes process of negotiating peace, the doubts cast, the fear generated, and the anger held. Dialogue between Evelyn and commanders and between Kony and his mother illuminate how personal, intimate relations shape such highly charged political discussions. Her recall reveals the possibilities of women's roles in peace talks but also the limitations. Evelyn and Kony's mother hold great moral and emotional influence over him and appeal to him to return peacefully. But, ultimately, Kony dismisses Evelyn and his mother, even mocking them. It is, in Kony's words, "he who will decide, not them," and the disparity between Kony and Evelyn is once more brought into sharp relief. When the talks fail, Evelyn returns to Gulu and seeks to remake life in a context she barely recognizes anymore, taking us into the final chapter of her life in Gulu.

Studies of survivor testimonies have indicated the way violence eludes language and pain, rendering one unable to speak.[20] In her diaries, Evelyn describes sleepless nights, overwhelming feelings of sorrow and loss, moments of disassociation, humiliation, low self-esteem, and somatization. Evelyn lives with these memories. They are not tucked away in a drawer to be brought out when she chooses but are daily reminders—a scar on her leg, a car that backfires, the police chasing a boy, the process of registering her children for school—that abruptly resurface Evelyn's memories of traumatic events. In chapter 7, "Daily Life," Evelyn presents the challenges of raising her children alone after the war. Her daily life revolves around housework, attending to her children, and, as expected of the eldest child, the care of her younger siblings. She does so in a world that has radically changed since her abduction: she missed the opportunity to complete primary and secondary school, so what job is available? How can she help the children with their homework? She has no land or reservoir of savings, so how to pay for the endless medical bills, her rent, her children's food? Important occasions—such as the marriage of a neighbor or her registering to vote—remind Evelyn of what she has lost and what she might have had had she never been abducted: "I was thinking a lot. I was thinking of the past. I was thinking that, if I had not been abducted, I would not be going through all this." She pauses in the diaries to make sense of why she survived and concludes, "It was to tell this story."

NOTES

1. I borrow these insights on reclaiming stories from indigenous studies and as inspired by Sam McKegney, who writes about the narrative strategies used by survivors of the Indian Residential Schools in Canada to reclaim histories in *Magic Weapons: Aboriginal Writers Remaking Community after Residential School* (Winnipeg: University of Manitoba Press, 2011).

2. Veena Das, *Life and Words: Violence and the Descent into the Ordinary* (Oakland: University of California Press, 2007).

3. Michael Jackson, *The Politics of Storytelling: Violence, Transgression, and Intersubjectivity* (Copenhagen: Museum Tusculanum Press, 2002); Erin Baines and Beth Stewart, "'I Cannot Accept What I Have Not Done': Storytelling, Gender and Transitional Justice," *Journal of Human Rights Practice* 3, no. 3 (2011): 245–63.

4. Swati Parashar, "What Wars and 'War Bodies' Know about International Relations," *Cambridge Review of International Affairs* 26, no. 4 (2013): 615–30.

5. Chandra Talpade Mohanty, "Under Western Eyes: Feminist Scholarship and Colonial Discourses," *Feminist Review* 30 (1988): 61–88.

6. Micaela Frulli, "Advancing International Criminal Law: The Special Court for Sierra Leone Recognizes Forced Marriage as a 'New' Crime against Humanity," *Journal of International Criminal Justice* 6, no. 5 (2008): 1033–42.

7. Nicola Henry, "The Impossibility of Bearing Witness: Wartime Rape and the Promise of Justice," *Violence against Women* 16, no. 10 (2010): 1098–119; Jonneke Koomen, "'Without These Women, the Tribunal Cannot Do Anything': The Politics of Witness Testimony on Sexual Violence at the International Criminal Tribunal for Rwanda," *Signs* 38, no. 2 (2013): 253–77.

8. For more on the importance of complicating these terms, see Sarah Soh, *The Comfort Women: Sexual Violence and Postcolonial Memory in Korea and Japan* (Chicago: University of Chicago Press, 2008).

9. On this point, see also Chris Coulter, *Bush Wives and Girl Soldiers: Women's Lives through War and Peace in Sierra Leone* (Ithaca: Cornell University Press, 2009); Megan Mackenzie, *Female Soldiers in Sierra Leone: Sex, Security, and Post-Conflict Development* (New York: New York University Press, 2012).

10. Chiseche Salome Mibenge, *Sex and International Tribunals: The Erasure of Gender from the War Narrative* (Philadephia: University of Pennsylvania Press, 2013).

11. It is common for Acholi parents to name their child after a significant event at the time of their birth. The Acholi live in northern Uganda, in the Acholi sub-region (sometimes referred to as Acholiland), and, according to the 2002 Census, they

constitute close to 1.17 million people. On the historical origins of the Acholi, see Ronald Atkinson, *The Roots of Ethnicity: The Origins of the Acholi of Uganda before 1800* (Philadelphia: University of Pennsylvania Press, 1994).

12. Atiak was a central route to Sudan, where the rebels sought refuge and arms.

13. Erin Baines and Emily Paddon, "'This Is How We Survived': Civilian Agency and Humanitarian Protection," *Security Dialogue* 43, no. 3 (2012): 231–47.

14. Tzvetan Todorov, *Facing the Extreme: Moral Life in the Concentration Camps* (London: Macmillan, 1997); Primo Levi, *The Drowned and the Saved* (New York: Random House, 1988).

15. For further discussion of the LRA's strategy of indoctrinating children through violence and creation of dependence, see Opiyo Oloya, "Becoming a Child Soldier: A Cultural Perspective from Autobiographical Voices" (Diss., York University, 2010), 65–94; Chris Blattman and Jeannie Annan, "The Consequences of Child Soldiering," *Review of Economics and Statistics* 92, no. 4 (2010): 882–98. For a gender perspective, see Jeannie Annan, Chris Blattman, Kristopher Carlson, and Dyan Mazurana, "Civil War, Reintegration, and Gender in Northern Uganda," *Journal of Conflict Resolution* 55, no. 6 (2011): 884–85; a more general perspective is considered in Bernd Beber and Chris Blattman, "The Logic of Child Soldiering and Coercion," *International Organization* 67, no. 1 (2013): 65–104; Alcinda Honwana, *Child Soldiers in Africa* (Philadelphia: University of Pennsylvania Press, 2011). For a general discussion of the demographics of children abducted, length of stay, gender, age, and so on, see Phuong N. Pham, Patrick Vinck, and Eric Stover, "The Lord's Resistance Army and Forced Conscription in Northern Uganda," *Human Rights Quarterly* 30, no. 2 (2008): 404–11.

16. Annan et al., "Civil War, Reintegration, and Gender in Northern Uganda."

17. Erin Baines, "Forced Marriage as a Political Project: Sexual Rules and Relations in the Lord's Resistance Army," *Journal of Peace Research* 51, no. 3 (2014): 405–17.

18. Response of a former wife of a senior LRA commander, in response to my question of who was responsible for this war; interview, Gulu, n.d.

19. Quaker Peace and Social Witness and Conciliation Resources, *Coming Home— Understanding Why Commanders of the Lord's Resistance Army Chose to Return to Civilian Life* (Gulu, Uganda: Quaker Peace and Social Witness and Conciliation Resources, 2006).

20. Elaine Scarry, *The Body in Pain: The Making and Unmaking of the World* (Oxford: Oxford University Press, 1985); Yvonne Vera, *Under the Tongue* (Cape Town: New Africa Books, 1996).

Histories

In this overview of the historical events surrounding the war in northern Uganda, I want to outline for the reader the context in which Evelyn's story unfolded and to which she contributes a new understanding of the war from the perspective of a woman. I do so by piecing together key historical events found in the literature and by situating Evelyn's story within these elements. Evelyn's life story brings to light the complexities and nuances of this war as a lived experience.

The War and Its Origins

The roots of the Lord's Resistance Army rebellion can be traced to colonial rule (1894–1962) in Uganda.[1] The British displaced indigenous authority structures throughout Uganda, replacing them with local elites loyal to the colonialists and effectively governing Uganda through a policy of divide and rule.[2] The colonialists favored the socioeconomic development of the southwest, engaging the elite in the political administration of the country. This policy also stereotyped the north, specifically the Acholi, as "inferior" and better suited to assuming security positions; they were used to secure the authority of the colonial sovereign.[3] This strategy had the effect of politicizing ethnicity in postcolonial Uganda, creating a political system in which the military played a prominent role.[4] Thus, when Milton Obote, leader of the movement for independence, assumed the position of prime minister (1962–66) and then president (1966–71, 1980–85) of Uganda, he held onto power by forging fragile regional alliances and using violent force against the opposition. Yet it was his own general, Idi Amin Dada, who deposed Obote in 1971. Purging the national government of functionaries loyal to Obote, Amin replaced them with his own acolytes[5] while committing large-scale human rights abuses in the country to contain any opposition.[6]

The United National Liberation Army (UNLA), a coalition rebel group founded in exile with the support of the Tanzanian army,[7] overthrew Amin in 1979. However, not all segments of the UNLA were happy with the election results that ushered Obote back into power, claiming they were fraudulent.[8] Under the leadership of Yoweri Museveni, some former UNLA once more mobilized, intent on taking the presidency by force. The National Resistance Army (NRA), under Museveni's leadership, launched attacks against Obote in 1981, marking the beginning of the Ugandan bush war, which lasted through 1986. The war resulted in notable violations of civilian rights in Luwero, at the center of the war.[9] By 1985, a split had occurred within Uganda's national army, and Obote was once more deposed by one of his army generals, this time Tito Lutwa Okello. Under international pressure, Okello entered into peace talks with Museveni in Nairobi, reaching an agreement to end the war.[10] Museveni broke these agreements shortly thereafter, eventually capturing state power by force in 1986.

In the post-1986 victory, Museveni immediately began to rewrite the official histories of Uganda, deepening regional divisions sown in colonial times.[11] Following an interview with an Acholi elder on Ugandan politics, Dolan remarks that during colonial rule "no one group or subregion enjoyed both military and economic power simultaneously, and discourses of ethnic difference were established which live on to this day." Dolan continues: "The promotion of the Acholi to major positions in the security establishment for example, was, after independence, reframed as proving that they were militaristic," a position examined closely later in this essay for how it would shape regional relations and the beginning of the war.[12] At the time of this writing in 2015, Museveni remains as the head of state.

The Ugandan Bush War, 1981–86

Branch asserts, "The NRA rebellion [against Obote and then Okello] was the crucible in which the north-south divide was ethnicized and took a central place in national politics."[13] In order to shore up popular support for the NRA, Museveni politicized what he termed the "northern problem" during the bush war focused on Luwero. Following the end of the war, Museveni effectively exacerbated the idea of a north-south divide that originated in colonial discourse and governance practices.[14] The newly formed Ugandan state under Museveni effectively claimed to bring security to the country after more than twenty years of violent rule. Throughout his nearly thirty years of rule, Museveni has continuously identified the north as a site and source of political instability in the country.[15] Deposed UNLA soldiers from the north were accused of being solely responsible for the gravest abuses committed during the bush war, although the UNLA was not responsible for the start of the war and the Acholi did not compose the entirety of the national army.[16] Atkinson notes Museveni and the NRA "stoked ethnic and regional differences nationally" at this time by identifying military opponents during the Ugandan bush war not as the UNLA but specifically "as Nilotes (Lango and Acholi), or as Bacholi or Abacholi (the Bantu forms of Acholi)." Further, "This naming process . . . interchanged and conflated regional, linguistic, and specifically ethnic labels. . . . [W]hatever particular label, or combination of labels, was used, those to which it was applied were generalized as alien and dangerous others, accused of abuse and misrule in both the past and the present."[17] This portrayal of the north as a regional threat to security, other proponents argue, is a state-propagated "meta-narrative," invented to justify Museveni's prolonged stay in power and significant military spending.[18] So long as the north was perceived to be a threat to the security of the country as a whole, Museveni could justify military spending and his continued position as head of state for nearly three decades.[19]

The Start of the War in Northern Uganda

After Museveni assumed the presidential office following the NRA victory, Acholi soldiers in the UNLA fled north to seek safe haven. Acholi elders were willing to welcome the retreating soldiers so long as they agreed to be ritually cleansed, a gesture the soldiers rejected as an imposition of the elders' authority, and so they left, retreating further north, some crossing into Sudan to seek refuge.[20] As the NRA—now the national army under Museveni—consolidated control of the country and entered the north, Acholi elders sought to reduce the threat of war in the north through dialogue and negotiation. Their efforts failed when the NRA began to round up and detain individuals, dispossess people of their land, and commit crimes against people and their property.[21] In response, demobilized Acholi soldiers formed a new rebel group, known as the Ugandan People's Defense Army (UPDA), or colloquially as *cilil*.[22]

In the midst of this turmoil, an Acholi woman and spirit medium, Alice Auma (also known as Lakwena, Luo for "messenger"), was directed by the spirit world to lead the Acholi.[23] Lakwena's prophesies provided spiritual succor to a people still grappling with the memories of human rights abuses of past presidencies and the perceived and increasingly real threat of the new regime, and as such she quickly attracted supporters and followers.[24] Allen and Vlassenroot explain her popular support "partly as a consequence of dramatic social changes. . . . Local understandings about communication with the spirit world had expanded in ways that helped make sense of what was happening."[25] With the support of civilians affected by NRA violence, Alice Auma formed the Holy Spirit Mobile Forces (HSMF). The spirits instructed the HSMF to follow strict moral principles regulating social and sexual relations and to conduct ritual cleansing practices.[26] Such religious practices were not necessarily new to the region, but they took on a whole new meaning in the context of war.[27] The HSMF fought using unconventional military tactics; for instance, miracles were reportedly performed that transformed rocks into bombs and deflected bullets of the enemy. In contrast to the UPDA, Lakwena wished to fend off not merely foreign invaders (the NRA) but also internal enemies (such as uncleansed UPDA) through ritual purification and cleansing.[28] The NRA continued to commit mass human rights violations, some argue in retaliation for the perceived role of Acholi soldiers during the bush war. These violations included the by now well-known mass rape of men (*tek gungu*), the looting of cattle, the stealing and defacing of property, and the arbitrary arrest, detention, and torture of civilians accused of collusion with the UPDA, creating further civilian support for the HSMF.[29]

However, by late 1987 the HSMF was defeated militarily, and Alice Auma fled into exile in Kenya.[30] By 1988, most of the UPDA had also been defeated militarily, and many of its soldiers demobilized and returned to civilian life following a peace agreement in Pece, in northern Uganda.[31] Despite this, NRA abuses continued, and several high-profile UPDA men who had returned under the peace agreements were murdered. Furthermore, civilians continued to live in a state of crisis, having lost land and livestock and having endured several years of intense military fighting during which many were subject to violence.[32] As Atkinson observed of the period, the president continued to deride the Acholi, blaming the war on their "backwardness."[33] Evelyn was a toddler during this time, growing up in her father's village, her parents' first surviving child.

The Lord's Resistance Army

It was in this context of uncertainty and rapid change that Joseph Kony emerged as a spiritual and military leader in the region. Kony, a relative of Auma, had reportedly acted as a spiritual healer until some point in 1987, when the spirits instructed him to lead.[34] With remnants of former UPDA and HSMF, as well as devout civilians, Kony led a newly formed army—the United Democratic Christian Army—against the NRA.[35] Kony and his men reportedly regrouped in Kilak Hills, a hilly outcrop where it was possible to evade NRA detection and from where they could launch strategic attacks. There, Kony began to attract further supporters and gain influence as a spiritual leader, performing miracles and divinations that helped the rebel group in its efforts.[36] The NRA intensified its efforts to defeat Kony between 1988 and 1991 in a series of military campaigns but was unable to defeat the rebels,[37] who continued to carry out scattered counterattacks. In response, the NRA developed counterinsurgency techniques, targeting the civilian population, displacing up to 100,000 persons, and carrying out extrajudicial killings.[38]

In April 1991, the NRA launched a four-month military campaign, Operation North, restricting civilian movement and arresting suspected collaborators. At the same time, the Minister for the Pacification of the North, the Honorable Betty Bigombe, organized local defense units (known as "Arrow Groups"), arming and encouraging civilians to defend themselves and align with the NRA. According to Branch, this is precisely when Kony—who had by then renamed his group the Lord's

Resistance Army—began to intensify attacks against civilians as a form of "collective punishment."[39] The LRA mutilated (cutting ears, lips, and limbs), threatened, and killed persons they perceived to have betrayed them, reportedly to send a message regarding loyalty and strength. It is during this period that Evelyn's earliest memories of the war were formed as retold here, memories of a child who feared and fled both the NRA and the UPDA.

Militarization of the Region

Following this period of intensified violence, the two parties reached a détente. Having made its point to the population and the government, the LRA drew back to assess the situation. Museveni too reassessed and attempted a new tactic, implementing a developmental scheme for the north.[40] Bigombe worked to lay the groundwork to initiate peace talks, and by October 1993 the terms were set and the first meetings to negotiate a peace deal were held, with a formalized ceasefire in effect and strong indications that Kony was ready to come out of the bush with his fighters. LRA fighters moved freely throughout the region and town, and civilians enjoyed a brief respite.[41] When Kony asked for more time to assemble his fighters, the government accused him of deceit. On February 6, 1994, while visiting Gulu, the president announced that Kony had seven days to sign the peace agreements or face a renewed military campaign. Kony rejected the ultimatum.[42]

In August of the same year, a group of rebels abducted Evelyn on her return from school and took her to Kilak Hills, an LRA base that provided the rebels protection from detection because of its hilly terrain and lush vegetation. There, she worked as a porter to Kony until the time came for the LRA to relocate to Sudan, where it would enjoy the support of Omar Al-Bashir, the president of Sudan, which was fighting its own war against the Sudanese People's Liberation Army (SPLA). In exchange for Khartoum's support, the LRA fought the SPLA. Up to that time, Museveni had supported the SPLA in its efforts to liberate the south, and its leader, John Garang, was often seen moving around in Gulu.[43] Ugandan support for the SPLA and Sudanese support for the LRA effectively generated proxy warfare, adding a new, transnational dimension to the war in northern Uganda.[44]

Between 1994 and 2003, the LRA established expansive military bases in South Sudan, adjacent to those of the Sudanese armed forces.[45] Tens of thousands of children were abducted into the LRA in the mid-1990s, to train as soldiers but also to act as porters, laborers, and servants to help build and maintain homesteads. These children were placed in the homes of commanders; they referred to these commanders as "father" and to their first wife as "mother." They were told the LRA was their family now and that the ones they knew and loved in Acholiland were now dead, killed by Museveni. Evelyn, who served as one of Kony's escorts for several years, was eventually forced to become a servant to his first wife, Fatima, caring for and raising his eldest son, who was then just a baby. By 1997, Evelyn would be forced to become Kony's wife and have a child of her own.

In return for the refuge, continuous military support, and training extended to the LRA by Khartoum, the rebels fought in Sudan against the SPLA, which in turn was often joined by its ally, the Ugandan military. The LRA endured several defeats, including having to reestablish bases after their capture by the SPLA and the Ugandan army. At the same time, the leadership dispatched commanders and soldiers to go on "standby," short visits to northern Uganda made with the intention of abduction, looting, or retaliation.

In Uganda, Museveni set about consolidating political control over the country,[46] introducing a series of changes to the Constitution to extend his term in office on the grounds that he needed to first ensure political stability. Using memories of the Ugandan bush war to restoke fears of the perceived threat to national security and development posed by the Acholi, Museveni won the presidential elections in 1986 — although the majority of Acholi voted against him.[47] Following his win, he once more publicly devoted himself and the army's attention to the war in the north. To deprive the rebels of popular support, the military responded by creating more and more "protected villages," forcing up to 450,000 people into displacement camps. Responding to Museveni's repeated declarations that the war was nearly over, the LRA unleashed unprecedented violence against civilians in northern Uganda, including large-scale massacres of civilians.[48] Rather than redouble its efforts in the north as required to protect its population, the national army diverted its attention to the wider geopolitical dynamics. The NRA, now renamed the Ugandan People's Defense Force (UPDF), entered the Democratic Republic of Congo (DRC) to help armed opposition groups depose its president, thereby starting what would become known as Africa's Great War in 1998.[49]

In the post–Cold War era, the international community responded to the militarization of the region and the displacement of the population with alarm and pressured states to resolve the mounting devastation wrought by such wars. For instance, international donors to Uganda and the UN insisted that Museveni end Uganda's occupation of the DRC. A growing lobby, both an internal one formed within Uganda's civil society sector and an external group led by the Acholi diaspora and its allies, brought increased attention to Museveni's failure to provide protection and his seeming inability to end the war in Uganda.[50] By the late 1990s, local Acholi leaders had organized regionally and trans-nationally[51] to pressure the government to pass an amnesty act[52] and to enter peace talks.[53] Activists for war-affected children took note of the situation in northern Uganda and Sudan, particularly after the now well-known abduction of 139 schoolgirls from St. Mary's School in Aboke in late 1996.[54] The story of the girls' abduction captured the imagination of the international media and led to increasing demands for regional states to end the war.[55]

Responding to varying appeals for international involvement, the Carter Center brokered an eleven-point agreement between Sudan and Uganda in 1999. The efforts reestablished diplomatic relations, paving the way for the UPDF to begin military operations inside Sudan against the LRA.[56] With waning support from the Sudanese government and the looming threat of a UPDF attack, the LRA entertained several efforts to initiate peace talks during this period, an issue on which the LRA leadership reportedly split. Some leaders wished to negotiate peace and return home, while others believed a military victory was still possible.[57] Kony reportedly insisted that only the spirits could decide their fate. Then Kony's second in command, Otti Lagony, dis-agreed with Kony, wishing to pursue talks and accusing Kony of falling out of favor with the spirits.[58] His plot to kill Kony in order to renew peace talks was discovered, and Otti Lagony was interrogated before being stoned to death.[59]

Operation Iron Fist

The September 11, 2001, attack on the United States paved the way for the legitimation and escalation of a military response against the LRA.[60] The Sudanese government—desiring to appease those who accused it of having harbored those responsible for 9/11—agreed to permit the UPDF to launch its largest operation yet in Sudan. Operation Iron First commenced in March 2002. Reportedly more than ten thousand Ugandan troops entered Sudan to "deliver a final blow" to the LRA.[61] The campaign effectively dislodged the LRA from its bases in Sudan, yet at a high cost to human life. Both UPDF and LRA soldiers experienced inordinate numbers of causalities, through combat but also through deprivation of water and food. As Evelyn describes in often painful detail, many of the "rebels" killed were children—either abducted or born into the LRA following the forced marriage and motherhood of abducted girls.

The campaign, moreover, dramatically escalated the level of violence unleashed on civilians, both in Sudan[62] and in Uganda. In Sudan, the LRA remained a useful ally of Khartoum, even if it had been forced to officially break off relations. Khartoum provided support to the LRA on and off again throughout Operation Iron First until the signing of the Comprehensive Peace Agreement in 2005,[63] which effectively ended the civil war in Sudan. Kony and a number of his commanders, along with their wives and children, remained in Sudan during the early years of Operation Iron Fist, wavering between assisting and fighting the Sudanese army, depending on relations. It was during this period that Evelyn recalls walking, sometimes for days on end, through the Imatong Mountains, where Kony sought refuge and respite from the advancing Ugandan military.

In northern and eastern Uganda, the LRA broke into smaller mobile units and carried out orders to abduct and press into fighting thousands of children: up to 8,200 were abducted in the first eighteen months alone.[64] Tens of thousands of children walked into town centers at night to sleep in temporary shelters (including in bus parks, under verandas, and in hospitals) to avoid abduction by rebels, susceptible to illness and abuse.[65] Civilians endured threats, beatings, loss of property, mutilation, torture, and murder at the hands of LRA, including large-scale massacres in unprotected, displaced persons camps.[66]

By 2005, the UPDF had forced up to 90 percent of the population (at the peak, between 1.3 and 1.5 million persons) into camps for internally displaced persons, resulting in large-scale loss of life.[67] Camps were poorly organized, overcrowded, and underserviced: people lacked access to basic resources such as clean water, food, and sanitation.[68] Further, they were subject to frequent attack; the UPDF and local defense units composed of civilians were poorly armed and trained, often unable to fend off LRA attacks on the camps. Men and women confined within the sprawling camps were constantly monitored by the military for possible collaboration with rebels and were subject to strict military regulations, curfews, restriction of movement outside and within the camps, exploitation of labor, and human rights violations (such as detention, rape, and beatings).[69] Deprivation, humiliation, and the breakdown of social and gender relations led to high rates of suicide, alcoholism, and sexual and domestic violence.[70] More than a thousand persons a week died from disease, starvation, or violence inside the confines of the camps.[71]

The sheer scale of human suffering led Jan Egeland, a top UN official, to announce that northern Uganda was "the worst, most forgotten humanitarian crisis on earth." "This senseless slaughter must end. It cannot and should not continue one day more."[72] With this declarative statement, Egeland triggered the mobilization of UN and state parties to respond to the crisis, calling upon Museveni to enter negotiations. Betty Bigombe returned to the north to assume the position of peace negotiator in 2004, but, although the LRA did speak to and meet with Bigombe, productive talks did not materialize. By 2005, following the signing of the Comprehensive Peace Agreement in Sudan and in view of the lack of any further possibility of support from Khartoum, the LRA began to relocate to the Democratic Republic of Congo. Evelyn was captured by the Ugandan military in January 2005, as she fled their advance, ten days after the birth of her third daughter.

The newly installed, semi-autonomous government of South Sudan, under the leadership of John Garang (who later in 2005 died in a helicopter crash), had no interest in a continuation of hostilities with the LRA and viewed the presence of more than ten thousand Ugandan soldiers in its land as potentially destabilizing.[73] Under the direction of Vice President Riek Machar, the government contacted the LRA to see whether it was possible to begin mediation under Machar's direction. By February 2006, terms of the negotiation were set, with groundwork quietly laid by civil society members.[74]

It was in the midst of attempts to reestablish talks that the International Criminal Court's chief prosecutor, in October 2005, unsealed arrest warrants for top LRA commanders.[75] The unsealing of the arrest warrants revealed a larger "truth" of the war: both state and internationally produced dominant narratives have long established the LRA as an "evil" and "senseless" party with whom negotiations were not possible.[76] While the arrest warrants galvanized the imaginations of Western and African publics alike regarding the possibilities of arrest and detention and the end of impunity, they masked the complexity of the conflict. In particular, they occluded the role of the Ugandan state, at times with the assistance, ironically, of aid agencies,[77] in the direct and indirect delay of peace and the perpetuation of suffering. Moreover, this binary understanding "ignores the fundamental complexity of the war and distorts the reality of those caught up in it. Indeed for many of the people of northern Uganda, and Acholi in particular there has been no black and white, no good choice to be made from among the often gruesome violence of the LRA, the often equally extensive and brutal violence of government troops, or the typically slower, quieter, but at least equally destructive structural violence of the camps."[78] If the facts and figures presented bring into focus this sobering historical reality of the war, then Evelyn's intimate recall of it from childhood to the present—the brutality of both parties, the grinding violence of daily life—bring to this history the voice of those subjected to the gray.

The Juba Peace Talks and Their Collapse

Some eighteen months after her capture by the UPDF and her reunion with her parents in January 2005, Evelyn boarded a plane to Juba, South Sudan to participate in the Juba peace talks, which took place between 2006 and 2008. Often considered the best opportunity to realize peace in the history of the war, the peace talks had their stops and starts.[79] Machar was considered a biased mediator, and more than once the

LRA delegation accused him of unequal treatment. LRA representatives protested by leaving the negotiation tables between January and April 2007, yet even the legitimacy of the delegates—many of whom were Acholi from the diaspora—to represent the LRA was unclear. Side negotiations took place, sowing internal confusion, distrust, and animosity within the LRA.[80] Kony fired his first delegation in 2007 and, suspecting that his second in command, Vincent Otti, was planning to undermine him, called for his execution and that of his supporters in October 2007. Thereafter the talks stalled for six months, before resuming again under the new leadership of David Matsanga.[81] Despite the halting process of the talks, several agreements—including the important Cessation of Hostilities Agreement—were reached and signed relatively swiftly. These agreements were considered to be both comprehensive and sophisticated in content.[82]

However, when the date came for Kony to sign the agreements, on April 10, 2008, he once more refused, seeking clarification from the elders in northern Uganda on questions related to demobilization and justice. The elders waited in vain for four days inside Kony's Garamba base camp in May 2008. Soon thereafter, it was reported that Kony had stated "he would rather die in the bush than turn himself in to the GoU [government of Uganda] or ICC 'to be hanged.'"[83] President Chissano (formerly of Mozambique), brought in as the UN special envoy to the talks, continued to pursue the possibility of renewing the negotiations, but, after months of disappointment and a final-ditch effort to extend the deadline, Kony again failed to show up.[84] Evelyn traveled between her home in Gulu and Garamba a total of six times, each time in great uncertainty, fear, and distrust. When she learned Kony had killed his second in command, Vincent Otti, she refused to go again, as she believed Kony was not sincere in the talks and perhaps knew before others did that the agreements would not be signed.

In July 2008, the DRC army, Forces Armées de la République Démocratique du Congo, began to surround the LRA in Congo, which the LRA interpreted as a sign of aggression. In December 2008, the war fully resumed with the launch of a multinational peace force, code-named Operation Lightning Thunder, composed of Ugandan, Congolese, and South Sudanese forces and supported by AFRICOM, the US Africa Command.[85] The operation, however, was largely led by the

Ugandan military, with other parties playing a nominal role. In a fashion typical of the LRA, it retaliated against civilians, committing large-scale massacres and abductions in that country.[86]

Today, the "new" LRA continues to live in mobile groups, moving throughout the regions of the DRC and in the neighboring Central African Republic and South Sudan.[87] Inside northern Uganda, a tentative peace has returned, despite political turmoil in recent years following an increasingly restrictive set of laws under the continued rule of Yoweri Museveni. The displaced-persons camps were dismantled and civilians returned home to start over again.[88] Kony remains at large at the time of writing, and the LRA is thought to have morphed into a "new" group, one that remains equally deadly, if diminished in numbers and cohesion. Evelyn, in the meantime, resumed her life as a mother and began a new one as an activist for the rights of war-affected persons in Uganda.

NOTES

1. "Misrepresentations and manipulations of ethnicity were part of the very creation of Uganda by the British." Ronald Atkinson, *The Roots of Ethnicity: The Origins of the Acholi of Uganda before 1800* (Philadelphia: University of Pennsylvania Press, 1994), 2. See 2–6 for a development of this argument.

2. Tarsis B. Kabwegyere, *The Politics of State Formation: The Nature and Effects of Colonialism in Uganda* (Nairobi: East African Literature Bureau, 1974); Adam Branch, "Exploring the Roots of LRA Violence: Political Crisis and Ethnic Politics in Acholiland," in *The Lord's Resistance Army: Myth and Reality*, edited by Tim Allen and Koen Vlassenroot (London: Zed Books, n.d.), 25–44; Sverker Finnström, *Living with Bad Surroundings: War, History, and Everyday Moments in Northern Uganda* (Durham: Duke University Press, 2008), chapter 1.

3. Atkinson, *The Roots of Ethnicity*, 2–6.

4. Amii Omara-Otunnu, "Politics and the Military in Uganda (1890–1979)" (Diss., University of Oxford, 1984); Frank Van Acker, "Uganda and the Lord's Resistance Army: The New Order No One Ordered," *African Affairs* 103, no. 412 (2004): 338–41.

5. Adam Branch, *Displacing Human Rights: War and Intervention in Northern Uganda* (Oxford: Oxford University Press, 2011), 56. Amin heavily recruited from his home area of West Nile. See Finnström, *Living with Bad Surroundings*, 65; also, Chris Dolan notes that the ethnic tensions in the country are not solely north-south, citing Amin's recruitment of soldiers from West Nile to persecute Acholi and Langi civilians. Dolan, *Social Torture: The Case of Northern Uganda* (Oxford: Berghahn Books, 2009), 43.

6. Peter F. B. Nayenga, "Myths and Realities of Idi Amin Dada's Uganda," *African Studies Review* (1979): 127–38; Ali A. Mazrui, "Between Development and Decay: Anarchy, Tyranny and Progress under Idi Amin," *Third World Quarterly* 2, no. 1 (1980): 50–51; Atkinson, *The Roots of Ethnicity*, 276–77.

7. Including FRONASA, the Front for National Salvation, led by Yoweri Museveni. See Ogenga Otunnu, "Causes and Consequences of the War in Acholiland," in *Protracted Conflict, Elusive Peace: Initiatives to End the Violence in Northern Uganda*, edited by Lucima Okello (London: Conciliation Resources in collaboration with Kacoke Madit, 2002); also available at http://www.c-r.org/.

8. Following the brief but ultimately failed rule of Yusef Lule (who lasted sixty-nine days in office) and then of Godfrey Binaisa (who ruled for nearly a year), elections were held in 1980, and Milton Obote once more assumed the presidency (1980–85). Ron Atkinson, "Afterward: A Perspective on the Last Thirty Years," in *The Roots of Ethnicity*, 278–79.

9. Museveni drew on the support of disaffected southern-based ethnocultural groups and of exiled Tutsi Rwandans living in Uganda to fight against the national army. Ondoga Ori Amaza, *Museveni's Long March from Guerrilla to Statesman* (Kampala: Fountain Press, 1998).

10. Atkinson, *The Roots of Ethnicity*, 278–81; Branch, *Displacing Human Rights*, 56–61; Finnström, *Living with Bad Surroundings*, 65–69; Bethuel Kiplagat, "Reaching the 1995 Nairobi Agreement," in Okello, *Protracted Conflict, Elusive Peace*, 24–27.

11. See Zachary Lomo and Lucy Hovil, *Behind the Violence: Causes, Consequences and the Search for Solutions to the War in Northern Uganda* (Refugee Law Project, Working Paper No. 11, 2004), 7–12.

12. Dolan, *Social Torture*, 42.

13. Branch, "Exploring the Roots of LRA Violence," 30.

14. Atkinson notes that Obote II's rule "fed into this collective NRM vilification" of the north, given that he drew "heavily but hardly exclusively, upon the northern Ugandan Acholi and Langi populations" for his army, in turn known for its reported organized revenge against civilians in West Nile, where Amin originated. *The Roots of Ethnicity*, 279–80.

15. Finnström rejects and complicates such meta-narratives; see *Living with Bad Surroundings*, 63–98.

16. Atkinson notes that eliding the Acholi with the UNLA "also ignored the significant presence . . . of non-northerners; indeed, Banyankore from western Uganda were second in the number in the UNLA after the Acholi"; see *The Roots of Ethnicity*, 280.

17. Atkinson, *The Roots of Ethnicity*, 280.

18. Andrew Mwenda, "Uganda's Politics of Foreign Aid and Violent Conflict: The Political Uses of the LRA Rebellion," in Allen and Vlassenroot, *The Lord's Resistance Army*, 45–58.

19. Morten Bøås, "Uganda in the Regional War Zone: Meta-Narratives, Pasts and Presents," *Journal of Contemporary African Studies* 22, no. 3 (2004): 283–303.

20. Branch, "Exploring the Roots of LRA Violence," 31. Branch argues that the war was born out of not only a national political crisis but also a crisis of authority within Acholi, where lineage-based authorities and elders, the middle class, and the political elite—already weakened by varying regimes of state violence—were further disrupted by the arrival of the UNLA.

21. Dolan, *Social Torture*, 43–44; Chris Dolan, "What Do You Remember: A Rough Guide to the War in Northern Uganda 1986–2000," *ACORD* (April 2000); Onenga Otunnu, "The Conflict in Northern Uganda: Causes and Dynamics," in Okello, *Protracted Conflict, Elusive Peace*, 13.

22. UPDA was composed of soldiers who had fled north following the overthrow of Obote in July 1985 and the fall of Okello in January 1986; Dolan, *Social Torture*, 43; see also Balam Nyeko and Lucima Okello, "Profiles of the Parties to the Conflict," in Okello, *Protracted Conflict, Elusive Peace*, 21–22.

23. A spirit medium in Acholi channels and speaks to spirits, providing a line of communication between the spirit and the material worlds.

24. Heike Behrend, *Alice Lakwena and the Spirits: War in Northern Uganda, 1985–96* (London: James Currey, 1999).

25. Tim Allen and Koen Vlassenroot, "Introduction," in Allen and Vlassenroot, *The Lord's Resistance Army*, 7–9.

26. Behrend, *Alice Lakwena*; also Rudy Doom and Koen Vlassenroot, "Kony's Message: A New Koine? The Lord's Resistance Army in Northern Uganda," *African Affairs* 98, no. 390 (1999): 18–19.

27. Kristof Titeca elaborates the strategic and functional effects of the new spiritual order in the LRA in "The Spiritual Order of the LRA," in Allen and Vlassenroot, *The Lord's Resistance Army*, 59–73.

28. Tim Allen, "Understanding Alice: Uganda's Holy Spirit Movement in Context," *Africa* 61, no. 3 (1991): 370–99.

29. Dolan, *Social Torture*, 44.

30. Allen, "Understanding Alice," 373.

31. Caroline Lamwaka, "The Peace Process in Northern Uganda, 1986–1999," in Okello, *Protracted Conflict, Elusive Peace*, 28–33.

32. As Dolan succinctly summarizes the ramifications of this phase of the war, "the toll on the economic and social fabric was beginning to be felt"; *Social Torture*, 45.

33. Atkinson, quoting Museveni, in *The Roots of Ethnicity*, 288.

34. On the origins of the LRA see Behrend, *Alice Lakwena*, 172–90; Van Acker, "Uganda and the Lord's Resistance Army," 348–51.

35. On the spiritual leadership of Kony, see Doom and Vlassenroot, "Kony's Message: A New Koine?," 21–24; Lomo and Hovil, *Behind the Violence*, 14–15.

36. In interviews, six original members of the LRA recalled countless stories of the miracles performed, including a story of defeating an NRA commander's powerful witch doctor. A similar story is told in Titeca, "The Spiritual Order of the LRA," 59–73.

37. Following Operation Fiaka Kufiaka in 1986 and Operation Sim Sim in 1987, the NRA launched Operation White Gold in 1987/88 and Operation North in 1991.

38. Atkinson, citing Amnesty International, *Breaking the Circle: Protecting Human Rights in the Northern War Zone* (London: Amnesty International, 1999), 11, in *The Roots of Ethnicity*, 289. See also Robert Gersony, "The Anguish of Northern Uganda: Result of a Field-Based Assessment of the Civil Conflicts in Northern Uganda" (1997), http://pdf.usaid.gov/pdf_docs/PNACC245.pdf.

39. Branch, cited in Atkinson, *The Roots of Ethnicity*, 290.

40. Atkinson, *The Roots of Ethnicity*, 291; see also Branch, *Displacing Human Rights*, 176–80; and Dolan, *Social Torture*, 45.

41. Dolan, *Social Torture*, 86–89.

42. Billie O'Kadameri, "LRA/Government Negotiations, 1993–1994," in Okello, *Protracted Conflict, Elusive Peace*, 41.

43. Museveni had gone to school with the leader of the SPLA, John Garang, in Tanzania, and the two enjoyed a close relationship until Garang's death in 2005.

44. Gerard Prunier, "Rebel Movements and Proxy Warfare: Uganda, Sudan and the Congo (1986–99)," *African Affairs* 103, no. 412 (2004): 359–83. The relationships in Sudan were, of course, more complicated than this introduction can elaborate. For a detailed analysis of varied rebel groups and alliances in the Sudanese war and the relationship to the LRA, see Mareike Schomerus and Emily Walmsley, *The Lord's Resistance Army in Sudan: A History and Overview* (Geneva: Small Arms Survey, 2007); for a broader analysis of the war in Sudan, see Douglas Hamilton Johnson, *The Root Causes of Sudan's Civil Wars* (Bloomington: Indiana University Press, 2003).

45. This period is referred to by former LRA as "settled life," where commanders constructed homesteads and established gardens and daily routines.

46. In 1995, the Ugandan government introduced a new constitution, which set the terms of the presidency. The first democratic elections since the contested 1980 elections were then held. Over the course of this decade, the government decentralized its powers, which served to extend Museveni's political reach throughout the country. Aili Mari Tripp, *Museveni's Uganda: Paradoxes of Power in a Hybrid Regime* (Boulder, CO: Lynne Rienner, 2010), 111–26.

47. Atkinson reproduces a series of public statements that "reveal the mindset of the President" during this period in *The Roots of Ethnicity*, 288–89.

48. The LRA led a series of attacks against civilians, including massacres in Atiak (1995), Achol-pi (July 1996), and Palabek (January 1997); they also began a campaign of mass abduction of children from private schools in 1996 and 1997, as documented by Amnesty International, *Breaking God's Commandments* (London: Amnesty International, 1997), and Human Rights Watch, *Scars of Death: Children Abducted by the Lord's Resistance Army in Uganda* (London, New York: Human Rights Watch, 1997). On massacres, see Justice and Reconciliation Project, "Remembering the Atiak Massacre: April 20, 1995," Gulu, Uganda, Field Note IV (2007); Justice and Reconciliation Project, "When a Gunman Speaks You Listen: Victims' Experiences and Memories of Conflict in *Palabek* Sub-County, Lamwo District," Gulu, Uganda, Field Note XV (2012).

49. Gerard Prunier, *Africa's World War: Congo, the Rwandan Genocide, and the Making of a Continental Catastrophe* (Oxford: Oxford University Press, 2008); Tripp, *Museveni's Uganda*, 172–77. Museveni began to support the efforts of the rebel leader Laurent Kabila in the neighboring Democratic Republic of Congo, triggering the first of two regional wars in that country, which led to millions of deaths and the plundering and exploitation of resources by the Ugandan military.

50. Kacoke Madit organized several conferences between 1997 and 2000, providing an important space to bring different parties into dialogue with one another and pressing for negotiation. Kacoke Madit, *Meeting the Challenges of Building Sustainable Peace in Northern Uganda* (2000), and Kacoke Madit, *The Quest for Peace in Northern Uganda* (London: The MK Secretariat, 2000).

51. In 1997, the Acholi Religious Leaders Peace Initiative (ARLPI) was formally founded by an interdenominational network of religious leaders who sought to end the "leadership impasse over the conflict" and to initiate contact with the LRA with the goals of arranging peace talks. Over the next decade and a half, ARLPI would release repeated statements calling for a peaceful end to the conflict, meet with national and international dignitaries, and conduct face-to-face talks with LRA commanders. See USAID, *The Role of the Acholi Religious Leader Peace Initiative (ARLPI) in Peace Building in Northern Uganda* (Washington, DC: USAID, 2001).

52. The amnesty was viewed as one way to settle the conflict peacefully while giving persons at large a means to return home. For a discussion of the Amnesty Act as a strategy for ending the war, see Manisuli Ssenyonjo, "Accountability of Non-State Actors in Uganda for War Crimes and Human Rights Violations: Between Amnesty and the International Criminal Court," *Journal of Conflict and Security Law* 10, no. 3 (2005): 405–34; Kasaija Phillip Apuuli, "Amnesty and International Law: The Case of the Lord's Resistance Army Insurgents in Northern Uganda," *African Journal on Conflict Resolution* 5, no. 2 (2007): 33–61.

53. International allies, including Human Rights Watch and Amnesty International, lent their resources to the call, issuing influential reports and calls for action. Amnesty International, *Breaking the Circle* (1999); Human Rights Watch, *Uprooted and Forgotten: Impunity and Human Rights Abuses in Uganda*, vol. 17, no. 12a (2005).

54. Els de Temmerman, *Aboke Girls: Children Abducted in Northern Uganda* (Kampala: Fountain, 2001).

55. The adoption of various UN Protocols to stop the use of child soldiers following Graca Machel's study of the situation reinforced transnational lobbying to stop the use of child soldiers. Graca Machel, *Impact of Armed Conflict on Children* (New York: United Nations, 1996).

56. Joyce Neu, "Restoring Relations between Uganda and Sudan: The Carter Centre Process," in Okello, *Protracted Conflict, Elusive Peace*, 46–51.

57. Author interviews with former LRA commanders, Gulu town, 2010, 2011, 2012.

58. Lagony took over the position of second in command in 1997, following the death of Omona Field.

59. According to one former senior wife in the LRA, Lagony was impotent and could not produce children. He had gone to Kony and accused him of having many children but not helping him with medicine to conceive his own children. Kony had mocked him, stating it was his mother who had cursed him as a child and that he, Kony, was not responsible for helping anyone. The same woman argued that Lagony wanted to negotiate peace and return under the amnesty since he had no family and therefore saw no future for himself in the LRA. Reportedly, Kony announced following Lagony's execution that any commander or soldier who wanted to accept amnesty could, and notable defections occurred. Author interview, Gulu, 2011.

60. The LRA was placed on the US Terrorist Watchlist, the government of Uganda passed a terrorism act, and the UPDF began to receive training and support from the United States; Branch argues that US-based support to Uganda—disguised as a desire to protect civilians—constitutes a continuation of the war on terror by creating "new forms of transnational political authority, specifically unaccountable, militarized administration networks that bring together state, international, and sub-state actors and institutions." See Adam Branch, "The Paradoxes of Protection: Aligning against the Lord's Resistance Army," *African Security* 5, no. 3–4 (2012): 160–78.

61. Atkinson, *The Roots of Ethnicity*, 300.

62. Schomerus argues that the UPDF presence in South Sudan resulted in the mass abuse of civilian human rights. See Mareike Schomerus, "'They Forget What They Came For': Uganda's Army in Sudan," *Journal of Eastern African Studies* 6, no. 1 (2012): 124–53.

63. Atkinson, "The Realists in Juba?," in Allen and Vlassenroot, *The Lord's Resistance Army*.

64. Human Rights Watch, *Abducted and Abused: Renewed Conflict in Northern Uganda*, vol. 15, no. 12a (July 2003), 3.

65. Ibid. Also see BBC News, "In Pictures: Night Commuters," http://news.bbc .co.uk/2/shared/spl/hi/picture_gallery/05/africa_night_commuters/html/1.htm.

66. Phuong N. Pham et al., *Forgotten Voices: A Population-Based Survey of Attitudes about Peace and Justice in Northern Uganda* (Berkeley: Human Rights Centre, 2005), available online at http://escholarship.org/uc/item/4qr346xh; Justice and Reconciliation Project, *Kill Every Living Thing: The Barlonyo Massacre* (Gulu, JRP, Uganda, 2009), available online at http://justiceandreconciliation.com/2009/02/kill-every-living-thing-the-barlonyo-massacre-fn-ix/.

67. Often the UPDF provided civilians with only forty-eight-hours notice that they were being moved to the camps. Human Rights Watch, *Uprooted and Forgotten*; Morten Bøås and Anne Hatløy, "Northern Uganda Internally Displaced Persons Profiling Study," Office of the Prime Minister, Department of Disaster Preparedness and Refugees (Kampala, Uganda, 2006).

68. HURIFO, *Between Two Fires: The Plight of IDPs in Northern Uganda* (Gulu Town: Human Rights Focus, 2002), 59–68.

69. HURIFO, *Between Two Fires*, 43–54; Bøås and Hatløy, "Northern Uganda Internally Displaced Persons Profiling Study."

70. Dolan, *Social Torture*, 159–218; Moses Chrispus Okello and Lucy Hovil, "Confronting the Reality of Gender-Based Violence in Northern Uganda," *International Journal of Transitional Justice* 1, no. 3 (2007): 433–43; Jeannie Annan and Moriah Bier, "The Risk of Return: Intimate Partner Violence in Northern Uganda's Armed Conflict," *Social Science and Medicine* 70, no. 1 (2010): 152–59; Erin Baines and Lara Rosenoff Gauvin, "Motherhood and Social Repair after War and Displacement in Northern Uganda," *Journal of Refugee Studies* 27, no. 2 (2014): 282–300.

71. Republic of Uganda, Ministry of Health, "Health and Mortality Survey among Internally Displaced Persons in Gulu, Kitgum and Pader Districts, Northern Uganda" (Kampala: Ministry of Health, 2005), ii.

72. Agence France-Presse, "War in Northern Uganda World's Worst Forgotten Crisis: UN," *Reliefweb* (2003), http://reliefweb.int/report/uganda/war-northern-uganda-worlds-worst-forgotten-crisis-un.

73. Atkinson, "The Realists in Juba?," 206; Dylan Hendrickson and Kennedy Tumutegyereize, "Dealing with Complexity in Peace Negotiations: Reflections on the Lord's Resistance Army and the Juba Talks," *Conciliation Resources* (2012), http://www.c-r.org/sites/default/files/Dealingwithcomplexity_201201.pdf.

74. Simon Simonse, Willemijn Verkoren, and Gerd Junne, "NGO Involvement in the Juba Peace Talks: The Role and Dilemmas of IKV Pax Christi," in Allen and Vlassenroot, *The Lord's Resistance Army*, 223–27.

75. Warrants were issued for Joseph Kony, Vincent Otti, Okot Odhiambo, Raska Lukwiya, and Dominic Ongwen for war crimes and crimes against humanity; for an account of how ARLPI contested ICC indictments to preserve the possibility of peace talks, see Kasaija Phillip Apuuli, "Peace over Justice: The Acholi Religious Leaders Peace Initiative (ARLPI) vs. The International Criminal Court (ICC) in Northern Uganda," *Studies in Ethnicity and Nationalism* 11, no. 1 (2011): 116–29; Adam Branch, "Uganda's Civil War and the Politics of ICC Intervention," *Ethics and International Affairs* 21, no. 2 (2007): 179–98.

76. On the contrary, Sverker Finnström argues that the LRA had a political agenda. Sverker Finnström, "An African Hell of Colonial Imagination?," *Politique Africaine* 4 (2008): 119–39; see also Sverker Finnström, "Reconciliation Grown Bitter?," in *Localizing Transitional Justice: Interventions and Priorities after Mass Violence*, edited by Rosalind Shaw, Lars Waldorf, and Pierre Hazan (Palo Alto: Stanford University Press, 2010).

The international community was invested in this narrative as part of the pursuit of a liberal human rights agenda (to protect children from recruitment) and to link it to the global war on terror; the narrative legitimizes this global war and support to states that help fight it. See Jonathan Fisher, "Framing Kony: Uganda's War, Obama's Advisers and the Nature of 'Influence' in Western Foreign Policy Making," *Third World Quarterly* 35, no. 4 (2014): 686–704; Nicole Laliberté, "In Pursuit of a Monster: Militarisation and (In) Security in Northern Uganda," *Geopolitics* 18, no. 4 (2013): 875–94.

77. Adam Branch, "Against Humanitarian Impunity: Rethinking Responsibility for Displacement and Disaster in Northern Uganda," *Journal of Intervention and State-building* 2, no. 2 (2008): 151–73.

78. Atkinson, *The Roots of Ethnicity*, 307.

79. Michael Otim and Marieke Wierda, "Justice at Juba: International Obligations and Local Demands in Northern Uganda," in *Courting Conflict? Justice, Peace and the ICC in Africa*, edited by Nicholas Waddell, Phil Clark, and Mariana Goetz (London: Royal African Society, 2008), 21–29.

80. Including an effort by Salim Saleh, the president's brother and once head of the army, to hold side talks in Mombasa, Kenya — an initiative that some viewed as an attempt to divide the LRA.

81. For an analysis of this process and recommendations, see Hendrickson and Tumutegyereize, "Dealing with Complexity in Peace Negotiations," 17 30.

82. Atkinson, *The Roots of Ethnicity*, 313, refers to the agreements as "truly landmarks."

83. Quoted in Atkinson, *The Roots of Ethnicity*, 313.

84. For a comprehensive analysis of the reasons behind the failure of the talks — and the possibilities they realized — see Mareike Schomerus, "Even Eating You Can Bite Your Tongue: Dynamics and Challenges of the Juba Peace Talks with the Lord's Resistance Army" (London: London School of Economics and Political Science [LSE], 2012).

85. Several analysts and specialists have considered the military and civilian implications of Operation Lightning Thunder and subsequent multinational pursuits: Ronald Atkinson et al., "Do No Harm: Assessing a Military Approach to the Lord's Resistance Army," *Journal of Eastern African Studies* 6, no. 2 (2012): 371–82; Mareike Schomerus and Kennedy Tumutegyereize, "After Operation Lightning Thunder: Protecting Communities and Building Peace" (London: Conciliation Resources, 2009); see Branch, *Displacing Human Rights*, chapter 7, for an analysis of the geopolitical interests driving the military strategy in the region; also Ronald Atkinson, "From Uganda to the Congo and Beyond: Pursuing the Lord's Resistance Army" (New York: International Peace Institute, 2009).

86. Human Rights Watch, *The Christmas Massacres: LRA Attacks on Civilians in Northern Congo* (New York: Human Rights Watch, 2009); Ledio Cakaj, "Between a Rock and a Hard Place: LRA Attacks and Congolese Army Abuses in Northeastern Congo" (Washington, DC: Enough Project, 2010).

87. Ledio Cakaj, *The Lord's Resistance Army: An Architecture* (2013), http://ssrn .com/abstract=2253458; Kristof Titeca, *The Lord's Resistance Army in the Democratic Republic of Congo: Diverging Interest and Actions* (2013), http://papers.ssrn.com/so13 /papers.cfm?abstract_id=2253474.

88. Internal Displacement Monitoring Group, "Uganda: Need to Focus on Returnees and Remaining IDPs in Transition to Development" (2012), http://www .internal-displacement.org/countries/Uganda.

Africa. Illustration by Chrissie Arnold.

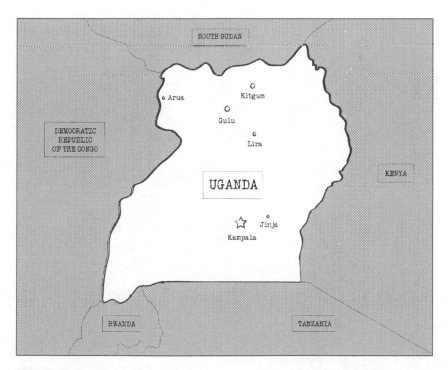

Uganda. Illustration by Chrissie Arnold.

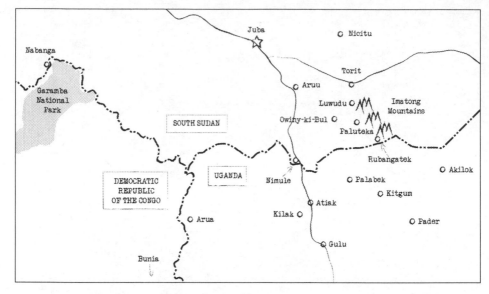

The border region of Uganda, South Sudan, and Democratic Republic of the Congo. Illustration by Chrissie Arnold.

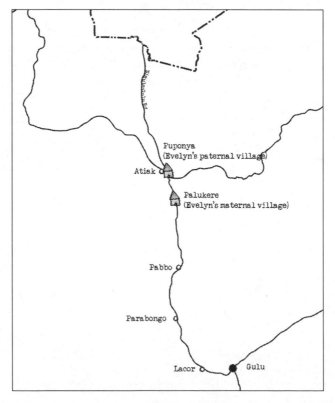

Places in Evelyn's childhood. Illustration by Chrissie Arnold.

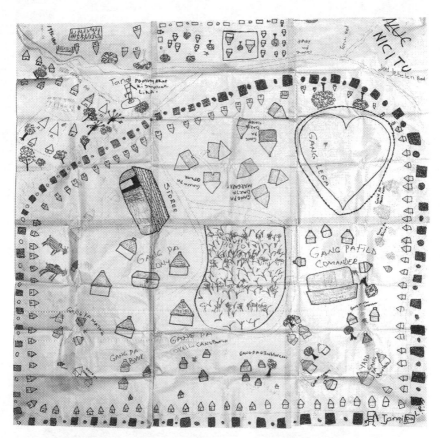

Nicitu, LRA defense in South Sudan. Located adjacent to a Sudanese military base, Nicitu was largely used as a safe area for mothers, children of rebels, and the injured. Pictured within the *adaki* (the protected base, indicated by darkened squares around its perimeter) are a hospital, a church with a heart-shaped yard for prayers, top commanders' homes, a garden, and livestock. Documented as part of a research project on forced marriage in Gulu, Uganda, 2010.

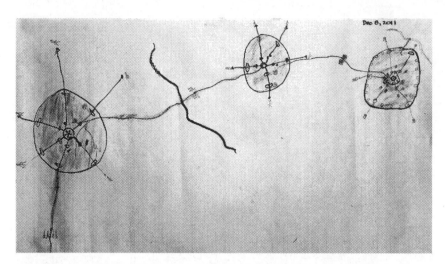

Configuration of an LRA position while on mobile. The three circles indicate a "position." Within, a commander would set up a temporary base and his officers would surround him. While the majority rested, soldiers would move around the perimeter of the position and set up a lookout guard some distance along the rail—the path where the LRA had walked single file (indicated by a line in the figure). The LRA would set up in the morning, afternoon, and evening to drink, eat, and rest but continued on mobile when outside their bases. Documented as part of a research project on forced marriage in Gulu, Uganda, 2010.

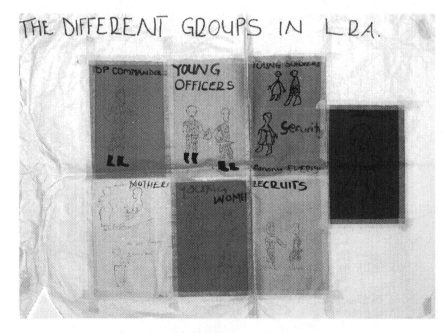

The different groups in the LRA: top commanders, young officers, young soldiers, security, mothers, young women, recruits, children. Documented as part of a research project on forced marriage in Gulu, Uganda, 2010.

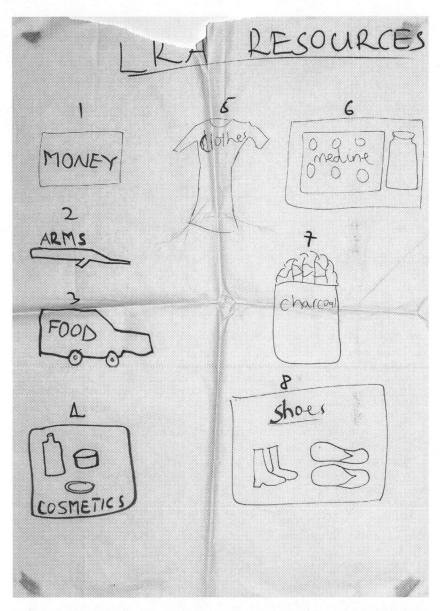

LRA resources: money, arms, food, cosmetics, clothes, medicine, charcoal, shoes. Documented as part of a research project on forced marriage in Gulu, Uganda, 2010.

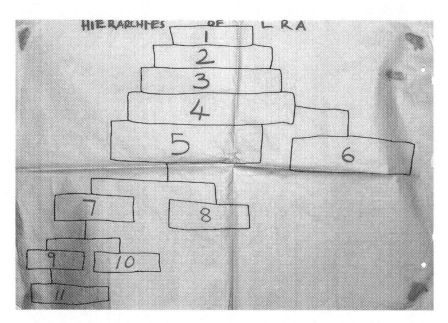

Military hierarchy of the LRA: 1. Chairman (Commander-in-Chief and General); 2. Vice Chairman (Chief of Operations); 3. Department Chiefs (Controller, Administration, Political, Intelligence, Security, Medical); 4. Brigadier General (in charge of the brigades); 5. Brigadier (in charge of one of the four brigades); 6. Colonel (in charge of one of the three battalions per brigade); 7. Major (in charge of a *coy* [company]); 8. Captain; 9. Second Lieutenant; 10. Lieutenant; 11. Private, Sergeant Major, Deputy Sergeant Major, Corporal, Lance Corporal. Missing are the *kuruts* (new recruits), who had no rank or official standing in the LRA. Documented as part of a research project on forced marriage in Gulu, Uganda, 2010.

I Am Evelyn Amony

1

Childhood

The Happiest Memories I Have

My name is Evelyn Amony. I was born on November 25, 1982, in my father's village of Pawiro Ato, Pupwonya Parish, in Atiak subcounty, Gulu District, Uganda. My parents' names are Marcelino and Margaret. Throughout most of my childhood, I witnessed the misery of war, and I think that is why my parents named me Amony. In Luo, my language, "Amony" means a period of war. I spent most of my childhood in my mother's village in Kalalo A, Palukere Parish, before I was taken to live with my father in his village, Pawiro Ato, when I was ten.

The happiest memory I have is when I received the second-highest grade in my class in Primary Four, at Pupwonya Primary School in Atiak subcounty. When my dad heard the news, he slaughtered a goat and gave me the liver. In Acholi, the liver is usually reserved for the elders; it is so delicious. We ate and drank sodas together like a party; my grandmother came and my cousins, too. The next term, I was abducted by the rebels, so I did not get to attend Primary Five.

When I was growing up, I wanted to become a nurse or a doctor. My best subject was science. Even my teachers knew I was good at it. Mathematics used to give me a headache. My highest score in math was only 70 percent, and this used to worry me so much. I loved to study, but the conflict spoiled it all. You never know, I might be blaming my spoiled education on the conflict, but I probably would not have continued with my education anyway; it was a struggle for my parents to pay school fees.

As I was growing up, my favorite food was *boo lakolong* [fried greens]. Even if you prepared the most delicious meat, I would prefer to eat *boo*. If I spent two weeks without eating *boo*, then life was not good.

We were five children in total to my mother, but my elder sister, Nancy, died when she was still young, before I was even born. So I was the eldest of three other children. My father brought a second wife into our home, and although she gave birth to ten children, only seven survived. So I am the oldest of ten other children in total. My mum was my dad's first wife.

My mum was not a jealous person. She even used to take care of orphans without any segregation; it was difficult for someone to tell which children belonged to her and which ones did not. My mother raised my uncle's children after he and his wife passed away. This is one reason why I am taking care of orphans today.

My mother used to teach me very many things. She used to say that even if we meet a lame person, a person with leprosy, we should not insult them. She told me that I could even dine with a person with leprosy, that I should have no fear. I remember one day she made us eat together with a man who had leprosy. I did not want to share a meal with him and cried very bitterly. She spoke to me afterward and told me not to fear because I would not contract the disease. I will never forget that incident. My mum taught me how to live with people well.

My mother walked us to and from school every day. She was always very happy to see me. On the way home from school she used to ask me what the teacher had taught us that day. My mum instilled in me the importance of education. She used to tell me that I should be a disciplined girl at school and that, instead of playing about, I should take my studies seriously. She used to say that if she ever learned that I had missed school I would be in serious trouble. She made me value studies, and so I took them seriously. That is why at the moment I try my best to ensure that my own children go to school. I also want to teach them everything my mum taught me concerning studies.

In school I was actively involved in athletics. I was a star in most of the races; it was only the one-hundred-meter race that used to challenge me. I used to compete with both boys and girls. Because of my success in running, so many people loved me. I had a lot of friends in school, but my best friend was a girl called Grace. When Grace was absent from school, I would find life difficult. She made me happy. She was nice. Another friend was a boy named Daniel. All of the other children would run away from him because he had a big wound that stank. One day he came to me and asked, "All the others won't let me sit with them. Can I share a desk with you?" So I let him, and we became good friends. I liked him because he was a very bright boy. I was his friend up until I was abducted. I have not seen him since I was taken. After I escaped I looked for him, but I was told he is now in Kampala. I saw Grace's daughter at her mother's house but was told that Grace is now married and living in Moyo district.

When I was abducted and taken into captivity, I used to worry a lot about my mum. I used to miss the way she would take good care of me, the way she would cook for me, prepare my bed at night, and help me to wash my clothes. When I was in captivity, the kind of women I met made me miss my mum even more. Kony's wives would beat me so much; they would call me so many names, and I had no one to talk to. Yet, when I was still at home, my mum would never do such things to me. My mum was so important to me; I miss her so much, and I think of her every day. Life from home was sweet.

My Grandfather

In Primary Three, my maternal granddad asked my dad to send my siblings and me to live with him. The old man did not have any young children to help him with his animals on his farm; most of his own children had already died. My mum used to say that my granddad had money and a lot of property. He was the *jago* [the parish chief] in Atiak and used to trade in hides and skins in Jinja. Life at his place was truly enjoyable except we were forced to look after his cattle. Being young, we saw this job as a punishment as it was hard work. He did not want us to go back to our dad's home or to go to school. Instead, he got us grandchildren to look after his cattle.

The cattle were kept a mile toward the sunset away from the main road. He had so many cattle! Very early every morning we had to herd his cattle to the fields, watch over them, and then herd them back in the evening. We felt it was a burden to us and that we were too young to do this. So, one day, we hatched a plan to drive the cattle into a neighbor's garden so that they would ruin the crop and force my granddad to pay for the damage. We thought that if we did this, he would no longer insist that we tend to his cattle. So one morning we drove the cattle into a nearby garden and then climbed into a tree and watched as they destroyed the millet and maize growing there. We waited until the sun began to set before heading back home, but the owner of the garden came and captured three cows that he planned to keep as compensation for the cows that destroyed his millet.

As we drove the remaining cattle home, we came up with a story: "If granddad asks us what happened, then we shall tell him that we were bathing when the animals went and destroyed the crops." So, when we reached home, that is what we told him, but he was upset and started knocking our heads and said that we were the ones that were going to pay for the detained animals. He said we purposely drove the cattle there and that we were very much aware that there were gardens up the hill, so why else would we have taken the cattle to graze there?

Our grandmother stepped in and told him to first wait for those who had detained the cattle because they would definitely come. It was not long before the owner of the garden and his wife came over to discuss the issue of the cows. When cows destroyed people's gardens it was considered a very big crime, and so many people gathered at our place. We were accused of intentionally driving the cattle into that garden. We just kept denying it.

Finally I decided to speak the truth, and I narrated what happened. Everyone agreed with me that "This is how people should be, when someone does wrong, she should say the truth and acknowledge it." They said our granddad should pay for the damage caused in the garden, and he paid for it with one cow, which the owner of the garden gladly took.

My Grandmother

My maternal grandmother tells me that when I was a girl, I used to love to work. I would wake up very early in the morning and dig in the garden before I went to school. I was never late for school like my friends were.

Typical of village life, one had to dig and fetch water before going to school, unlike in town here where a child wakes up and just goes to school without doing any house chores first.

Despite the fact that I was still young, my grandmother had taught me how to do nearly everything. That is why my grandmother said I loved to work. Even after school, when most of the children my age preferred to play games, I would go straight home to begin to fetch water. I wouldn't get to play until the moon had risen. But as much as my grandmother took me to be a very hardworking person, I felt she used to overload me with work. She made me prepare dishes like meat or very delicious edible rat. Just as everything was prepared and ready to serve, she would send me back to the kitchen to begin grinding millet. As everyone else was feasting, I would start to grind flour for the following day. I would eat only much later on.

My grandmother said she did that to make us responsible people in the future. She wanted us to know how to do lots of things. When grandmother found you grinding millet flour, she would get a small portion and throw it on the wall, and if it scattered on the floor, it was not fine enough. She would hold your hands hard on the grinding stone, and that is how I learned how to grind so well. Grinding millet was much simpler than grinding *sim sim* [sesame seeds]. So whenever I was sent to grind *sim sim*, I would collect some and throw into the drum to reduce the quantity that had to be ground. But there was this day when my grandmother came looking for something in the drum and there she found the discarded *sim sim*—it had never crossed my mind that I should instead throw these things out rather than put them in the drum because she might check in there. To me that was the best hiding place.

Swimming

In Pawiro Ato, I used to love swimming. There was a swamp in our area called *opara*, and that is where I would go swimming. One day, some girl who used to stay close by our place tried to strangle me under this water. I drank a lot of water; my whole eyes were very red. Ever since then, I have feared water. I got to know that water is dangerous. We were just kids, and to her it was a game, not a fight. She thought by pushing me into the water, she was just hiding me. I drank a lot of water, and when I reached home, my eyes were still red, and I fell very sick just a few days after. That is how I abandoned swimming altogether. I had a great phobia of water. When I was abducted, there was no choice; you had to enter water to cross a river when they told you to. Even if you were to say, "I hate water," you had to cross deep rivers and swim to the other side.

Auction Day

One day my dad took me to a tailor at the trading center in Atiak to make a new school uniform for me. This was around 1992. It was the month when children report back to school for first term. During this time, the bushes are burned and fresh grass begins to grow. It was auction day, and the surrounding villages had brought their livestock to sell in the trading center.

Soldiers were everywhere. We were allowed to enter the market, but soldiers did not permit anyone to leave. The NRA commander in charge was named Okot. He was an Acholi who hailed from Kitgum, a neighboring district to Atiak. Okot began to shout. He asked people to bring him the relatives of the rebels, but everyone just ignored him. He then spoke in parable. He said, "The heads of silver fish can make a meal for many people." When I heard his statement, I took it literally and wondered, "Given the small size of silver fish's head, can it really be cooked?!" People laughed at Okot and did not take him seriously.

Okot continued to speak, insisting people identify the mothers and relatives of the rebels. He said that those who did not help him would soon know for sure that silver fish's heads can make a meal for a multitude. My father and I remained quiet as the tailor made my uniform.

Around 4:00 P.M. more soldiers arrived. Okot kept calling for the relatives: "If you know Opiyo Tong, come here; if you know Vincent Otti, come here." He mentioned several names of people who hailed from Atiak and were in the bush with the LRA. In reality, even if you had a relative in the bush, it was not you who gave them permission to go there. They did not consult you before going. The LRA just abducted people and forced them to join regardless of age. One could be an old man, but, once abducted, he was a recruit and had to do as he was told.

Okot pleaded in vain for the mother of Vincent Otti to come out. He called for Vincent Otti's sister, but she was nowhere. He then coughed very loudly and intentionally. One of the NRA soldiers from Atiak started shouting, "The people of Atiak are very stubborn. and the majority are in the bush!" That soldier talked as though he was not from Atiak, yet it was where he was born. Okot kept coughing. When he coughed hard, I was with an uncle from my father's side. He sold clothing in the market. My uncle said the soldiers were just wasting our time because now they had spent the whole day without being able to sell anything.

Okot coughed again, and immediately the soldiers started shooting people. They started with the tomato vendors. They shot innocent civilians who did not own a gun, mere tomato vendors. Eight women who were selling tomatoes were killed instantly. That day Okot acted as though he wasn't an Acholi.

My uncle was a well-built man. When bullets started to fly, he carried me and covered me with clothes in his market stall. He also lay close by me. He told me not to run. I was so terrified I just jumped up and started to run, but my uncle stopped me. A government soldier and his wife appeared and started sorting through clothes. The soldier would show different pieces of clothing to his wife as my uncle and I sat there watching them. My uncle suddenly jumped up and kicked the soldier, and he managed to take his gun. He then walked over to the woman and began to strangle her, saying he was ready to die that day.

If you had seen how people died in Atiak on that day! So many people were injured or killed. As my uncle was fighting, I took to my heels and ran. I thought the soldiers were going to kill both of us. As I was running, I pulled a muscle in my leg and fell down. All I could do was kick my legs and turn around in the same spot. An NRA soldier came and stepped on me. This soldier was running ahead of civilians trying to flee. As soon as he was far enough in front of them, he would turn back and shoot them dead. I watched him from where I fell do it again and again. As a girl ran past me, he shot her. She fell dead on an anthill.

This same NRA soldier then doubled back and picked me up. He carried me into the NRA barracks located not far from the town center. He started telling other soldiers that I was from his tribe. I was so afraid

I said nothing. He would hold my hair and whisper to me, "There is no Acholi who is as beautiful as you. You belong to my tribe." He spoke in broken Acholi. He asked me where my mother stayed, but I just cried. I had heard that this group belonged to the *tek gungu* group.[1] These were soldiers known for raping men and women during this time. I was very afraid.

The commander in charge, Okot, arrived in the barracks with soldiers who carried goods looted from the market. They started talking about how the massacre was the fault of the rebels. When things calmed down, these very same soldiers moved through the town and told civilians that the rebels had attacked and killed these people and that they were now there to protect them. It was so painful to listen to the very persons who had shot and killed those in the market now sweet-talking the civilians, as if they had saved them from the rebels. They said the rebels had come for Vincent Otti's relatives.

After the shooting at the trading center, someone had run to our home and reported to my family that my father and I were among the dead. In actual fact, I did not know if my father was alive or dead, nor did he know if I was alive still or not. This is common in war. People learn what happened to each other only afterward. My own father ran and hid and then made his way back home.

In the barracks, my aunt who was married to a government soldier in the barracks discovered that I was there. She was very tough and did not fear the soldier who held me. She told him to release me at once and then told me to run home. I started to move back the way I came, but as I neared the trading center the sight was unbearable, so I ducked back into the bush and made my way home. When I finally entered my father's compound, I found people weeping. They all thought I had been killed. All the food that had been prepared that day for supper just sat there, uneaten.

My family and I shifted a lot following the massacre, sleeping in different areas in the bush, but the insecurity was everywhere. Some days we fled NRA soldiers. Other days, we fled the LRA.

---

1. *Tek gungu* (to bend over hard, to kneel hard) was an infamous government practice of raping civilian men.

Escape from Gulu Town

One day my parents sent my sister and me to live in Gulu town with my uncle and his wife. I stayed there for nearly a year and attended Primary Three at Holy Rosary Primary School. My uncle's wife seriously mistreated us.

On weekends we would fetch water from morning until sunset on empty stomachs; I did not taste a single bite of food. If my auntie decided that Saturday should be for fetching water, then that is what we did for the entire day. Then on Sunday we might be told to do laundry for the whole day, and we might eat food only at 10:00 P.M. My aunt would feed her children, but not my sister and me as we worked. My uncle's wife would say that we were not her husband's children, so she did not know why she should be caring for us. If by any chance my uncle returned home during the day, she would tell him that we had finished eating and yet the reality was that we had eaten nothing. I said nothing to my uncle; I just kept quiet.

My aunt resented that my mother had left my father and returned to her parents' village. My mother told us we had gone home to take care of my grandmother, that it was her responsibility to care for her mother being the first born, but I knew in reality she wanted to just escape her co-wife. My uncle's wife saw this as a burden to her, and she resented it. She said that she had not married my uncle to come and look after so many people, and that is what made her behave the way she did toward us. She mistreated us so that we would flee her home.

Life at the hands of my uncle's wife was just too hard. One day, one of the neighbors even asked me why I stayed with them and suffered like a housemaid. I thought long about what this neighbor said to me. If even she could see that the way I was treated was harsh and unfair, then I needed to leave. That is when I decide to walk all the way home from Gulu town to Atiak. I knew that all I had to do was follow the main road all the way back. I could not get lost. I knew it was only the one straight road, as we had driven it many times.

I first ran along that road. I ran between Gulu town and Lacor. I would run and walk, run and walk. I continued to Awer and then rested a bit, then continued again to Parabongo. From Parabongo I went up to Agole Primary School, and then I reached Pabbo, where I met one of my relatives. When he met me, he asked me, "Why are you so dusty?" Then I told him that "I am on my way back to Atiak from town."

I explained to him how my aunt had treated me and that I had decided to just walk home. My relative became so overwhelmed and began to shed tears. He wondered how I could walk on foot all the way from town.

He told me, "Let's first go to my place and spend the night, and since tomorrow I am going to trade in Atiak, I will take you back to your grandmother's home in a vehicle." I stayed with him, and early in the morning we boarded a vehicle back home.

When we reached home, my grandmother was husking millet. She welcomed us, and then my relative started narrating to her what happened, and she vowed that I would never go back to town. Yet we also could not stay there at my grandmother's home. My uncle came one day and insisted that I return with him to Gulu, but my grandmother said no, that I should go to my father's home and get to know his family since this was my paternal clan. Later on, my uncle was killed by the LRA. As he was traveling between Gulu town and Atiak to sell his goods, he was caught in crossfire between the rebels and the soldiers and was shot dead.

That NRA Uncle of Mine

There was another uncle of mine who was an NRA officer. He was my grandmother's brother. He was based in Kotido, but, you know, soldiers move frequently. So one night he and his wife arrived in Kalalo A, in Palukere, and stayed in our home. He had four military escorts with him. That evening around six o'clock my grandmother told me to grind cassava to put in alcohol. There were three pestles. There was one that was heavy, another one that was fairly heavy, and another one that was light. I looked for the one that was light and then began pounding cassava. Our home was directly in line with the road. I saw people coming, carrying heavy loads. The LRA had arrived.

They entered the compound and found me pounding the cassava. I immediately thought to run into the house to warn my uncle that the LRA had arrived in our compound, but my legs would not move beneath me. The LRA began to ask me questions about where the NRA had put up their base.

My uncle overheard them talking to me from inside the house. The military escorts to my uncle were behind the house on the other side, and they did not know what was happening. Our home was big. The LRA began to raid our property when my uncle began to shoot them from inside the house.

My uncle's escorts suddenly appeared and began to shoot the rebels. Four LRA soldiers were shot and fell right in front of my eyes. Two women and a man were shot and killed right on the spot, while a fourth was injured.

One of the LRA soldiers picked me up and ran with me. They moved some distance and left me with a young LRA girl to guard me, but she was distracted, and so I ran. The LRA soldiers chased me, but I dodged them and hid behind some rocks. I was so afraid and thought I was going to die that day, but they ran past where I was hiding. I overheard them talking about the rebels who had been shot at my home. I spent the night hiding in the bush alone.

The [soldiers in the] NRA barracks nearby had heard gunshots and came to our home, where they engaged the LRA. The rebels had thrown what they had looted as they ran away, and I actually followed the trail of our belongings as I made my way home. As I ran, a stick had lodged itself in my leg; actually, it entered one side of my leg and came out another. So I just had to drag myself home. The pain in my leg was unbearable, yet I had to run for a long distance. I got a long stick to help me limp. I began to limp with the stick slowly. I came and crossed the road.

My mother was looking for me. My grandmother was also looking for me. My uncle was also looking for me. Before I reached home, my grandmother saw me. She realized I was injured and called the others to come and carry me. They all thought I had been shot, but it was only the stick that had pierced my leg. The more I tried to walk, the more swollen my leg became.

My grandmother asked a man to go and inform my father that I had been injured in an attack. He left by vehicle to go to the Atiak trading center, and, as he did not know what had happened to me, he told my father that I had been shot and needed to go to the hospital. Before long my father arrived on a bicycle. He rushed to come and carry me. My leg was swollen, and I could not sit on the bicycle. It was so swollen.

I was taken to Atiak hospital, but there was no doctor there, so we had to spend a night in the trading center before returning in the morning. I stayed at the home of my mother's cousin. My father left me there to recover.

This lady boiled water and nursed my leg. The water was very hot. She began to nurse my leg, but it only made it swell more. Later on, pieces of the stick were removed from my leg. I do not know how they managed to do it. I stayed at in the trading center until my leg healed, then returned to my grandmother's home.

Can you imagine that that NRA uncle of mine ran away and left us unprotected? We worried that the Holy [the LRA often referred to soldiers as "the Holy"] would retaliate against us because so many had been killed and injured by the soldiers at our home. They always took revenge.

My Grandmother Said We Should Die in Silence

One day the government soldiers and the rebels were around my mother's village in Kalalo A. One of my cousins was a rebel; his name was Simon. He and his men used to cook around our village. One day, the government soldiers came to our compound looking for my cousin by name. My grandmother and I were there. We denied that we knew him, but this only angered the NRA soldiers. They told us to get our things together and that they were going to take us to the church.

As we moved along the path with them, they stopped and asked our neighbors, "Who is a child of Simon?" My neighbor pointed at me and said, "This is the cousin of Simon, and that one is his aunt."

They separated my grandmother and me from the other civilians they had also forced to march with them to the church and told us to walk ahead. We were very frightened. When we reached the next compound, they locked us inside a grass-thatched hut. They threatened to set the hut on fire unless we told them the whereabouts of Simon. They would shout, "Where is Simon? Why did you deny knowing him? Are you also rebels?" After this discussion, they set the hut we were in ablaze, blocking the door.

My grandmother said we should die in silence. She told me not to cry, but the heat from the flame had become too hot to bear and I started shouting and crying. My chest was on fire. I felt as though I would die any minute. The whole hut was filled with smoke, and you could no longer even see where the door was. Before the fire consumed us completely, a Ugandan army commander kicked the door open and told us to run. As soon as we stumbled outside the hut, the roof collapsed, and we had burns on us from the embers and ash. My skin was blistered from the heat.

The commander was angry with the soldier who had locked us in the hut. He dragged him to a granary and tied him there, shouting angry words in a language that I could not understand. He set the granary on fire and continued to yell angry words. The soldier screamed in terror. They then untied him and began to beat him terribly. My grandmother understood this language and later told me that they had been angry at him for torturing us and wanted him to experience what he had done to us, warning him not to treat civilians in such a way.

Things then grew confusing quickly. The rebels attacked. My grandmother and I hid behind a nearby tree in fear of the bullets. We watched some of the soldiers get shot and fall to the ground. Once it was quiet, we came out of our hiding place and again started to run. Unfortunately, we ran straight into the soldier who had put us in the hut and set it on fire. He was alone, and the commander who had rescued us was not there. He looked at us with revenge. He stripped me of my shirt and used it to tie my arms behind my back. He then took off with my grandmother and left me there in the tall grass. I think he tied me up like that with the intention that I would be shot by one of the bullets that had again started to fly between the soldiers and the rebels. I would try to get up to run, but my arms were tied so tightly that I kept falling over.

Eventually the fight moved on, and the sound of bullets faded into the distance. A man who used to help my father with the cattle found me. He untied me and took me home. My grandmother had been beaten terribly by the government soldiers. She said they had argued about whether or not to force her to go with them to western Uganda to become a birth attendant for the military. It was their commander who stopped them and let her go.

Even though I was abducted and eventually spent so much time in the bush, I remember my childhood as the most important part of my life. So much happened to me from my childhood to the time when I was abducted and taken to the bush. Actually throughout my life there were very few pleasant moments that happened to me.

Abduction

The rebels arrived in my grandmother's compound in Kalalo A in the late afternoon. It was a day in late August 1994. I was still eleven years old. They were wearing combat gear and had just arrived from Sudan. They had been sent to collect young boys and girls, thirteen years old and younger. Earlier in the day, the rebels had captured a young boy and told him to give them the names of children who would be returning home from school later on. The boy did that and then led them to my compound.

They were waiting for us when we arrived. I went into the hut to remove my school uniform, when I could hear them call my name. They said, "Which one is Evelyn Amony?" When I heard my name, I did not say anything. They called my name again and looked at me. I told them, "I am not the one. My name is Betty Ato."

I thought they would not abduct me if I could convince them I was someone else. But they did, and Betty Ato would become my name for the next eleven years.

As I knew the footpaths well and they were from a different part of Uganda, they asked me to show them the way. I started moving to show them the way. They had taken me, my best friend, Grace, and my cousin Moses, who was only a boy. They later released Grace because she was fat and the rebels said they did not want fat people.

As we started to move, I saw my grandmother and ran to her. The rebels got a big stick and started beating my grandmother. We began to move on, but my grandmother followed us; she did not want the rebels to take me. We moved a little further before the rebels stopped her and started to talk to her, telling her to go home. She continued to insist they release me. The rebels drew a line in the dirt and told her that if she crossed it, they would kill her.

They were carrying all of my grandmother's clothing, having looted it from our home. She told the rebels that they should go with all her things but to leave me behind since I was the only child she had to help her.

The rebels challenged her. They asked her, "How about us? Do you not think our grandmother asked for us? Do you even know how many we are in our family? Our mother did not give birth to many of us, and the rebels left them with no children in the home." My grandmother crossed the line and pled some more. They drew a new line. She again crossed it. The rebels grabbed my grandmum at once and tied her to a tree trunk very tightly. I was so worried when I saw her being tied on the tree; I thought they would kill her. As she cried out for us, the rebels forced us to move ahead and left her alive.

We eventually reached another compound, which happened to be that of my teacher. He was relaxing by the fire with his wife, and our sudden arrival surprised him. He was wearing gumboots, so the rebels thought he was a government soldier and just started shooting at him. He and his wife were fast; they ran and avoided being caught.

We moved further along now in the dark and crossed Ayugi River. At that point, I was given goods to carry on my head. When this happened, I started to cry. I cried and cried, and they went and got a cassava stem and started to beat me. We then continued moving. We would run and walk and duck when we were on major roads to avoid soldiers. We reached somewhere and started cooking food, and the next day we would keep moving.

We walked from place to place for more than two weeks without any purpose or sense until we arrived at Te Kilak and joined a brigade called Stockree. That was when we found a big commander called Raska Lukwiya, who started telling us that we are going for a rendezvous with the other battalions.

As he finished speaking to each of us, the soldiers alerted him that one of the newly abducted girls had tried to escape but that they had caught her and asked what should they do? Raska told them to take the new recruits for training so that the idea of escaping would leave our minds for good. Raska sent one of the young boys to go and cut branches from a tree and distribute them to us for "training."

We did not know that we were being sent to go and kill the young girl who had earlier attempted escape. We were taken somewhere and told to kill that girl, using the branches we were given, but by the time we got there she had already been killed by children who arrived before us. The place was close to a river; very many newly abducted children were gathered there.

As we had missed killing her, a new boy was brought before us to kill. I stood far from the boy and prayed and avoided hitting the child with a stick. I never touched him. Other children beat him until he died. When he was dead, we all went back to the position where Raska was, where we prepared for the rendezvous. We spent this last night in Te Kilak. In the morning we were told to go and bathe. After bathing, we were given a bag with clothes, bed sheets, and soap and left to meet the rest of the LRA.

2

Kurut

Pouring Sorghum

I had not yet been in the bush for long when the new recruits and I were told we would carry foodstuffs to Te Kilak, the location of the central LRA sick bay inside Uganda. Before we left, the leader of the LRA, Joseph Kony, assembled all of the new recruits and warned us that if we lost any of the food along the way, then we would face it rough. *Ladit* [an Acholi-Luo term of respect for a male elder] Kony told us that this was the only food the LRA had. He said that even if government soldiers attacked us along the way, we should not drop a single piece of food. He said that those who dropped food would be killed. *Ladit* Kony was very angry because some soldiers he had sent to loot food in the Atiak trading center had been shot dead by the Ugandan army. He said he would kill many people for this loss. I wondered if this rebel leader thought that people were hens that could be killed at any moment.

We walked and reached the position [a term used by the LRA to refer to a temporary or permanent base where the LRA rested while on mobile or that was established as a defense or hospital in the bush]. I carried sorghum in a basket on top of my head all the way to Te Kilak without incident. As I removed the basket from my head to put it down, some of the sorghum poured onto the ground. Around two cups of sorghum poured down.

One of the female commanders asked me who I thought was going to collect more food for the LRA. When *Ladit* [Kony] overheard the commander ask me that, he got up from where he was sitting beneath a tree and came to us. He asked me, "Young girl, are you the one who poured this sorghum?" I said, "When I was removing the sorghum from my head, it poured. I did not do it intentionally." *Ladit* Kony asked, "If all these people are taken to your mother, will she give enough sorghum for everyone to eat?" I thought that it was okay to answer him. I said, "If we are to go to our home right now, she will give you sorghum. There is a lot of sorghum in our home."

He asked me how much sorghum we had at home. I told him, "We have four granaries full of sorghum. If we are to go now, my mother can give around two full granaries of sorghum." I was reprimanded for answering him back. Kony sent for the young boys they called *youngus*. He told the *youngus* to beat me. He told them that if I cried, they should beat me with twice the number of strokes. He told them that if I even lifted my head in pain, they should shoot me dead.

A heap of sticks was brought. I was told to lie down. I lay down, and the *youngus* began to beat me. I did not cry or move. I do not know what happened to me because I did not react to the beatings. I felt an excruciating pain, and my body began to swell. My backside was swollen and bruised. Blood flowed out of my bruised skin and seeped into my clothing, gluing it to my body. When they were done beating my backside, they beat my neck.

I was given so many strokes on the neck and my backside. My neck was swollen. My backside was also swollen. When they were finished, I was told to get up, but I was unable to do so. I was so dizzy I could not do anything. I was told again to get up, but I could not. I could not stand up. My back made me so weak. I felt my strength deteriorate. My whole body was in pain. I couldn't do anything.

Later on in the night, *Ladit* brought me medicine and told me to take it. I was weak but decided not to take the medicine. I held the medicine in my hands. I was given water to take with the medicine. I pretended as though I had swallowed it but had not. I thought, "You have beaten me and now want to give me medicine to live? I would rather die. Was I really beaten for the little sorghum that I poured?"

When I remember this story, I feel heartbroken. It is painful to talk about, but I will do so. I was told to lie down. I lay down, and I must have passed out because the next thing I knew the sun was out. Kony sent a boy to check on me, to see if I was still alive.

One of the *youngu* who had beaten me, named Onek, pulled me up, but I just lay down again. I was told to sit up, but I could not. So, instead, I kneeled. *Ladit* wanted to see me, so I told Onek to hold my hand and take me to Kony. Onek held my hand, but as I tried to get up I fell down. My body began to shake. *Ladit* came and observed my state. He ordered someone to bring me porridge.

I was given fifty strokes on the neck, and it was painful. My neck was in pain. My backside was so injured that I could not sit. I prayed to God to let the soldiers attack us so that we would all die. I thought if we were attacked, at least one of the *youngu* who had beaten me would be killed. We stayed in the position for three days. I kept on praying.

Despite the fact that my neck was swollen, the *youngu* insisted that I grind rice because they wanted to eat rice bread. My neck pained a lot as I was grinding. When I went to bathe, I could not remove my knickers from my body because of the swelling. The threads of my knickers were stuck into the wounds. I called a girl named Stella to help me bathe. She boiled water and then poured it over my wounds. That was how the knickers slowly loosened from my wounds. Stella slowly removed the threads one by one. When Onek saw this, he just cried, even if he was the one who beat me. He said, "Is this how people are really beaten? For just sorghum!" We both cried. We were almost the same age.

Onek brought shea nut oil and fats from a python. Stella put the oil on my wounds; the pain cooled, and the swelling reduced. I could not move my neck. If I had to turn around, I had to move my whole body. My ears were also swollen where the sticks had landed. My hands were not beaten because I did not try to protect myself. Kony said people were beaten from the bush to make them brilliant. He said, "We want to make them clever so that they can be wise. There is no food here, and that is why we beat those who pour food. At home you cannot be beaten because of pouring food because there is plenty of food."

Kony annoyed me so much with those words. I have never told anyone this story. I did not even tell my mother about it because it is extremely painful to remember, but I feel I should talk about it so that people know what I went through.

How I Narrowly Missed Death

In Te Kilak one of the commanders insisted that I go to his home. I knew what he wanted, and so I hid. The commander called some young boys and ordered them to beat me to death for refusing to go to sleep in his home. As they began to beat me, you could hear *Ladit* Kony approaching; he was laughing with a high voice. At first I did not know it was Kony, and I wondered who could laugh just as another is about to die?

So many *youngu* had begun to run toward me to participate in killing me. The boys started whispering to each other that "Baba [father] is coming, Baba is coming." They threw down their sticks and ran away. *Ladit* came and found me alone. He looked at me and asked, "*Anyaka* [young girl], how are you?" I responded that I was fine. He asked, "Where is your home?" and I responded that I came from Atiak. He ordered his escorts to come and help me walk to the sick bay, where I was treated for my injuries.

Later on Kony ordered all those young boys who had been sent to kill me to come before him to explain what had happened. The commander who had ordered my death was arrested and brought to Kony to be questioned. Although he denied any involvement, the commander was beaten.

After I recovered, *Ladit* Kony took me to live in Otti Lagony's compound in Te Kilak. Lagony was one of the senior commanders. I stayed there for nearly a month before Kony sent some of his wives to come pick me up to bring me to his compound to live as a *ting ting* [LRA name given to helpers]. I refused to go. I had heard from other girls that Kony's wives were cruel and abusive and that they would turn me into their slave. I would be the one to wash all their clothes, cook their food, and do everything while they sat and did nothing. So I refused to go with the wives.

Kony had to come himself to pick me up. He told me I would become his son's babysitter and that I should not be afraid. I thought if I cried, he would leave me alone. Kony told me to "remove that civilian way of thinking from your mind; you shouldn't be crying like that." He told me his wives would take good care of me, and his escorts picked me up and carried me to their home.

Kony's wives began to mistreat me that very same day. One of his wives told me to go with her to the well to bathe. When we reached the well, she pushed me into the river. She told me, "You girl, you behave as if you are very special. You are bigheaded. I am going to teach you a lesson." She told me to give her my bag, and I did. She unpacked everything from the bag, my knickers, my soap, and my bed sheets, and took them as her own. I remained without anything.

Later on, in the middle of the night, when it started to rain, this very same wife threw me out of the house and told me to sleep in the rain. She said it was for my own good, to train me as a soldier and to remove the civilian way of thinking from my mind. She did this every night that it rained. I would sleep in the trench where running water would flow over my body. My body became pale.

Kony's wives would knock my head all the time. If *Ladit* called me and told me to take the baby to him to see, they would knock my head very painfully before I took the child to him. They would punish me anytime they felt like it, even if I had done nothing wrong. They used to say that *Ladit* liked me very much because he would call me all the time to do things for him. They told me that if *Ladit* called upon me to help him, I should not respond. I felt stranded. I feared that *Ladit* would punish me if I did not respond; yet if I did respond and go to him, his wives would beat me terribly upon return.

I wanted to escape, but it was difficult because security was so tight in *Ladit*'s home. It wasn't easy to escape that home, so I just stayed. I could not stop worrying and thinking about my home. I became sick, and *Ladit* accused me of planning to escape, that he could see it in my behavior. He told me to stop thinking about home. He told me that if I attempted to escape, I would become lost and just keep moving around Te Kilak in circles until I found myself back with them again. So I just continued living like that, with all that pain.

The Long Walk to Sudan

We left Te Kilak after celebrating Independence Day in October 1994. Kony told us that we were going to start a new life in Sudan. At the beginning of our journey, we had to cross the River Aswa, which was flooded due to the rain. We used to cross rivers by holding onto a rope tied between two trees on opposite sides of the river. As I crossed the River Aswa, I was pulled under as my jerry cans filled with water. Onek, the boy who had been forced to beat me, was also drowning.

As I was taken under the water, Kony and another man jumped into the river and rescued the boy and me. I had drunk a lot of water, and my stomach was full. They carried us across the river, and when we reached the shore the soldiers began to step on my stomach to make me vomit. I thought that they were trying to kill me.

Ladit ordered some people to "carry this *ting ting* and take her to the position," which was not far from the river. They brought a *kitar* [a makeshift stretcher] and carried me to the position. When we reached it, *Ladit* told one of his wives to make me diluted porridge to eat. My whole body was just shaking.

It was time to move again. *Ladit* asked me if I was able to walk, and I told him that I could, so we started moving toward Palabek. There were rules during that journey. Each brigade was supposed to move in a straight line called the rail; walking like this made it easier to move through the bush as those ahead formed a path, but it also allowed them to watch us. If you strayed from the rail or created a gap between yourself and the person ahead of you, you were pulled out of the line, taken to the bush, and killed. We continued to move like that the whole night. I would hear them say to *kuruts* [new recruits] who fell behind on the rail, "You should rest because you are tired and it has created a gap in the convoy." Those who were tired were taken to the bush and killed.

Every *kurut* was watched by a commanding officer. If you had to relieve yourself, you had to ask for permission from the officer, and he had to accompany you. If you tried to relieve yourself without permission, you were beaten, and sometimes you were killed. Those who didn't follow the rules of the journey would be sorted out of the line and taken away.

At times, I could hear people being beaten to death in the bush as I passed them on the rail.

One day we found a homestead, where the granaries were full of *sim sim*, rice, and groundnuts. There were also bananas. We spent a night in this homestead, and in the morning each of us was given foodstuff to carry; I was given two basins of rice and a basin of millet. It was very heavy, and I struggled to carry it without creating a gap in the line.

Ladit Kony met me on the way, and, after seeing me struggle, he took one of the basins from me and said that it was better if he carried it himself. His soldiers immediately removed the load from him. Kony told me to stay close to him; otherwise, I would fall behind and be killed.

We ran out of food before we reached Sudan. We bumped into a civilian homestead before reaching Pajok, where the owner had planted bitter cassava. People began to uproot and eat raw cassava. We also ate certain fruits called *oceyo*, but that fruit caused people to vomit like nothing. That is what people ate during that time.

Most of the children I moved along the rail with died of cholera, hunger, or thirst. Others died when they fell behind on the rail. In the morning, you could wake up and find your friend had died in the night. They would look as if they were asleep. They resembled edible rats that had died from poison. People in Uganda said that the LRA abducted their children and exchanged them with guns in Sudan, but the truth is that they died of cholera. Many children died. We were all so tired. Kony encouraged us to continue walking. He would say, "Walk. You are about to rest."

By the time we arrived in Luwudu, an LRA base in Sudan, I could barely walk. My feet were swollen, with open wounds. I was told to go to Kony's compound to be a *ting ting* for his wives. I could no longer walk and had to crawl everywhere I wanted to go. Despite the pain I was in, his wives insisted that I cut grass needed to construct the rook of their huts. I cut grass from morning to late evening. I would cut the grass, tie it and put on my head, and then crawl with it back to Kony's compound. I could not take a single step, I was in such pain. I suffered so much in the hands of these women.

There were male soldiers at *Ladit*'s place who were a bit kind to me. One day a soldier named Odora saw my feet and started asking Kony's wives why they were sending me to cut grass when there were people who are healthy. "Can't you see that her feet are swollen?" They responded, "If she doesn't do it, who will do it for her? Who came here to do work for her? Everyone walked to Sudan; who is she with swollen feet?"

I just tried to stay alone, by myself. I would sleep under a certain tree alone. One day my cousin managed to come and see me. She told me not to be hurt by the actions or words of Kony's wives and that things would soon improve. She was able to see me only once; it was against the rules to speak to your relatives. There were also rules against visiting another person's home. If you were caught, the LRA would question what you were looking for in another person's compound. No one was allowed to go inside *Ladit*'s home. If my cousin had come and been caught, she would have been killed. Kony's wives were deadly. They could have done something bad to her.

At some point, *Ladit* Kony realized the condition I was in, and he took me to one of the commanders, named Bogi. Kony told Bogi to look at how swollen my feet were, and Bogi became disgusted by Kony's wives. "These sisters of mine are evil, they behave like Satan, they never mind about their colleagues." My feet were cleaned, and I was taken to the hospital immediately, where I was injected every morning. Bogi took me there every morning. We were from the same village. Bogi was from Atiak Pacilo, and I am from Atiak Pupwonya, but in the bush we lived as relatives.

Military Training

In Luwudu, we began training. We learned to march and how to use a gun. On the days we marched, I would wrap Kony's son in a cloth and tie him to my back. When it came to cleaning the guns and trying them out, I left the baby at home because Kony told me that an accident could easily happen during training as some people were just learning how to fire a gun. We would clean, dismantle, and reassemble the guns once a week, every Friday. From Monday to Thursday we would march.

The trainers woke us up at 5:00 A.M., and we would march up to 9:00 A.M. Then we would go for *fallen* [assembly], where all soldiers would attend a roll call and be assigned work. The training lasted two months, and everyone did it, whether you were new or experienced. After the training, people were given guns. I was also given a gun. I was completely afraid of guns, and the training was difficult. We were all so hungry; as *kuruts* we had little to eat. People died like nothing in Luwudu due to starvation. If you were found stealing food, you were punished.

The worst thing that happened during that time was portering *tin* [ammunition] and food. The Sudanese leaders supplied us with food and fighting weapons, so we needed to walk long distances to meet the

Arabs in Torit and then carry supplies back to the LRA base. I carried these things on my head until my hair fell out and I developed open wounds that became infected. If I did anything wrong, it was that bald head of mine that would be knocked. My feet were not any better.

However much I tried to tell those people [LRA commanders] that I was in pain, they never once let me rest but constantly sent me to carry *tin*. It was one of the most painful periods of my life. I had just arrived in Sudan and was newly abducted, but I had to work and work. I walked until my feet healed in the process of walking. It reached a point when the pain disappeared on its own. I tried to escape when we were in Luwudu, but I was caught and beaten severely. The people who beat me are all now dead from battle. Many people tried to escape, but if you were unlucky and they caught you, they beat you to the extent that you couldn't even sit.

Gong

Eventually I was relocated to a new base in Sudan called Gong, a place that was flat. There I had guard duty and had to stay awake all night long. As a *kurut* you were not allowed to cover yourself with anything at night. The officers used to say that the gun was our bed sheet. There was a bathroom. A tunnel was dug to allow water to flow out from the bathroom. I slept in that tunnel. I put my feet in the tunnel and covered myself with a sack. The sack was my bed sheet. There were so many mosquitoes, and I had bites all over my body. The sack made my body itch.

The older recruits would walk around at night to monitor the younger ones, and if they found you asleep they would take your gun. When your gun was taken in the LRA, you were imprisoned in the military [prison] and beaten. This was to discourage you from sleeping in the night. I slept in the bathroom to avoid being caught. No one would ever imagine that a person could sleep in such a place. I slept like a dog.

I was so thin, and my head was still bald from carrying *tin*. The boys in *Ladit*'s home nicknamed me "bitch" because it was hard to differentiate between me and a dog. They said that even if I was to become a wife, I would give birth to puppies. I had rashes, and my head was bald. If you have never been a rebel, you cannot imagine what I went through. Someone finally realized that I covered myself with a sack and took it away. While I lived in Gong, I used to pray that God would take my life quickly. I will never forget about that sack. I used to think about my mum, I used to think about home, but I knew there was nothing I could do.

There was no food. The pain from hunger made me steal. Rules against stealing in the LRA were very strict. Another girl and I would steal food and hide it in the tall grass. When we were sent to cut grass we would eat it. We promised each other not to tell anyone about it. Eventually a hut was built for the *ting ting* to sleep in, in Kony's compound, and we could rest. All of this happened when we were in Gong.

The Work of a *Ting Ting*

After Gong, I was moved to a base in Palutaka. The LRA had captured this base from Sudanese rebels [referred to as the Dinka, or SPLA]. It had brick buildings, a hospital, streets, and an airfield. The houses had an iron roof. *Ladit* placed each *ting ting* into one of the homes of each of his four senior wives. We were told that wherever these big women went, we had to go with them as escorts. Even if these women were going to fetch water, we had to move with them and carry their guns.

I was assigned to the house of Kony's first wife, Fatima. She had two young children, both of whom were boys. I had to do everything for those boys. I had to bathe them, wash their clothes, feed them, and so on. Their mother did nothing. Luckily enough, Fatima's children were not bad. They did not cry as long as they were healthy. The only problem was that the younger one sometimes bit me. He once bit me so hard that I could still have a scar up to now. He wanted to be carried everywhere. If I put him down, he would cry, and Fatima would become so angry with me. I never punished him for biting me for fear that Fatima would beat me.

The work was so heavy. In the mornings I had to wash clothes for the children. When I finished washing their clothes, I would go and fetch water. I would then clean Fatima's house. After I finished mopping the house, I fetched more water. I would scrub the saucepans clean, even very dirty ones that had been cooked black. As a *ting ting*, I had to make sure everything was spotless and that there was always enough water. I had to sweep the compound each morning and fold the bed sheets that had been used the night before. Some days I woke up very early in the morning and would go with the other *ting ting* to fetch firewood. After the morning work was done, we would begin cooking; I would then pick the clothes that I had earlier on washed and iron them. Fatima would not give me any soap to wash the clothes, but I was expected to clean them very well or I would be beaten. When Kony discovered how the *ting ting* were being abused, he called us together and accused his wives of being lazy.

The Battle of Owiny-ki-Bul

One day Kony announced an attack against the SPLA in Owiny-ki-Bul. Kony was angry because the SPLA had killed many of his commanders at another base, called Pajok. I was still a coward who had never fought, but I wanted to avoid the continuing mistreatment of Fatima. In my heart I felt that if I was to die then I should die in Owiny-ki-Bul.

The LRA united together with the Arabs [the Sudanese Army], and we left in six large lorries. The Arabs said that they were fighting with us so that we could return home to Uganda. They said we were going to overthrow the government of Uganda. A lot of weapons were brought. Morale was very high. We entered the region of Owiny-ki-Bul around 9:30 in the morning. Kony himself traveled with the convoy, and he ordered his men to shoot rounds in the air to show the SPLA that we were strong.

As we approached the defense, we saw that the SPLA had tied corpses to poles to make it appear as if they were soldiers standing on guard. The corpses had uniforms and guns in their hands as though they were shooting at you. We fought at Owiny-ki-Bul for three days before the Ugandan soldiers came. They began to shoot us very early in the morning on the banks of the Atebi River. I was among the first people in the battalion to go to the riverside to defend the LRA.

When I reached there, a soldier shot me with a rapid gun. I dived and fell down. From where I lay on the ground, I started to shoot him. I do not know if it was me who shot him or someone else, but the soldier fell dead. I removed his guns, gumboots, and clothing. You know, in order to prove to LRA commanders that you fought you have to charge [take items belonging to the soldier you killed]. I took the soldier's gun and uniform and returned to the base. When *Ladit* Kony saw me, he told me to go away and not to return until I had put on the dead soldier's uniform, yet it was covered in blood. He told me that the uniform now belonged to me.

I went to the Atebi River and began to wash the uniform, but I was scared. I felt nauseated by the smell of blood. There was a girl called Aturu. She came and said, "Betty, you are a coward." She then washed the uniform. In the evening, when I was ironing the uniform, it still smelled of blood. I ironed the uniform and then hung it up. After we captured Owiny-ki-Bul, we rested, but you could not eat because the smell of the corpses was unbearable. Dogs carried parts of dead people. Being a soldier is funny. You cannot eat if you are not strong. You will refuse food until you reach a point when hunger overtakes you and you finally begin to eat.

The *Katusa*

We lived in Owiny-ki-Bul for several months before I was selected to go and train. *Ladit* Kony said I should learn how to use every gun starting from the mine to the B-10 and even the weapon used for shooting an airplane, called the *katusa*. The *katusa* looks like a computer. You first selected the number of bullets you wanted to fire and the pattern you wanted to fire them in; you then pressed a button, and it would fire. We traveled by car and parked some distance from a Dinka detach [military outpost], got out, and fired a shell from the *katusa* into the detach. We watched what was happening using binoculars. The Dinka retaliated and shot bombs, which fell near me. The soldiers I had come with jumped in the car and drove off very fast, leaving me behind. I had no other choice but to walk back alone along the road to Owiny-ki-Bul. Every time a car drove past, I squatted on the road side and hid. It became very late, and I was feeling hungry before I finally reached the defense.

In the morning, an Arab plane came to bomb the Dinka. It was an antinob. When an antinob detonates a bomb, it digs a huge hole. That day the Arabs accidently dropped bombs on the LRA and the Arabs in Owiny-ki-Bul, instead of on the Dinka. I was at the well when the first plane came. I had gone with a woman called Major Aol. I was still fetching water, while the Major was climbing a hill carrying her water.

The hill was slippery, so I warned her not to fall. I told her, "You will fall; the banks of Atebi are slippery." She said, "Do not worry, I am going to climb it, Betty." Just as she said this, a bomb detonated. Those in the plane thought that we were the Dinka. The bomb detonated on the very spot Major Aol stood. I saw Major's clothes on the tree. Her flesh scattered all over. That day I ran and stayed for three days without defecating. I lost all the feces from my bowels. There was nothing completely. I could not even eat. I was mourning that woman. If mourning could make people come back to life, then Major would have come back to life. When you see people's flesh scattered by bombs, then you will never eat meat again. It got dark after a short time. I went back to the defense, and everyone was in the *adaki* [defense around the perimeter of a base or position where soldiers live and sleep]. I could not even sit. My body was shaking.

Information about Major Aol was conveyed to the central command, and *Ladit* Kony and Lagony arrived to discuss the matter. You know, Lagony was a person who stared a lot. When you served him food, he looked at you from head to toe. If you had not combed your hair, he would not eat your food. If you had not cut your nails, he would not eat your food. That man was so different. The day Lagony came, he started looking at me. I also decided to look at him, so that we were both staring at each other. I looked at him so much that I decided that I had also become bad. I then left.

That day the antinob killed more than three hundred people in Owiny-ki-Bul. When the Arabs learned that their plane had accidently dropped bombs on the LRA and their own soldiers instead of the Dinka, they were so annoyed. They sent their soldiers to the river banks in Atebi and fought the Dinka. They said that they were going to fight until we reached Uganda. When the battle was over, the Arabs looked for the bodies of the commanders and carried them away, but the corpses of privates were all put in one grave. So many people were buried in one grave.

Soldiering in Uganda

After the battles in Owiny-ki-Bul, we returned to Uganda in a convoy. We constantly moved from place to place, from Kitgum to Te Kilak and to a place called Akilok. Wherever the sun set we spent the night. We fought the UPDF, not every day but often.

Sometimes it was calm, and we would spend a whole week in one place. We moved in lines; each line was a brigade, and together we were a convoy. When we left a place, you could tell that the number of people was huge because the people leading the lines would arrive in the position and be finished cooking by the time the last one in the line had arrived.

The brigade I was in was called Control Altar, with Kony. When we fought, the women also participated in battles because the UPDF did not differentiate between the LRA and the abducted; they would just shoot anyone. The journey was very hard. It is because God loves me that I survived. Others died of hunger and thirst. The only person that was kind to me in the bush during this time was Kony.

He Did Not Laugh Anyhow

There was an LRA commander in Uganda called Ocii. He was ruthless. He had no respect for people; whether you were a mother or a father, he treated everyone in the LRA equally. I remember once he beat me because I had made a gap in the line. People remarked to him, "You beat the *Ladit*'s *ting ting*. You are bigheaded." He said, "Everyone is a soldier when they are on the way."

The man was rude and tough. He did not spend a day without beating his wives. During battles he beat people to go and fight on the front line. He said, "Run! Run! Run! Go to the front line." There are rude people and there are humble people; each has a different leadership style. A person who handled the *kuruts* in a good way was liked, but a rude person like Ocii was hated. No one wanted to live in Ocii's home. He was never merciful. People in the LRA had different characters just like at home. It was Ocii's character to be rude.

Every person is different. Whenever I was told to beat someone, I always cried. I knew that he or she would feel pain from the beatings just like I did. I used to cry so much after I was beaten. I found it painful. I never cried when I was being beaten, but later, when I was alone. If you started crying as you were beaten, they would double their efforts. If you were to receive fifty strokes and you cried, they would start counting from the beginning again. You were beaten afresh. You were beaten until you could no longer sit. I feared beating any one, and it was painful when Ocii beat people. He even pointed guns at his fellow officers. That was the life we led from the bush.

There was a time Ocii was shot in the head and chest. People said that he should be left to die so that we could rest. Imagine, if he exercised such violence on those who were in the bush, then what was the level of violence he exercised on civilians? If he did not have mercy on people he walked and lived with—even his wives—then how did he treat a civilian? These are the things I remember about Ocii. He did not laugh anyhow. He was always sad. Those who knew him from his home said that was also his character as a child. These are some of the few things that I knew about Ocii.

Attempting Escape

One day we moved to Lango, reaching there after four days of walking without rest. Even vehicles rest during a long journey! We moved day and night. At times we would walk while sleeping. You would not say that you are tired. You would just sleep, and when the guards came they would carry you.

Along the way, I tried to escape. As we crossed a road, I remained behind and hid among the trees. I told myself that my legs would return me home. We crossed the road at around five o'clock. I decided to lie down and escape after the LRA had left. As I waited, I fell asleep.

When Vincent Otti noticed that I was not among those who had crossed the road, he came to look for me with eight of his men. All of them were commanders. I woke up and could hear them speaking to each other. Vincent Otti told the others that what I had done was very dangerous because if the government soldiers had found me, they would have killed me.

I kept quiet. Vincent Otti was saying, "Betty's sick leg must have made her stop somewhere. Betty cannot escape. If am to find her, I will cane her even if she is sick."

When I heard him talk like that, I got up and went toward where they were, but the government soldiers came and began to shoot me. I just started to walk away slowly as if I were not a rebel. The government soldiers started to approach me, but when they saw that I was dressed as a rebel they began to shoot me again.

One of the LRA commanders who had come to look for me ran toward me. He took my gun and began to shoot at the government soldiers. They began to exchange bullets. I could not run. The commander told me to run, but I could not. My legs would not carry me. I had given up on life. I told God to take away my life if possible. My legs were so swollen. The government soldiers soon retreated, and Vincent Otti and the other commanders carried me to the position.

I had a wound in the middle of my foot. My legs were swollen, and I could not remove the gumboots. My legs were in pain. Vincent Otti told his wife to boil water. You know, when the evening comes gumboots stiffen, so I had to heat the gumboots until they softened and I was able to remove them. My legs had swelled. My feet smelled. I had moved for three days without removing my gumboots. Vincent Otti began to nurse my legs. Eight penicillin tablets were crushed and put in my wound. I thought that my wound would never heal. He nursed my wound, and I was given tea.

One of *Ladit* Kony's escorts told him that I was at Vincent Otti's place. *Ladit* asked what I was doing there. He worried that Vincent Otti would think that he was not taking good care of me and told the escort to bring me back. The escort came and told me that *Ladit* had sent for me. Vincent Otti said that he had just put medicine on my wound. He told the escort to wait for the medicine to dry, and then I could leave. Vincent Otti removed the sandals from his wife's feet and gave them to me to put on. He told me not to bandage my leg before the wound healed.

When *Ladit* saw me, he felt ashamed. He began to tell his escorts, "How can Vincent Otti nurse Betty's wounds as though you are not around? It is your work to nurse her wounds. She cannot even walk. If she were to die it would be because of you. You are not giving her attention. You are all soldiers. You can get wounded any time. As long as you are still rebels, you can get wounded. You need to help your colleagues. They can get hurt any time. You can wake up when you are fine but then get wounded at any time. You can walk absentminded when someone has put bullets in the magazine waiting to shoot you." I do not know whether it was because Vincent Otti and I are from the same village that he helped me, or what.

Protecting Kony

I was one of those people who were so afraid of being on the front line and afraid of even holding a gun. One day we were moving toward

Atiak when the government soldiers [by then the NRA had been re-named the Ugandan People's Defense Forces, or UPDF] attacked our convoy. So many people were shooting at each other in all directions. A bomb detonated close to me, throwing me into the air. I ran for approximately a mile and hid.

When things had cooled, I went back to pick up my bed sheets that I had thrown; bed sheets were so important to protect yourself from the cold at night. As I searched for them, people started firing again, and the battle was tense. The bombs fell here and there. You know, soldiers never want the other side to be the last to fire, so they keep firing back and forth at each other.

I escaped death three times that day. I started running, and four of us separated from the rest of the group: a young girl, a boy, *Ladit* Kony, and myself. We needed to hide. The UPDF must have captured someone from the LRA side and learned that Kony was part of the group, so they were not going to give up looking for him. Two government planes arrived and began to shoot, but they kept accidently shooting UPDF soldiers.

At about 2:00 P.M., I climbed a tree to see what was going on. To my surprise, I discovered that where we were hiding was just next to an area where the UPDF was sheltering wounded soldiers. I slowly climbed down the tree and thought, "God, I wish you could give me wisdom and a way through." I went to *Ladit* Kony and said, "*Lapwony* [teacher], we are very close to our enemies; remain here as I climb back on the tree." I climbed, and I could see the UPDF below as they began to carry the injured soldiers to a new location. The plane returned and started shooting . . . *gwing* . . . *crrrooom* . . . *bimb* . . . those were the sounds of the big bombs; you could also hear the small ones sounding like *tattaaatata* . . . *taratara* . . . *rarara* shooting line by line. I had to climb down the tree and hide.

From where I was hiding, I could see the plane swoop down closer to the ground. I had an SMG [submachine gun] and started shooting at the plane, I hit it . . . *twa twa twa* . . . then the plane stopped shooting so it could dive down to a lower altitude to identify my location. I started shooting them rapidly . . . *tata tata tata tata* and the plane went away. I rolled very fast and shifted from where I was. Two planes came this time and descended close to the group and started firing and bombing;

they bombed the tree where I was and uprooted it. I said, "God, you still want me to live . . ." I shifted to another place. I moved a bit, and the plane again started shooting . . . *krim kroom krim kroom*. When the plane shot, you could see gas . . . something like tear gas . . . it was very dusty. We used to call it *muganga*.

I left and went to *Ladit* and told him, "*Ladit*, you know what? It seems we are now on our own; let's leave this place. You first remain here as I go and patrol the place." I checked the area and found a place we could pass through. I came and told *Ladit* it was time to go. So we started moving; we moved a bit, then I stopped *Ladit* and said, "First stop here and wait for me." I entered a homestead that had been abandoned, and I found so many things. There were sweet potatoes being peeled in the compound; chickens were all over the place. I did not mind about these things but told God that I am only looking for *moo yaa*—shea nut oil.

I entered the house and found where they had just been making the shea nut oil! I found an Oxfam container and filled it with the *moo yaa*. I tied a black plastic bag around the container, and we started moving. The LRA were on the other side of Unyama River, and I was the one leading the way in our group. *Ladit* was right behind me. Suddenly, a certain boy called Okello just jumped into the road in front of us and started firing rapidly at me. He asked me, "*Mimi kitu gani*" [Kiswahili slang—meaning, whatever, what is up?]. I kept quiet. We had a certain way of talking to each other; for example, if you heard someone say "*gunya*" [chimpanzee], you were expected to respond, "*wayo gwok*" [a dog's aunt]. Then I immediately said, "*Gunya*," and he responded, "*Wayo gwok*." When we realized we were both LRA, we ran to each other.

The boy thought that I was alone, and he asked me, "Where is *Ladit*?" I told him that *Ladit* was there. As soon as he saw *Ladit* approach us, he threw his gun to the ground and said that he had never missed, he always hit his target when shooting, and that his plan was to shoot me and shoot whoever was behind me. But he said, "It's great that I missed hitting you; that means God hasn't yet planned that I be the one to kill *Ladit*. I could have killed him today!" He threw away the gun and said he never wanted to use one again.

We reached the position by nightfall. There were so many injured people, and many more had been captured. When people saw me, they started to run to me and say, "*Mego* [Acholi-Luo word for mother] Betty has come, *Ama* [term of respect for a mother] Betty has come . . ." because they knew that I was together with *Ladit*. Then Kony also appeared. He discovered that the boys from our home were being beaten for failing to protect Kony. He told them not to beat them. "Don't beat anyone for what happens during a battle. What will you do when you hear that I have died? How much will you beat your friends? It is God who plans death." We all went to some home nearby, and *Ladit* started telling everyone how I worked hard that day. "Betty worked very hard today," he said. My whole body was cut with grass, and my pants were all torn; I walked like a crazy person. This is how I walked through the bush that day.

In the evening, we went and cooked food somewhere, and *Ladit* said that the injured should be taken to the sick bay and those okay should proceed in the convoy. So that was when I started realizing, "Oh, the gun is also a good thing because it helps you." That was the point I started calling the gun Margaret, my mum's name, because I felt that my gun was like my mum. The only thing is that the gun doesn't tell you stories.

3

Becoming a Mother

How Can I Be Your Wife?

I had just turned fourteen years old when I became Kony's wife. It was in January 1997, in one of the LRA bases in Sudan called Aruu. One day Kony called all of his wives to the house and told them that I was to be his wife. He told me that I could not refuse. He said that I should be the one to prepare food for him now so that I could get used to him. All of the older wives were prevented from cooking for him. I felt so bad.

One day I asked him, "How can I be your wife when up until this point you have called me your child?" He said, "You have no choice, you must be my wife. If you don't want it, then you can go back to your mother's house." But he was just teasing me because he knew my mother was so far away.

He called me into his house. I didn't know why he had called me, but he said, "Today I am going to share this bed with you." My reaction was to just run, to escape, so I did.

Kony sent his bodyguards after me, and they caned me fifty strokes on the back and buttocks to punish me for embarrassing him before others. After they were done with beating me, Kony said that it was my parents' fault for giving birth to such a beautiful girl. He told me to go and to nurse my wounds.

Some time passed, and I thought he would leave me alone, but he called me again and said that I had to make the choice between life and death. If I wanted to live, I had to be his wife.

I told him that I wanted to live. He said, "From now on you are my wife. If I tell you that it's your turn to spend the night in my house, you have to."

I went to Vincent Otti and asked him to help me. He told me that he could do nothing to help me. He said Kony was the highest-ranking person in the LRA and that they could help only those involved with lower-ranking commanders. I felt so helpless. I had to start living in Kony's house as husband and wife.

The very first time I spent the night with Kony I conceived. I wasn't amused. Kony was an old man, almost my father's age-mate, and yet I had to sleep with him as his wife. When he learned that I was pregnant, he had me taken to the hospital in Juba for a medical checkup. When I got there, the hospital staff said that I was too young and that my husband had to report to the hospital before they would give me any treatment. It was very odd for such a young girl to be pregnant, and when I reached the hospital a crowd gathered to stare at me. The escorts called Kony to come to the hospital, but he refused. Instead, he sent one of his young bodyguards to register me as his wife at the hospital.

I stayed in Juba during my pregnancy, in Kony's home inside a base for the Arabs, because Kony was too embarrassed for me to be seen among his commanders. The other leaders complained that I was too young to become Kony's wife and that he should have given me time to mature and grow. So I stayed in Juba until it was time for me to give birth, and then I returned.

I wanted to get rid of the baby. There was an old Congolese woman who ground lots of red peppers very finely and told me to drink them. I drank it all, but the baby didn't come out. Instead, I experienced horrible pains in my waist and had to be taken back to the hospital. The hospital suspected that I had taken some drugs, so they tested me. The pain was so much, my waist pained for a whole month. Kony said that if they could prove I had taken drugs, he would just kill me on the spot. But no drugs were ever found in the tests, and I never told anyone what I had done.

The Jacket

There was a time *Ladit* Kony went to Khartoum and returned with a jacket that he gave me as a gift. If there was a time to escape, then that should have been it. The elder wives were angry that *Ladit* had given *me* a jacket.

We were living in Aruu by then. I put on the jacket to go to get water from the well. Fatima [Kony's first wife] and the elder wives were waiting for me there. They started to beat me, asking why I had been given this jacket as a gift from Kony. I told them that it is *Ladit* who gave it to me. Then they told me, "Every time you are saying it is *Ladit*, it's *Ladit*, how special are you? You who take yourself as if your pussy has been fried with onions, cooking oil, and spices; today you will see. We are going to beat you and slice your vagina completely."

Some boys and women were watching. Kony's wives slapped me one at a time; they beat me and insulted me before all these people. I came back home with red and swollen cheeks. My ears had been pinched to the extent that I had fingerprints on them. In my heart, I vowed to continue wearing the jacket for which I had been beaten.

When I reached the compound, all the other *ting ting* were so angry when they saw how I was beaten. They felt so hurt. They started to incite me to shoot Fatima in the head the next time she dared to do such a thing to me.

My ears were aching, and my head was in pain. I was lying down when Fatima came and told me, "Get up and bathe yourself. If you are taught a lesson once, you should not get angry at people. Don't you see how officers were angry with you? You are very young and something nice is given to you, yet we wives who are officers have nothing. So if you are given a lesson, why can't you learn? Don't even tell *Ladit* what happened even if he asks you."

I just kept quiet, but the older girls reported the issue to *Ladit*. So when *Ladit* called me and asked me to narrate to him what had happened, I had to tell him everything. He called Fatima and told her to pack her bags and leave for Juba, as the house there were a total mess and he wanted her to organize it. She left for Juba without knowing that Kony really just wanted to separate us. The other *ting ting* ran after the car and threw clumps of dirt at it and wished she would never return again.

The next day Kony told our driver that I had been beaten terribly because of the jacket that he had given me. The driver could not keep quiet. He went to Juba and told Fatima that she was sent away because of what she did to me. She was furious and decided to return to Aruu.

Our jubilation didn't last long. Fatima returned and told Kony the weather in Juba was so hot and the baby could not withstand the heat. *Ladit* forbid her from returning, but when Omona Field, the second in command, who was also Fatima's uncle, was departing for Aruu, Fatima jumped into the vehicle and refused to get out. When she arrived in Aruu, I went to greet her, but she just jeered at me without saying a word. So I just left and went back to our house, even though all along she had purposely returned to face me.

Confronting Fatima

I did everything for Fatima's baby. I fed him, bathed him, and washed his clothes. Fatima didn't do a thing for that baby. I was expected to take the baby to her to breastfeed, and as soon as he was satisfied, I took him away from her. If I didn't wash the baby's shit, I was beaten.

When I was pregnant, Fatima accused me of taking over her husband, saying that I was even going to have her husband's child. She would insult me with all kinds of bad language.

I remember a day when *Ladit* was going to Juba; he told me that I should slaughter a hen and prepare it for him to eat. He even chose the hen that he wanted and told me, "Betty, get some boys and tell them to get hold of this chicken, and you prepare it for me." Immediately I called the boys, who came and grabbed the hen while Fatima just sat watching quietly. She always wanted to be consulted whenever any chicken was to be slaughtered.

When I had already removed the hen's feathers, Fatima came to me and said, "Heh, this home has now become yours, has it? Since when did you become the first wife of this home to the extent that you can even decide to slaughter a chicken? This pregnancy of yours has really made you bigheaded. You are going to die with it; if you don't die, then that means I am not a daughter of Kitgum."

Then I told her, "Hey! Why do you blame me for all this? Why don't you tell *Ladit* to die with his baby? Why don't you complain to

Ladit about it? Why utter all that to me?" She jeered at me for answering back at her.

I cooked the chicken, but *Ladit* told me that it was getting late and he had been called to go to Juba. I put the food in a flask for him, and he said he would eat it from Juba. I called Fatima to come and serve the food, but she refused. In our culture, it is always the first wife who serves the food when it is cooked, especially to the husband. Fatima refused to serve the food and also forbade the second co-wife from serving it. At the same time, *Ladit* was telling me that I should hurry, as he wanted to leave. So I went and served the food very fast in the flask and gave it to him. I left only one piece for Fatima's son.

When Kony left in the vehicle, Fatima came to me and asked me what I expected her to eat since I had served all the food. You know, she used to eat the same food that *Ladit* ate [where culturally men were served meat and the best foodstuffs]. She started insulting and slapping me. She immediately called the young boys to hold me down and beat me.

When I saw the boys coming, I hurried and got hold of my gun. She had tied a *bitenge* [a colorful textile] and had a bare chest [an act that is considered *kir*, an abomination meant to insult and curse and to draw public attention to an offense]. One of the co-wives started shouting at Fatima, telling her that she had pushed us too far. Fatima looked at me and said that there was no way I could shoot her, that if I did, I would see what would happen to me.

On my side, I loaded the bullets in and put the gun on *sema* [took the safety off], ready to shoot Fatima. I then took aim and fired a bullet just above her head. I fired a second shot. I did not want to kill her, but I wanted to scare her. I wanted to let her know that the gun isn't afraid of anything, even if you are powerful. The security men came and stopped me while Fatima fell down and started crawling away.

We were both arrested and taken to the military. Kony was informed of what happened, and he woke up very early in the morning and came back from Juba. Very many people, including officers, came. They thought that *Ladit* would come and beat me up, but he didn't. Instead, he sat the two of us down and asked what had happened.

Fatima wanted me to speak first, but *Ladit* told her, "How can Betty be the first to talk? You are her elder and my first wife. You start by telling us what brought these misunderstandings among you." She said that she had only asked me why I didn't leave food for the children and that I had just decided to go and pick up the gun to shoot her.

When Fatima finished telling her part of the story, I narrated everything in detail, including how she mistreats people generally. I said all this in front of all of the commanders. When I was finished speaking, Omona Field said that I should have killed Fatima. He said her only purpose was to mistreat people and that everyone was tired of her work. Meanwhile, Omona Field was her uncle. When Omona Field talked like that, Fatima started to cry; she asked how her uncle could talk like that. How would *Ladit* treat her now that he was hearing all that?

Ladit called Fatima a bad woman; he said he had not been aware of what was happening. Then he said that from that time on, he didn't want to find me washing clothes or doing anything for Fatima or their son. He said I was already a wife and pregnant, so Fatima should give me respect. From that moment on, I decided not to talk to Fatima. Even if she called me to her, I would not go or respond. I shifted out of the house we shared and in with another co-wife. *Ladit* also stopped visiting Fatima in her house.

Eventually Fatima came to me and said that it is not good for us to continue living like that, angry and without speaking. She said that when something goes wrong, we have to forgive one another. I feared what Fatima had said to me earlier: that I would die with my pregnancy. I feared that she would actually do something to me so that I wouldn't survive my pregnancy, and that is why I wanted to avoid her.

When Fatima came to ask for forgiveness, she told me that we should live as one. She said that we should be helpful to one another. She said she had already forgiven me long ago, and she wondered why I did not forgive her.

I told her that if she wanted to resolve the issue, we had to inform *Ladit*, that we cannot resolve these things on our own. I told her that if she wanted to improve her character, she should declare this in front of *Ladit*.

You know Fatima found life very difficult without my help. There was no one to help her with domestic work or to look after her children. Her baby boy would cry for me, but I would chase him away when he came. I had lost my head. Fatima used to torture me as a girl, but I had also become big, and she should have respected me too.

Sister Rakelle Comes for the Aboke Girls

In 1996, the LRA abducted a group of schoolgirls from St. Mary's College in Aboke. It put a lot of pressure on the LRA because the girls were from a very good Catholic school, and a nun named Rakelle from Italy insisted on the return of the girls. It was on BBC Radio, and even the Pope appealed to Kony to release the girls.

One day when *Ladit* was in Khartoum, he informed us that Sister Rakelle was coming to Nicitu with some others to find the Aboke girls. He told us to leave Juba and go to the Arabs' barracks to hide.

In the morning, LRA soldiers moved throughout the barracks, warning those of us hiding there that Sister Rakelle had arrived and that we were not to speak a word of Acholi or English. We were to speak only Arabic. If you did not know Arabic, you were not to open your mouth at all. All of the *kuruts* were told to hide. The Arabs did not want us to be found. We did not even cook that day. Instead, we were made to hide behind the barracks in a military cemetery where thieves were taken and killed.

There was one boy from Kitgum. Sister Rakelle came and began to speak to him in Acholi, asking, "Are you hungry?" The boy replied in Acholi that food would be prepared and brought for them. When Sister Rakelle heard the boy speak in Acholi, she hugged him and asked, "Have you heard about the Aboke girls?" The boy said he had not. She asked him where Kony's camp was, and the boy replied that he did not know Kony but that he was a refugee from the war in Uganda. The boy did not say anything bad, but he was taken away. I later heard people say that the boy had been killed.

The day Sister Rakelle came, we hid in the cemetery. We were bitten by mosquitoes. When they finally left the base, we went home, prepared food to eat, and then returned to the barracks around ten o'clock at night. Very early in the morning we were taken back to the cemetery to hide again.

I thought we were going to be killed in that cemetery so that we did not reveal ourselves to Sister Rakelle. The way I see it, the Arabs have no mercy. They took us to where they kill people and then showed us very big knives and told us to remain quiet. I said all kinds of prayers as so many different thoughts went through my mind. I feared being killed in such a gruesome way when I was pregnant and prayed that God did not make me be abducted to die such a terrible death in that place. I cried the whole day.

By late afternoon the Arabs came and took us to our compound inside the base so that we could cook. Suddenly a commander ran into the compound and warned us that Sister Rakelle had arrived!

We were warned again not to speak a word. I remember that I was wearing a pink pregnancy dress. I was sitting on a mat, about to drink tea, when Sister Rakelle rushed up to me and asked if I had heard of the Aboke girls captured by Kony. She was speaking Acholi in a *munu*'s [a foreigner's] accent. I kept quiet. She ran behind the house and started to call out one of the Aboke girls' name, Palma. She shouted, "Palma! Palma! Palma!" That was how the *munu* shouted Palma's name. She then called for more Aboke girls, "Silvia! Alaba!" She was calling their names as if they would respond, but they were not on that compound.

As Sister Rakelle ran around, she knocked over the tea, and I whispered to one of the other women how careless she was, jumping all over the compound. Sister Rakelle heard me speak in Acholi and shouted that she was not careless but was looking for the Aboke girls. She then sat down beside us and would not leave our side. She spoke to us in Acholi. I responded in Arabic, "I do not understand your language. What are you saying? I do not want to hear what you are saying. If you continue with what you are saying I will cry." You know when there is fear you act differently; if we knew that these people could bring us back home, then we would have come out with the truth, but the fact was the LRA was killing anyone that spoke to them.

After Sister Rakelle left, some of us began to think. We wondered if we were not important because the Sister looked only for the Aboke girls, not us. All of us were abducted, but no one followed us up to Sudan to try to find us. Why were the Aboke girls followed? Were they the only ones who were useful? Who had blood in their veins? We talked a lot about this afterward, about why no one looked for us. We concluded that it was because they had an education. We concluded that children who had some education were more important than us. What about the rest of us? We used to think about it. As children, this is what we thought about.

Water for Bathing

While I was still expecting Bakita [my first daughter], I remember *Ladit* used to move a lot. Sometimes he would go to Khartoum, and there were times he went to London; he once stayed in London for one month. As he was coming back, he sent a message that I should be the one to go to welcome him in Juba. He sent this communication through the radio call and said that if I was still in Aruu, I should leave and go to Juba, since he was about to return. Then Fatima started complaining, "Why does *Ladit* want you to be the one to welcome him while there are older wives too?" To avoid trouble, I decided not to go.

When *Ladit* arrived in Juba and learned I was not there, he sent a car to pick me up from Aruu and bring me to him straight away. When the car arrived, I started collecting my things, as did Fatima, although she hadn't been told to do so. We both entered the vehicle. She was so gloomy and refused to talk to me. The driver told me to sit in the front seat of the vehicle, but I refused. Fatima said that she would not go and sit in front; how would *Ladit* view that? She wasn't going to interfere with our good life, but she was going for her own mission. So we all sat in the back of the vehicle until we arrived in Juba without saying a word to each other.

When we arrived in Juba, *Ladit* told me to go and take for him water for bathing. But when I took the water to him, Fatima followed me and poured the water from the basin onto the ground. When *Ladit* went to bathe, he didn't find water.

He came back and asked me, "Huh, Betty, how come I didn't find water in the bathroom?" I told him that if he didn't find water, he should please ask Fatima. In the meantime, Fatima took her own water for *Ladit* to bathe, but he said that he wouldn't use that water for bathing; he said that I should take his water again. I was a bit hesitant but just decided at once to pour on the ground the water from the basin that Fatima had prepared for *Ladit*. I poured fresh water into the basin. Fatima immediately poured this water out and refilled the basin. That day, we did that several times until *Ladit* just decided to go and pour his own bathing water.

After he finished bathing, Kony called us to his house. He told us that he did not want that kind of satanic behavior in his home. I told him that I have respected Fatima to the extent that I have become tired. You asked me to take for you bathing water, but she went ahead and poured it; again you told me to take the water, and she still poured it. Maybe it is the excitement of seeing you back that is making us behave like this, I do not know.

Fatima said that if she wanted to beat me, she would do so terribly and when she wanted to. She then sarcastically asked me who was Kony's first wife, she or I? I told her that if she was to uncover my back, she would find scars that I had attained as a result of her beatings, but she wouldn't find any scar from Kony. "If you are to look at my scars, you will realize that it was you who used to beat me. Those scars prove that I indeed respected you." *Ladit* told Fatima that she would remember how helpful I was only when it was too late. *Ladit* asked her to go to spend the night in his house, and she went.

In the morning, *Ladit* asked me to go and prepare for him bathing water. "You have started again today with your bathing water?" said Fatima. I told her, "Can't you see this big tummy of mine? Do you think I will come to sleep in your house? What is wrong with me taking water? Is there a problem if I take for him water and he bathes?"

Ladit called me and said, "Betty, go and buy fresh fish and prepare it for me, but don't buy omel as I do not like it. Buy a different kind of fish." So I left with one of his escorts, who drove the car to the riverbanks. Fishing used to take place at the riverbank in Juba. So we went and didn't find very good fish; we found omel, the kind that he didn't like, and a few others, like tilapia. But by then fish was so scarce. We had gone with only ten shillings; we bought a heap of fish and returned with them.

Fatima said, "Betty doesn't even know how to prepare fish. Let me first see how she will prepare this fish." Inside my heart, I sighed and said, "This woman really underrates me." So I decided to just go ahead and cook; I removed the scales of the fish, cooked and served it for the big men — *Ludito* [playful variation of *Ladit*]. They ate it all and asked me to add some more.

I did and then Fatima said that, "Now they are eating poison and they think they are enjoying the food. That food is not nice because she has added something in it. This kind of eating is unusual. A full bowl of food was first served and all eaten, again the second one was served, and all has been eaten? I don't believe it. It must be influenced by other factors." I went and collected everything that had been used for eating by these people. After I collected the things, I felt so tired; I bathed and went to lie down to rest.

In the evening *Ladit* asked, "Where has Betty gone?" Fatima replied, "Do I know where she usually goes? Maybe she has gone to the Arabs' homes [implying an affair with an Arab soldier]." Then *Ladit* asked, "Does she always go visit the Arabs?" She said, "*Afande* [soldier], it seems you still don't know the characters of your women; they always go to visit soldiers."

I was sleeping in the house. I heard everything that they discussed. *Ladit* entered the house and found me lying down. He called me, but I pretended I was asleep. Again he came back inside and called me; then I got up and sat. Kony asked me, "What is wrong with you?" I told him that I was just feeling sleepy and had decided to rest. Then he said, "All this time, you have been sleeping here?" I told him, "Yes." Kony said, "I was told that they found you with some Arab man a few minutes ago."

I told him that was a lie. I told him to tell the person who saw me with the Arabs to take us there. "If you believe such small untruths, I should just leave and go live with the Arabs. You are a big person, Kony. You shouldn't even pay attention to gossip. If you think I have been sleeping with the Arabs, then just let me go and live with them."

I immediately started packing my belongings. I picked my maternity dress and put it on. I went to Omona Field and informed him that I was tired of gossip and was leaving to go live with the Arabs. Fatima began to ask me why I was behaving like that. I told her that she was the one who brought all this mess.

Fatima then said, "Do you even know that men can also be confused [implying Kony was mistaken]?" She said that she never said anything. I told her, "It was you who said all these things, and I heard you say them outside my home!" She denied it and said that my ears were mistaken, that I didn't hear very well. *Ladit* Kony just walked away.

The next morning, *Ladit* said that Fatima should remain in Juba, while he and I returned to Aruu. We had spent only one night in Aruu when Fatima boarded a lorry and came there. *Ladit* at this point didn't want me and Fatima to share a home in the same base. So when Fatima arrived, *Ladit* told me to return to Juba using the same lorry that Fatima had used to travel to Aruu. I boarded the lorry and returned to Juba, while Fatima remained in Aruu. *Ladit* prepared and left for Uganda.

Vincent Otti Is Captured and Tortured

During a battle in one of the LRA bases, called Palutaka, Vincent Otti was captured by the Lutugu [a tribe in South Sudan], who hated the LRA. The Lutugu tied Vincent Otti and his escorts up, then undressed and beat them. Vincent Otti was then separated from his men and said he could hear the Lutugu kill his soldiers one by one. He said his men would beg for their lives and then be shot. Vincent Otti managed to untie himself and run as the Lutugu pursued him. He entered a certain river called Kinete and followed the water. The Lutugu followed him, but he hid well, and they never found him. He then ran until he reached a place called Torit, where the Arabs had a large base.

The *Arabu* [Arabs] sent a message to *Ladit* Kony that they had found Vincent Otti, who was by then a valuable commander in the LRA. They took him to Juba Hospital for treatment. When we arrived and first saw him, it was shocking. He looked like a *kurut*. As soon as *Ladit* saw the condition he was in, he began to cry. Vincent Otti's legs were wounded the way a *kurut*'s would be due to long walks. The wounds were rotting, and the stench was very bad. The sight of Vincent Otti's feet was frightening. They had turned black, and they even had maggots.

If you were not stronghearted, you wouldn't go near him. Tears rolled down my cheeks when I saw Vincent Otti. He told me that I shouldn't cry as he was going to live. I was told to boil water and nurse his wounds. I even injected him with medicine. I also made for him tea, and he took it. He had been served food, but he said he did not want to eat the food; he only cried. Every time he saw *Ladit* Kony, he would begin to cry again.

My Firstborn

One morning, I awoke in the house to find that a bird called *okok* had entered. I felt it was a bad sign and reported it to the commanders. I felt that something was very wrong, but the commanders told me that it was hard to tell what the bird meant. I started feeling labor pains and began to fetch water, avoiding everyone. Kony's driver, Lapeko, arrived in the compound and insisted that I return to Juba with him that very day; he said that *Ladit* was waiting for me to arrive. I told him that I was waiting for something and we should leave tomorrow.

The labor pains increased. I continued to fetch water, and each time I returned from the well the pain increased. The pain spread from my waist to my back. I was worried. I was unsure of how I would give birth. Finally, I asked one lady how it was the baby would come out of me. She said, "The way you conceived the child is the way you will give birth." She said I asked stupid questions.

I kept quiet. The pains continued to increase. Lapeko kept checking on me. He asked me what was wrong with me that day. I told him there was nothing wrong with me. "What do you want me to do so that you know I am fine?" He said, "No problem." The women had cooked and served food. It was hard to dodge going to eat. I said that a pillow should be brought for me, and it was brought. I leaned on the pillow and tried to eat. I got a small piece of bread and a lot of sauce. I chewed the food when the pains stopped. They said, "Betty, you eat." I said, "I do not know. I find my stomach is full. I took tea earlier on. When my stomach is lighter I will eat."

I stayed for some time and then went to sleep in *Ladit*'s house. I stayed for very long in *Ladit*'s house before I went to bathe. The pains increased. I prayed, "God, if you want me to give birth today, then let me give birth in the latrine. I do not want this child. How will I begin to take care of this child?" My other heart told me, "If you continue to talk like that, then you will both die while giving birth." I stayed in the latrine for almost one hour. No one went to the latrine. I stayed in the latrine until I felt I smelt of feces. I tried to push the child, but the pains on my waist increased. I decided to leave the toilet. I still had my knickers on; I did not think of removing them. I left the latrine and went to the cassava garden when the pains increased so much.

One of my co-wives thought I was a thief in the garden and began to sound the alarm; sometimes the Lutugu would come and steal our cassava. Another one of my co-wives stopped her, as she recognized my dress. They started to run toward me. They asked me what was happening, but all I could reply was that my head was spinning and I could not walk. They helped me to reach the house, and as soon as I entered it my water broke. They ran to get the midwife, and no sooner had she come than I gave birth. They removed the knickers by force. I thought that I should give birth with the knickers on, that they would prevent the child from falling on the ground and getting dirty. That was what I was thinking of. The birth attendant tore the knickers from me and immediately my baby came out. I asked the sex of the child before the umbilical cord was cut. It was a girl.

My whole body shook. I burst out crying with fear. I did not know that you experienced pain when you gave birth. I thought the pain was a bad sign that might mean the baby would die. When the birth attendants saw how much water I had collected that day, they exclaimed, "No wonder this woman fetched a lot of water today. She knew that she was going to give birth!"

They boiled water to wash the child and me and then began to massage my stomach. I was so scared. I thought, "My! Is this suffering! Let this be the last time I give birth. Here I am burning with water, but *Ladit* is moving in Uganda." That was what I was thinking. I stayed for some time like that. They kept on bathing me with hot water.

I stayed for one week without eating. I had no milk in my breasts, not even a little. Word about it was sent to *Ladit*. They told him I was not eating and had no breast milk for the child. They told him the child was being fed on sugar that was mixed with water. *Ladit* said the controller [a spiritual diviner] should be called so that he could talk to him.

The controller put medicine on my breasts and squeezed them. I will never forget the pain I felt from him squeezing the breasts forcefully. Finally, milk began to flow. I feared people watching me breastfeed. I was frightened. I thought it was weird. I felt like hiding. I was just stranded.

I was afraid to carry the baby, so for the first week only other people held her until it was time for her to sleep or eat. She was a good baby and never cried. As long as she had been bathed and was feeling fresh, she didn't cry. People liked my child very much. She had a lot of hair. Kony named that child Bakita.

Fatima loved the baby so much and carried her everywhere. She had only sons, so she loved my child. She said she was her daughter, yet when I was pregnant she hated me so much. Fatima even carried the baby to her baptism ceremony. I just walked along empty-handed.

One day I heard *Ladit* Kony tell Fatima to watch me around the child, because I had a funny mind and might abandon the baby. When I heard him say that my mind was funny, I said, "Good, if he says my mind is funny, then I will show them that my mind is really funny." I went to play. The child cried, and I forgot about it. I went to the well and found young girls of my age, and we played at the well. *Ladit* said that if I was found playing again, I was to be beaten. He told me that I should know that I am a mother now and that I can no longer play foolishly. He told me that I should do things like a wife and erase thinking that I am a child. He asked me how a young child could give birth to a baby?

Confronting Kony

Bakita was still young when she became very ill. We were staying in Nicitu. She was vomiting and had diarrhea to the extent that I thought she might lose her life. *Ladit* Kony said that if the child died, he would also kill me. He said that I should find my own way of taking the child to Juba Hospital; he was so annoyed. Yet I had no way to reach Juba with such a sick child. I could not just walk there and carry her in my arms. *Ladit* forbade me to use his car. I became so sad and told him, "You have many children. You will not lose anything if this girl dies. Some of your children are still in the womb, while others are being born. You are going to impregnate one of your wives tonight. Children are not important to you. If God wants my child to survive, then she will, but if He wants her to die, then she will die."

Eventually I traveled using a lorry that carries charcoal. I sat on top with the child. One of the soldiers told me to give him the child so that he could sit with her in the front. He was also sick. I gave him the child, and they sat in the front seat. I managed to reach the hospital in Juba. Bakita was admitted for three days, and then we were discharged. I was hurt because of *Ladit*'s words. He said he did not love me and was mistakenly staying with me. He told me I was brought to this marriage by the gun, that there was never a proper courtship between us.

I stayed for three months without doing anything for Kony. I never made him even a cup of tea when he came to my home. I never greeted him or responded when he talked to me. He had said that we should both lead separate lives. I wanted him to kill me because he was the one who impregnated me and caused the problems I was going through. He wanted me to hide when I was pregnant, yet he was the one responsible for it. He wanted me to stay in Juba because it would be a disgrace for the rebel leaders to know that I was his wife and because Vincent Otti would find out that I was pregnant or had a child. People were not happy with him because I was still young and he had impregnated me. I told him I did not want to be his wife. I told him to let me just live in his compound and work as a slave.

Kony asked me why I talked to him like that. He said no woman had ever spoken such words to him before. He said, "From today onward I do not want you. You can stay in my home but not as my wife. Stay alone. I, Nora's son, will never stay with you as a husband." He is the kind of person who does not put what he has said into action. I did what he said. I stayed in his compound, nursing Bakita, but I refused to bring him water when he sent me to do so; that is work for a wife.

I refused to do anything he asked me to do. You know, Kony is funny; even when you are down, he will insist you cook for him or bring him bathing water. In Nicitu, I had my own house. He came to my house and asked me what was wrong. He said, "Betty, what is wrong with you? Who has hurt you? You do not bring me drinking water if I send you to do so. You do not want to do anything I ask you to do. Who do you want to listen to? Who is your husband? You do not want to come to my house when I send for you?"

I asked him, "Why do you forget what you said? You said that I should no longer respond to any of your requests. You said from that day onward that I was not your wife and that I was going to stay in your home like a soldier. I will not make the mistake of doing what you say. If I do, then people will blame me if anything happens to you. I will not do anything you tell me to do. If you want, you can beat or kill me. I have made up my mind. You can kill me if you want. Here is your child. You can do anything you decide to do to me."

He said that he did not want to hear such stupid words because he was not a child. He asked me what had happened to make him utter such words. I told him, "You know what happened! I am not the one to tell you. Ask those who were there to remind you of what you said. Ask the driver to tell you. I will not tell you what happened. I will not do anything for you. You will not bathe with my water."

He asked, "Do you know a gun?" He came and held my head and asked me if I knew how to shoot a gun. I told him, "How many people have died in the bush? How many children from Atiak have died from the bush? I can also die and follow them. Besides, my family is dead. Everyone in my family was killed. Even if I am to be alive tomorrow, where will I stay when I go home? Even if you oust the government, I will not have a place to stay."

He said, "You have exaggerated what I said. I was joking, but you took it seriously. You are now annoyed. You take everything too seriously." I said, "*Afande*, I am only following what you told me. I will do what you said. That is what you should know. If anything happens to you, the LRA will kill me. I will not do anything for you."

Kony said, "Today you are going to sleep in my house. I am going to share a bed with you to show you that you are my wife."

I said, "I will not share a bed with you."

He said that he was going to stay in my house. I told him that there was not enough space for both of us in my house. He went and got his towel and came. He poured water into a basin for bathing in front of my house and then went to bathe. The LRA had made it a point that *Ladit* should not do anything for himself or carry his water because he is a big person. His escort saw him carry his water and came. He said, "*Ladit*, let me help you carry your water." *Ladit* refused to be helped. He said, "No, let me go and bathe." He went and bathed. He came back and told me to give him a comb. I sat quietly. He barked at me, saying, "Get up and bring me a comb from the house." I did not get up.

The escort was the one who brought him a comb. *Ladit* combed his hair and asked me how I wanted him to talk to me. He said that I should know that he is my husband, and when we go back home, I will not stay with any other man. He said I began to stay with him before I knew anything to do with a man and he was the one who taught me until I gave birth. He promised to kill me if I continued behaving this way.

I said, "*Ladit*, what you said hurt me so much. Let me be like a soldier or a maid for the women in your home. I will do anything you say, but I will not stay with you as a spouse. The only child I will have with you is

Bakita because of what you said. I have been a slave in your home before. Look at how I suffered at the hands of your wives. They beat me and slapped me at their will. I have done everything you tell me to do. I was a babysitter in your home. I took care of the children in your home. Their mothers never washed even their faces. I was the one who did it. If today you think that I am a bad person, then no problem. I was abducted to be a slave in your home. A slave is comfortable as long as she eats. God had planned for me to experience what I am going through. Let me tolerate what God planned for me to go through so that it passes."

Ladit came and held me. He said, "Tell me what is wrong. I will not repeat the same mistake. From now onward I want to stay with you. You can use anything of mine the way you used to." I continued to refuse. I left him and returned to my house and locked the door. Kony followed me and knocked on the door. I was quiet. He walked and went back to his house and slept.

Ladit sent for his top commanders, like Lagony, Vincent Otti, and Matata, to come in the morning. He said that he wanted them to come to his home to help him solve the matter. It was a very cold morning.

The LRA leaders came to my house and sat. I was the only woman among all the commanders. I carried my child on my lap. *Ladit* told the leaders how I had hurt him. *Ladit* said that I was careless and was not taking good care of his child.

I was so angry and began to cry. Vincent Otti told me to stop crying because they had come to solve the matter. *Ladit* thought that the rebel leaders were going to support him and that I was the one that would be blamed.

The leaders then told me to tell them my version of the story. I told them, "I was staying alone in Juba and decided to come live in Nicutu. A week later the child fell sick. When I asked *Ladit* if I could go back to Juba, he refused. He asked me why I had left Juba to come to Nicitu in the first place. He told me he was not going to let me use his vehicle and that my child could die. He told me to walk up to Juba." I was hurt when I was talking. "I told him that he was lucky because he had many children and would impregnate someone that night. I told him he was good at giving birth to children but that Bakita is my only child. I told him to let my child die if he wished, but if God wants Bakita to live and help me in the future, she would live."

I told Vincent Otti, "Ever since I was abducted, Kony's wives beat me. They said I was going to take over their husband. The man they beat me for also mistreated me. I did not know what to do." Vincent Otti shed tears. He said, "*Ladit*, this girl is still young. You have to be patient with her. She does not know how to take care of the child. It is up to you to help her. You cannot tell her to find her own way. If she is to escape and die or get killed by the Arabs, what will you say? It will bring bad luck to the family. What you did is bad. You should not have made her pregnant. If she was going to give birth, it should been three years from now. She is only a child and has given birth. It is painful. I am not quarrelling, but I am trying to amend the matter."

Vincent Otti reprimanded *Ladit* and then began to talk to me. He said, "My daughter, what you did was wrong. When a man talks to you, you have to be polite. Men are to be seduced. You should have prepared for him a meal even when he had said that he didn't want you to cook. This would have shown that you are a good woman."

That day my tongue slipped, and I said, "*Ladit* is a big person. In actual sense he could be my father, but he handles me in a bad way." That is what I told the commanders.

Everyone supported me. I made tea, and they took. *Ladit* also got the courage to tell me to take for him bathing water. I wanted to put the baby on my back, and he told me to take her to him. I brought him the baby, and he carried her. I began to stay with him from that day onward. He told me to forgive him. He said such issues embarrass people from home. He said my parents might know of what happened and say that he mistreated me. He said he stayed with me when I was still young, and he wanted to take good care of me.

He said there were times when his mind was taken up with other things and he could become rude. He promised not to mistreat me from that day onward. That day he told me many stories so that I would forget what happened. We did not sleep till one o'clock in the morning. In my heart I was thinking that, if I were a witch, I would have flown away with the child.

In the morning he told me to go to live in the house in Juba. He said he would be coming to check on me from time to time. He said he would stay in Juba and then come back here. He told me to go back because he didn't want me to stay together with Fatima because she disturbed me a lot. This is one of the experiences I had when I was with Kony. He told me to stay with Acellam Caesar [head of LRA Intelligence]. I stayed for a long time in Juba. Bakita learned to walk when I was in Juba.

From the bush there were also marital problems. We had domestic fights. I was so stressed during this time. If I had the capacity, I would have escaped. It was a difficult period. After quarrelling with *Ladit*, I got pregnant with my second daughter, Winnie. From the time that we had that fight, *Ladit* liked me a lot. He thought I could not fathom telling all he had done wrong to the elders [the senior commanders], but I did. I was not scared of telling the leaders anything.

When I went to Juba, he changed his attitude toward me. He checked on me every two or three days. He began to provide for my needs. He bought soap and put it in the house. He also gave me money so that I could buy food and have a balanced diet. He said I had to eat well because I had a baby. We were given cowpeas and beans to eat as soldiers, but *Ladit* gave me money so that I could buy beef, fish, and vegetables in the market. He told me to buy these things and eat.

If I had not been abducted and were living in my village, I would have refused this man for good. He said so many things to hurt me before he moved me to Juba. What hurt me most was when he said that he had given me a child but there was no marriage. He had made my breasts flat from breastfeeding, but he was not obligated to me. He also told me one day that my mother's gap in the teeth was as smooth as a small stone for grinding. From home it would have been an offense to talk about someone's mother. He would have faced it rough. This is what happened. I have talked about how men lived with their wives in the bush. This was how I lived with Joseph Kony.

Yellow Fever

When I was pregnant with Winnie, I was told to go to Juba as *Ladit* was sick in the hospital and wanted to see me. Indeed, *Ladit* was in a critical condition when I was brought from Juba; his whole body had turned yellow. He had yellow fever and had not been eating any food. So when I came, we spent one night together, and the next day he started telling me that he had sent for me because he wasn't sure if he would survive.

He told me that I should come sit close to him, as there were certain things that he wanted to share with me before he died.

Then I told him, "Aah, why are you talking like that? How sure are you that you are going to die?" He said that he was feeling so weak to the extent that he doubted if his sickness would spare his life, because since he was born, he had never been that sick. Then I told him, "You will get well, there are worse diseases than this, you will recover." He continued to say that he is so hurt because he knows that as soon as he dies, his very commanders will take me over as their wife and that hurts him so much.

I told him, "We all have different dates of dying; we can't die on the same day. One person has to die first and leave the other. God didn't plan our dates for dying to be the same." He immediately started crying after I told him that. When I saw him crying, I came and called one of the senior commanders, John Matata.

Matata asked *Ladit* what the problem was, but Kony did not answer. He asked again, but again *Ladit* again did not answer. Kony's condition worsened during the night. He said that everyone should leave his hospital room; he didn't want noise. We all started shifting our beddings outside, but he told Fatima that I should go back and sleep inside the room with him, so I went. All along I didn't know that *Ladit* had a bad plan. He was thinking that since he was going to die, he should stab me to death. He had a very sharp knife.

He started by saying, "Min Bakita [mother of Bakita], first come." Then I told him, "*Afande*, you relax, is there a problem?" He told me, "Put for me a pillow." He continued, "Bring another pillow; I want my head high up." And I did. So all along he wanted to get enough strength. I had no idea that he had a knife. He at once picked the knife and stabbed the edge of the bed as I leaned over him to fix his pillow.

I started running away as I shouted. People came running into the room, and they thought that I was crying because *Ladit* had died. People started asking me, "What is the problem?" I told them that I don't know what was happening with *Ladit*; he wanted to stab me with a knife, but instead he stabbed the bed.

Kony said he was feeling hurt. He said that if he died, he wanted me dead too. He said he did not want to leave me behind for other men to enjoy when he was the one who raised me, that I grew up in his hands and he was the first man I knew and started life with as a husband. He said that if he died, I might live with another man and give birth to another man's children. He talked of very many bad things and started crying. I felt empathetic, but I was also angry. I told myself, "From today onwards, I won't ever step inside *Ladit*'s house again, since he wants me dead."

The next morning, he again sent people to come and tell me to prepare for him pumpkin leaves. I said no, I won't enter *Ladit*'s room. I told them I might be in the process of serving food when Kony could decide to stab me! So I refused to go to Kony. Those commanders started saying, "Take for him food; we shall be there when you are serving the food and protect you." So I prepared the food, but when I served it I was so afraid. He kept asking me to lean toward him because he could not sit up properly to eat it.

The sickness really tortured Kony. It took away all his strength. After he received injections, his condition began to improve. He started gaining weight, but his attempt to kill me couldn't be erased from my mind. I remember asking him, "What would you do if you had actually killed me and yet you end up surviving the sickness? You would have killed me for no reason." He just laughed.

There was a day he told me that the only way I would outlive him is if he was shot dead during a battle. He said that as we watched some movie where Chuck Norris . . . no . . . Rambo tried to kill himself after his wife's death. Kony told me that before he dies, he will first kill me and his favorite son, Kony, so that he dies happy. He said he could not accept to leave us alive in this world to suffer without him. He said he doesn't want anyone to inherit me as their wife. He would talk as if he had mental problems.

Lagony Is Killed

After Omona Field died, Kony appointed Otti Lagony to take his place as second in command. By 1999, Lagony had started dividing the soldiers. He wanted to surrender with some of the soldiers but their plan was to kill Kony before surrendering. Among their plans, my name was also written; they said that for Kony's assassination to be easy, they should first do away with me or maybe recruit me to kill Kony myself.

He had written all of his plans down in a letter, but it was dropped in the gardens and found by one of the women, who gave it to Kony. They had planned to kill Kony, myself, Fatima, and one other co-wife! They thought the three of us were so close to Kony and that we knew all of his secrets. They had a plan on how to kill each of us; for me, they planned to kill me on the way to the well. I was so hurt and told myself, "Me, a very young girl, how could Lagony draw a plan to murder me? On the other hand, Kony himself attempted to murder me by stabbing me. What should I do in this world?" I used to feel so hurt, I became so weak, and on top of that there was the pregnancy. Eventually *Ladit* sent me to the hospital. *Ladit* sent me with three security men, he was so afraid that someone would try to kill me. As I was taken to the hospital, Lagony and his conspirators were arrested. They were stripped naked, and their guns and shoes were removed. They stayed in the prison for almost one month as they were interrogated, and then they were killed. They were stoned to death naked and left to rot in the sun.

A Real Human Being

I remember very well the day they killed Stella. The picture of that girl and what happened to her will forever be in my mind. Stella used to live at Lagony's place. You know, despite the fact that we were abducted, sometimes you just got used to the man you were with. For example, even if you were given to a very tough man and you were softhearted, it would reach a point when you got used to him and life just went on. Stella had grown accustomed to staying with Lagony. When Lagony was executed and she was taken to live with another senior commander, Ocan Bunia, she tried to escape the LRA. Stella had made her way to the Juba Airport when the LRA found and arrested her. She was taken back to Nicitu.

I was still expecting Winnie. When Stella was brought to Nicitu, a whistle was blown and a message was passed that instructed every woman to assemble in the yard, whether you were pregnant or not. This girl was beaten before all of us to the point of open wounds on her backside. I started crying when I saw the pain she was in. I felt that she should have escaped, because I knew she had been going through difficulties in the bush.

When asked why she attempted escape, Stella said that usually when everyone goes to pray, Bunia would always want to have sex with her, and yet she feels that she is still very young. He would want to sleep with her even during broad daylight. She told us that there was a day that she had gone to bathe and Bunia followed her to the bathroom and wanted her to bathe as he watched. She found this so difficult to do, and, worst of all, Bunia is a big man, not fit to be her husband.

One of the commanders, Livingstone, asked us, "You women, first see the actions that this girl took, what judgment do you make? This girl is just running away from love. Who told you that people run away from love? If everyone just ran away when loved, then who would love? Stella should just swallow and withstand that love and be with that man." I felt very hurt; I looked at the big men and wondered why such acts were not punished. Instead of acknowledging that what Bunia was doing was bad, these people decided to support his actions and claim that the man was just in love with Stella.

In reality, if you were forced to be with someone you didn't get along with, definitely you found life in the LRA hard. After I left the assembly, I went and lay behind the house as I continued to cry for Stella. Tears overwhelmed me. Then *Ladit* came and asked one of his sisters, called Atila Joyce, "Why is Betty crying? Why is your brother's wife crying?" Then Atila said, "I don't know why she is crying, I also just saw her come, lie down, and begin crying." Then he asked me, "What is happening to you?" I told him that there was nothing except that my back was paining due to the pregnancy. So I continued crying like that and kept worrying about this girl.

After being beaten, this girl was carried and taken to the military. At about 7:00 P.M., I heard gunshots. Little did I know that Stella had already been shot dead. The girl was shot rapid. Then *Ladit* started saying, "Now they have shot that girl and yet I told them not to kill her." He immediately called those commanders to come to him with a walkie-talkie, and they came. They told *Ladit* the girl was hard to deal with. She had told them that she would rather die than go back to Bunia. They said that since death was what she wanted, they helped her die.

I really worried about Stella. She was such a beautiful girl with very white teeth. It is not good to kill someone who has committed no wrong. If something makes your life difficult, you have to talk about it. And yet when you say your troubles out loud in the LRA, you are killed for it. So this really happened very painfully. It made me hate Livingstone so much to the extent that even if I met him on the way, I wouldn't say hello to him. I felt that he had a plot to kill that girl. I never liked any of those big men for what they did.

For us humans, we sometimes do wrong; some people even attempt to escape, but they are forgiven. For Stella, she was killed unjustly. Stella had a lot of hair, with white teeth. I think about every woman who was brutally killed from the bush, and I keep thinking that their families back home miss them, the same way my parents used to worry about me. Some of these things sometimes make us believe that women were useless to the movement. The commanders would even tell us that they didn't know the real reason why they abducted us but that, truthfully, it was because they could not have sex with animals. They needed to have sex with women. Other than that, women were useless to them. Then I really wonder if a real human being can be useless.

A Chance to Escape

I gave birth to Winnie in 2000. I spent most of my pregnancy in Juba Hospital. The doctors said the baby was big and that I wouldn't be able to push, so they recommended a Caesarean. My husband was supposed to go to the hospital to sign the form for the Caesarean. At the time, the LRA and the Arabs were in a conflict, so *Ladit* was not able to go to the hospital in Juba because he feared he would be arrested. He said that if God has planned for me to have a normal birth, then that would happen. While I was staying in the hospital, I met a nun from the mission who was from Uganda; she would visit me there. She brought me many things to help take care of me, and a friendship developed. She promised to bring me back to Uganda on the plane. I told her that I could not return home without my daughter, Bakita.

It reached a point in the pregnancy when I became so weak that I couldn't even walk; I would just crawl. My legs were paralyzed; even my hands were stiff because of the drip. I couldn't even lift my hands to bathe myself. One day Kony came to visit me in the hospital, but, you know, in Juba they had tough rules. No soldier was to enter the maternity ward. When you had on the uniform, they never allowed you to enter the ward. When you had on civilian clothes, they allowed you to enter.

Kony came when he had dressed up in a military uniform. He had put on all his pips [stars indicating rank on lapels], so the medical doctors said he could not enter the hospital, so we had to talk to each other through the window. I was not supposed to leave the room, and he was also not to enter. He asked me how I was. I told him that I was fine, but my hand was becoming paralyzed. Indeed, my whole arm was becoming paralyzed. I had stayed for four days without bathing.

Ladit said he was going to send someone to take care of me, but I should know that it was not safe and that a war was going to break out between the LRA and Arabs at any moment. I told him, "I am not yet fine. I have no strength, and, second, the child is not playing in my womb. The doctor says the child is not lying in the right position. It is lying in the wrong position; therefore, they have to change it. That is why I cannot walk. My legs are swollen. They also said that the child is very big and I have to be taken for an operation. I have to be taken to Khartoum for that operation." Kony said that if I feel I have some strength, I should not go to Khartoum. He said that they might go to Uganda. I continued staying in the hospital.

A soldier named Lalere was brought to care for me. He was the one who cleaned me with a cloth. I could not eat while I was in the hospital during this time; I just took fluids. My body was swelling. I stayed in the hospital for one month. One day I told Lalere, "You are suffering with me as if you are my husband, yet Kony is there." I then began to cry. Lalere also started crying. He said, "*Mego*, be strong. I am a child from home. I am an Acholi. Atiak and Palabek are one. Be strong; there is nothing that will happen to you. I will not leave you."

On the day the nun had planned to put me on the plane back to Uganda, I was in pain. I could not go without Bakita, so I found a way to move back to the barracks to get her so that we could escape together. As I entered the barracks, the pain grew worse, and I ended up delivering alone. When some soldiers heard the baby crying, they called the medical personnel, who came and helped me cut the umbilical cord of the baby. Then they took me back to the hospital because the baby was so big. I became so weak that I was taken back to the hospital. I stayed there for some time until I gained strength; then I was discharged.

4

Leaving Sudan

Leaving Sudan

After Winnie was born, my co-wives and I worked in the gardens in Rubangatek until the relationship between the LRA and the Arabs soured and the LRA was no longer welcome in Sudan. The LRA first moved as one big group and crossed the border into Uganda, climbing the Isore Mountains before breaking into two different groups: commanders Vincent Otti and Raska Lukwiya moved together further into Uganda, while Kony and Kenneth Banya moved as a group back and forth across the Ugandan-Sudanese border. John Matata, who was appointed second in command after Otti Lagony was killed, broke his brigade into small units and moved around "in mobile" [an LRA term referring to when they are on mission and constantly moving from one position to another] throughout Sudan in order to distract the soldiers from pursuing the rest of us. In Uganda, Vincent Otti's group went toward Atiak and Raska Lukwiya's group headed for Agoro, while Brigadier John Lakati and Colonel Onen Kamdulu moved to Palabek.

I moved with Kony's group across the Isore Mountains to Agoro along the rail. Each person had to carry his or her own belongings. I carried an Oxfam container of sugar, a basin of sorghum, some wheat, my bag, and my baby girl, Winnie. Bakita walked beside me. We would stop only to cook quickly before packing up and moving on again. We had to keep moving because Ugandan soldiers had arrived in Agoro. If they saw smoke from our fires for cooking, they could trace our where-abouts and attack us.

One night we had to move in the mountains the whole night to escape the UPDF as they were following our group. Just as it was ap-proaching dawn, the UPDF caught up with us and attacked our group. I could hear gunshots, and then suddenly a bomb fell near me. Bakita and the boy who was carrying her fell down and slid into a crevice. I was also thrown into the crevice but held onto a tree to keep from falling further in. I thought that my children and I were going to die together that day, but God helped me.

It took some time, but eventually we caught up with *Ladit*. As soon as I arrived in the position, he called out to me, "Bakita's mother, are you still here? Keep moving; a plane is going to come." As soon as *Ladit* said those words, two planes came. The only advantage of being on a mountain is that those shooting from the planes are fearful that the bullets will refract from the mountainside and hit the plane. Rocks are like a magnet. They can hold the plane.

We moved for a long distance, zigzagging across the border and eventually reached Anyima, in northern Uganda. We spent the night there. We were so thirsty that people begged for each other's urine to drink.

I just collapsed on the road. *Ladit* ordered four of his men to double back and carry the children and me to the position. I told my cousin to carry the child but not me. "I cannot go on. Leave me behind. My day has come." I lay down and began to cry like a kid. I made a sound like a goat. Any person who passed me became sad. They thought that I was going to die. My chest pained.

The boys carried my children and belongings as I rested. Somehow after a while I found the strength and was able to continue to walk. When I reached the position, I found *Ladit* quarrelling with his soldiers for leaving me behind. I found one of my co-wives digging for water in the sand. My co-wife collected the water in an Oxfam container and gave it to me to drink. I drank all of it, and she started to complain that there was no water left. I asked her who would help her if I died.

I fell asleep in the sand, but I could hear *Ladit* calling me to him, so I got up. The water had given me strength to move. I went to him, and he asked me what the problem was. I told him that he definitely knew my problem. He told me, "There are some things that I distributed to people. This is your share." He gave me bed sheets, soap, Vaseline, and knickers. I told him, "There is no need for me to get these things because I want you to release me. Let these things help those who are going to remain behind."

Ladit just laughed at me. He said, "If you are to be released, then I will be the one to decide, not you. I will not allow you to go back home and suffer. I do not want you to die. I cannot let you go and die. If you are to go back, it will be to die. That is not good."

I told him, "I am talking to you as my husband. You are the father of my children. I gave birth to children with you. You are the one who has taught me everything that I know. I did not know how to live with a man before I met you. You are the one who guided me, and that is why I am your wife."

Ladit said, "I will be the one to decide whether or not to release you." This is what he said to me.

I then referred to Kony by his first name. I said, "Joseph, if you mind about us, if you want the children and me to live, then please release us. I have reached a point where I cannot go on. I am tired of this world. If you force me to stay, then I will not live."

He said, "You will not die. I am here for you. I will help you."

In the morning people began to move northward again. We walked and reached a river. They decided that we should stay on the riverbanks for one week. We stayed there for one week, and *Ladit* sent people to get food from Akilok [a trading center]. They brought two cows and goats. The cows were taken from the Karamojong. The goats were slaughtered first. There was plenty of cooking oil and other items.

Kony said, "Betty, I think that carrying your belongings is what is making you say that you should be released. I cannot release you and have you go back to your home. You are still going to give birth to many of my children."

I was so hurt by what he said, and I began to cry. I said, "The two children I have are enough. Giving birth does not mean anything. Are we in the bush to give birth?"

He said sarcastically, "No problem, I will release you tomorrow."

I made up my mind that I would escape. I decided to wean baby Winnie. *Ladit* became strict. He did not want me to move any distance away from him. He wanted me to move in his shadow. He made my life so hard. On the other hand, the other wives were talking negatively. They said that *Ladit* was acting as though we were going to share the same grave. He stopped me from going to distant wells. He sent boys to the well instead.

Fatima could not stand this attention toward me. She said *Ladit* was showing off for me, and it disgusted her. *Ladit* said I was not going anywhere. I kept on praying to God to open up a way so that I could escape with the children. I remember that many people escaped during this period, and we could later hear them speaking on the local radio station, telling us they were back home. I thought that escape was impossible. It was a difficult time, but it passed.

Life in the Bush Was Different

Life in the bush was different. If you were selected to go for a military operation, you had to go. There was no excuse for not going. When it was secure, a woman remained at home with the children, but when things were not fine, nobody cared if you were a woman or not; you had to fight. When the Arabs broke off relations with us, it was a difficult time.

We walked everywhere to find food. One day, as we picked food from a garden, a group of Dinka began to shoot at us. Five of us had gone to pick maize, but only three of us escaped alive; the other two were shot dead. I was the only one who escaped without an injury, as the other two survivors were shot but lived. That is the good thing God did for me that day.

I felt so discouraged. Just imagine: one moment you are chatting with a friend, and the next moment she is dead. I recall my friend that day had just said, "Hey, pass me that," and then she was shot.

Death from a gunshot is so painful. I find this a very hard thing to think about, but there is nothing to do about it. If I worry about it, nothing changes. If I begin to think about it, I cannot sleep. My brain works all the time.

Massacre and Pursuit

The Ugandan military launched a large attack against us in a place called Katira, near the Isore Mountains, where the Lutugu [an ethnic group in South Sudan] tribe lived. The UPDF had mobilized civilians to attack us with bows and arrows. Others had guns. We defeated them and captured the entire village of Lutugu. The LRA herded the villagers together into one spot. It was as though there were an auction. We had begun to eat when one of the Lutugu escaped. When this person escaped, Raska Lukwiya gave an order. We heard ululations. People were crying.

There was a deep hole. LRA soldiers were ordered to throw each and every person into the deep hole. I have never seen so many corpses in all of my life. These people were killed. Some were shot with arrows like they had shot us; others were cut. No firearm was used on them. You would see these LRA soldiers standing on the mountain and throwing people into the hole, one after another. By the time they hit the water below, they were dead. Even if someone had survived the fall, there was no escape from such a steep hole. I felt so disturbed that I could not eat for three or more days. Each time I tried to eat, I would see their faces and how they had died.

We stayed in this position for several days before the dead began to smell and we had to shift to another place. As we moved along the way, we realized the UPDF soldiers were following us, but Kony said not to double back to attack them. We knew the UPDF soldiers had no food, and the LRA wanted them to starve to death.

Those UPDF soldiers just died from starvation and thirst. I recall walking among their corpses. They would just be there seated by a tree or lying down, with their gumboots still on their feet. They died of hunger and exhaustion. They were trying to imitate the LRA by climbing the mountains, but you cannot imitate the LRA.

The LRA decided to perform a cleansing ceremony. Just as we began, the soldiers attacked us, but we overcame them. I watched the UPDF fall dead right in front of me. They had no strength at all. We moved ahead, leaving so many corpses behind. My dear, that was a battle! Very early the next morning, more soldiers arrived and began to shoot us. I heard a sound, "*twiiiiiuuh,*" and a bomb fell near me. Winnie ran toward me with her blanket, and I tied her to my back as gunshots were fired, "*trrrriring trrriring,*" and the *paa* [shells] sprinkled everywhere around us. When a single gun is shot, you heard this sound, "*taaacktuuk*" or "*tuuktuuk.*" When a rapid gun was shot, it made this sound: "*trrrrirring trrrrriring trrrriring.*" You would see dust. Motors and RPGs [rocket-propelled grenades] made this sound "*trruruungrrung*" when they were shot. As this was happening, people lamented loudly. We ran and escaped the battle. When we later returned, we found the UPDF soldiers had died not just of bullets but from eating poisonous fruit in the area.

None of them would ever return to Uganda. Some of them died with gumboots still on their feet. What annoyed me is that you found that Acholi or Alur boys were the ones who died. You would know because UPDF soldiers carry with them identification that identified who they were and what their tribe was.

Trriirin Cuuupcucuup Cuuupcuup

Very early one morning I went to pick bananas and saw a soldier on the mountain. I pretended not to see him and continued with what I was doing. He looked like one of our people but also did not look like one of us. Soon a number of soldiers appeared and began to approach where I stood under the banana tree. During that time there were *amuka* [civilians organized into militias] throughout northern Uganda. If the *amuka* found you, they did not spare you.

I warned my daughter, "Bakita, soldiers!" They immediately began to shoot us. There was a boy called Alex who used to carry Bakita. I remember he was a very good child. He lost his life that day; he was shot. I took Alex's gun and carried Winnie on my back.

When Bakita heard the gunshots, she put on her gumboots, picked up her bag and water, and ran. We ran into a cave, and the soldiers began to shoot bombs into the cave. In the confusion, I slowly crawled on my stomach out of the cave. I thought Bakita was right behind me, but she was not; we had been separated. I walked, walked, and walked before I finally found the position.

The LRA thought an RPG had killed me. I was relieved to see that Bakita had made her way back to the position. It started to rain. You know, when it rains on a mountain, it becomes very slippery and hard to walk. We stayed in that place. We spent a night there. We began to cook. We cooked that night and then slept. That day I survived. That man really shot at me. "*Trriirin cuuupcucuup cuuupcuupp.*"

Lucky to Be a Mother

One night a new recruit I was in charge of escaped. I was to be beaten for allowing this to happen. I said to the soldiers about to beat me, "Go ahead and punish me, but this can also happen to you. It was not my wish for this to happen. If I had a choice, I would not have allowed her to escape. I did not want her to escape. She escaped on her own. But go ahead and beat me the number of strokes you think I deserve." They began to beat me when *Ladit* stopped them. He said no mother should ever be beaten. He said that I was lucky to be a mother. He said that if I were not a mother, I would have been beaten.

In my heart I thought, "I used to think that when I give birth I will not be beaten. I am still beaten even after giving birth." I was hurt because we were beaten for every slight mistake we made. Women at home pack and leave when they have a fight with their husbands. From the bush we had no place to go. The gun was our life.

A Child's Bed Sheets

I was moving along the rail toward Akilok when I saw two soldiers. They began to shoot us with mortars. A mortar fell near me. I was covered in dust with the baby, Winnie. Bakita was with Kony. I got up and ran straight into a tree. I thought that Winnie had died. I saw her trying to get up. I picked her up and put her on my back. I ran and left my child's sheets. In the bush, there was nothing more important than a child's bed sheets. With sheets, you can run for a long distance without the child falling from your back. When you carry a child without sheets on your back, the child can easily fall. Bed sheets were very important in my life. When a bomb detonates, oh my God! The smoke can make you think that everyone is dead.

The Fire

For a short while, the Arabs and the LRA renewed their relationship, and we returned to Sudan. *Ladit* separated his wives and children into different groups as he left to speak to the Arabs. He left our children and me in the Isore Mountains to do farm work. In December, Kony returned and told us to stop what we were doing because he had learned that the government of Uganda had a new plan to attack us. Kony told us to prepare to return to Rubangatek in Sudan, but as I rushed to do so I fell down, and my knee was dislocated. I could not walk, so Kony decided we would spend one more night where we were.

The following day, it was Dominic Ongwen [one of the commanders indicted for war crimes] who carried me. I begged Kony to leave me behind, but he would not accept my request. We crossed Pajong Road, and we slept again for three nights, hoping that my knee would be okay to walk on.

Strange things started to happen. By Christmas day we had become lost in the forests. We crossed a river, but before long we had turned around and found ourselves once more at Pajong Road. Suddenly there was fire everywhere, blocking us from moving ahead or tracing our movements behind. Kony radio-called to Fatima to tell her that we would join them later on as it had become too difficult to pass.

After the call, Kony started speaking strangely. He insisted that I cook for him. As we began to move, he insisted he be the one to carry Bakita. He had never carried Bakita before, yet he put her on his shoulders. He said, "Betty, I have named Bakita after Fatima. Our daughter is the one that will remain, while Fatima will not. Bakita will replace Fatima." He said the name "Fatima" is for remembrance.

Kony's escorts insisted that *Ladit* give them Bakita to carry; it was shameful to them that Kony should carry a child. Kony said, "I want to carry her to my wife Fatima." Kony disappeared with Bakita, insisting we remain behind to cook. After cooking, we began following him slowly. The boys told me stories to distract me, because I was still in a great deal of pain.

As we drew closer to Rubangatek, we heard someone sounding an alarm. At first we thought it was to welcome Kony, but then you could smell the smoke. As we moved closer, we saw Kony sitting alone. We did not ask him or any of his escorts what had happened but could see their mood had changed.

One of Kony and Fatima's eldest sons ran up to me and said, "Mummy, everyone has burned to death!" I asked the child what had happened, and he said that a wildfire had spread so fast it had burned everyone in its path.

A commander came and ordered everyone to sit down in a line. They started counting people, and when they reached me, they told me to pick up my bag and go to Kony. When I reached Kony, he told me that his wives and children were badly off and that I should go and see what I could do to save them. He told me to take toothpaste and smear it on their wounds.

When I reached them, the site was shocking. One of Kony's younger sons was severely burned. He could no longer see, but he could talk. We carried him to a mattress as he cried. As we began to wash his body with water, he died. The sight of his burned body will remain in my mind forever.

Another of Kony and Fatima's sons was also injured. He kept crying to me, saying, "You are now my only mummy. You will be my mummy forever!"

Fatima was dead. The boy kept asking, "Who will be my mother? My mother is dead!" He kept crying and shouting. I tried to soothe him, and at the same time I asked him to show me where his mother lay; I thought perhaps she was still alive and he was just in shock. As he tried to guide me to her, another child came to show me where other children lay together with their mother. I saw one of my poor co-wives lying next to her three children. Her children had died in the fire, and my co-wife struggled to breathe.

The boy took me to the body of Fatima. The only part of her body that was recognizable was her fingernails on one hand. She was holding her ear on the side of her head. Her face was not recognizable. You could see a bone exposed from her leg, which was still on fire and smoking. I told the child to run and get water. He returned, and, as we poured water over Fatima, a sound escaped her. I think that was when she died.

In the morning, we began to bury the dead. In total, three wives, nine children, and an escort had died. A woman named Ajok also died.

I was later told that her husband had shouted at her when she tried to run from the fire that she should remain to cook for him and not fear the fire. He threatened to beat her if she dared to leave.

Grinding Stones

We left the immediate area and went to stay in nearby gardens, a farm close to Rubangatek. We constructed a tent to nurse those who had been burned but did not die and buried the dead. If you entered that space, you could hardly breathe. Their wounds had begun to rot, and the smell of that place was so terrible. Pythons kept entering the tent; they were attracted to the smell.

Everyone feared staying near Kony during this time. They thought he would do something bad. Some thought that he would shoot people. Others thought that he would shoot himself. This was the time I was closest to him. Kony did not want me to leave his side. Some people said that Kony might kill me and then commit suicide. I was not afraid of him. I thought that if he wants to kill me, let him kill me. Even the rebel commanders were scared to go near Kony. His officers removed all the guns from his compound. He would ask for his pistol endlessly. He asked me to search for another pistol. I tried, but not seriously. I told him I could not find one.

One day Kony called me to him and started to talk to me. He told me how he was so sad that his wife Fatima was dead. He said his youngest son named Kony—who was also Fatima's youngest son—should have been the one to succeed him when he dies. He said he loved his son very much. He said that his son Kony was his most beloved son and he trusted him very much, but God had separated them, so he just wanted to end his life. Kony said that the only thing that prevented him from doing so was that he knew he had many children he would leave behind and that if he died, there would be no one to take care of them.

He asked how he would care for his children now that Fatima was gone. I told him, "*Ladit*, recall that one day you said that it is more important to have a flat grinding stone than to have the small stone used for grinding. While it is difficult to find a flat stone, you can always find a small stone with which to grind. When you have no flat stone, there is nowhere to grind. Kony, if you leave us, the future for all these people will be lost. If you are not around, you will never have another child, but if you choose to live, you can have a new child whom you can name Kony." *Ladit* said that even if he were to have another son named Kony, he would not love him in the same way he loved his first son. I then told him, "If you die because of your wife and son, then you may as well kill everyone in the bush. They are here because of you. If you kill yourself, it is as good as killing all of them. No one here is capable of leading us home."

That day Kony told me to make him tea and juice. Kony said that everything in this world happens for a reason. He told me that he was not going to shoot me; he believed that I loved him and that I was strong. He said it is hard to be a prophet. He said that God had tempted him. We talked a lot. He said that one day we would overthrow the government and live a good life and that I would be the first wife in his home because I did not leave him when he was going through such a difficult time. He said he would try his best to take care of me so that my future would be bright. He said to have hope.

Kony said that he would not leave me during times of trouble or happiness. He said that I had faith. I told him that God could take away all your children at one time and then replace them all later on. I told him that I could die at any time, and he could, too. I told him that he could not predict the future. God might have planned that we should not grow old together. I gave him an example. One time we were going toward the area of Atiak. We met an old man and an old woman. The woman could not manage to do anything for herself. Her husband would crawl to collect firewood around the home. He would then crawl to collect water. They were very old. I asked him if he remembered that couple. He said that he did. I told him that if God has planned that I grow old with him, then it will happen just like it happened to the old couple, but if God has not planned that I grow old with him, then I will leave him, just like Fatima did. I reminded him that that was not the first time he saw death.

He said, "Betty, I have heard what you have said; I have lost many top commanders and child soldiers. There was no one who came to give me advice. In Acholi there is a saying that a female dog also catches animals [meaning perhaps that even women are important, where it might be assumed that only male dogs can be great hunters]. You are giving me advice when my own officers fear to even be close to me."

This was the time that I was close to Kony. I told him of my hope to return home to Uganda with the children. The rebels were releasing their wives at this time because the war had become so intense. Kony said that he was going to release all of his wives to return home. He said that he was going to remain in the bush with only men. I became happy. I thought he would release us and allow us to return home.

Imatong Mountains

It was not long after the fire that relations with the Arabs deteriorated again and we left to climb the Imatong Mountains. I was always falling behind on the rail [the single-file line the LRA walked in]. People would reach the position as I was still walking. I carried Winnie on my back and Bakita in my arms. I also had to carry our clothes and food. You might want to just throw those clothes away to make your load lighter, but it was very cold in the mountains at night. You might want to throw away the food, but then the children would cry of hunger and disturb you. They had to eat.

One day I was so exhausted that I kept falling asleep while walking and holding my children. I called out to God, "If you want me to die, let it be here," and then I put the children down and slept in between the mountains. The sun had not yet set; it was only around four o'clock, but I had no more strength. I recall that the place where we lay down had many bamboo sticks around.

I saw a certain brother of mine called Oling. I called him. I said, "Oling, Oling." He turned and saw me. He said, "What is wrong, my sister?" I told him, "I am going to die here. My chest is paining, and I have no strength. I cannot go anywhere." He said, "Get up." This is what Oling told me. I decided to try my level best because Oling said the Lutugu were pursuing the LRA. I could hear gunshots, but I had no strength. It took me time to reach the position.

Up until this point, we had had nothing to eat but cassava for more than a month, but that day the LRA raided some goats from a Lutugu village. We cooked those goats, and people ate. I bathed and sat down to rest. *Ladit* Kony said, "Betty, if you do not find the strength to walk quickly, then one day you will be killed along the way." I told him, "*Ladit*, if I die, it means my day has come. I find my chest paining because of carrying two children together with luggage." He replied, "You keep telling me about your children. Who told you to give birth to them? Do not tell me anything about children. Each and every one who gave birth here knows they have to struggle with them. Mine is a gun. If I had not given you children, then you would ask yourself if you are not a woman because you had not given birth."

I began to cry. I realized he was mocking me. I did not give birth to the children alone. I gave birth to them together with him, against my wish. I said, "*Afande*, are you the one talking like that? No problem. Tomorrow if they whistle [signal that the UPDF are around], then I will leave the children behind. I am the daughter of Atiak. I came here without any children, and that is how I will return." He said, "No problem. That will mean you are an enemy of the LRA, and I will treat you as my enemy. Too many people in my family are dead. If any woman plays around with my children, she will see how I will handle her."

At that precise moment, a bomb detonated beside the children and me. It made this sound: "*wiiiiiuuuuh*." *Ladit* ran away when the bomb was detonated. I heard him say, "The bomb has hit Betty with her children!" We were covered in dust. Another bomb was detonated, and it fell ahead, as if in a zigzag pattern. I began to crawl with the children, holding Winnie in one arm and Bakita in the other. Bakita had grabbed the bed sheets, but the rest of our clothing was left behind. There was nothing else we could do but run.

We hid in bamboo trees next to a camp of Ugandan soldiers for the night. That night I once more prayed to God, "If you want us to die, do it at once. Do not let us be injured and left behind to die." We survived the night.

In the morning I began to follow the rail. As we approached the position, I saw Kony and overheard him speaking to another commander, saying, "My wife and children are still missing."

When the bombs sounded, Kony ran without even knowing where his wife and children were. Now he said to the commander, "I do not know if she will come or not, but I know that if she is alive and finds us she will be very annoyed with me, but I will find a way to coax her to be fine." He then began bragging, "Women are just easily coaxed. That if you do not talk sweetly to your wife, she might escape. With this level of insecurity she may be captured and die blaming you for her death."

I just walked into the area and passed right by Kony. When I was passing, he said, "Betty, come here, bring me the children. What happened yesterday made us separate, my wife." That was what he said. I was very sad. He called Winnie. He said, "Winnie, Winnie, come." He picked up Winnie and went with her. I went and sat under a tree with Bakita. We sat there for some time before Kony said that we should cook for him. We cooked. I escaped death that day. When I look back on what happened during that time, I know that it was God who helped me. If it were not for God, I would have died a long time ago.

Bakita Gets Gumboots

One day as I struggled with the children through a narrow pass in the mountains, Bakita fell off the side and out of my view. I struggled to carry both children with the goods. I would carry Winnie and the goods, then return to get Bakita and carry her, and so on. When I went back for Bakita, she was gone. I scrambled down the side of the mountain to try to find my daughter. I had to find her by tracing her cry. I had to put down what I carried, and each item slipped down the side of the mountain behind me. By the time we climbed back up it was dark, and we spent the night along the path.

When I finally reached the position in the morning, *Ladit* immediately began to quarrel with me for spending the night away from him. Then I asked him if he thought it was proper for me to spend the night with my children in the wild as if they were just like any other children and not his. I was angry.

Later, *Ladit* ordered his men to give me a boy named Bosco to carry our children for me. He was embarrassed. After we were given Bosco to carry the children, Bakita's life improved. She was even given gumboots and other goods of her own because she was growing up and was able to walk. When there were battles, Bakita would run; she no longer needed someone to carry her. Bakita suffered a lot as a young girl; her life was so difficult, but as much as she suffered, she walked.

Koo

Imatong is one of the highest mountains in South Sudan. When you were at the top, you could hardly see what was at the bottom; everything was so far away. You could not make out human beings clearly. They looked very pale. The steepness on the slopes of the mountain would scare you to death, yet we had to move up and down the mountains endlessly.

One day as we descended the mountain, we reached a thick of bushes called Koo, and I ran out of energy. My legs got very weak. I was carrying Winnie, who was a heavy child. I actually collapsed and should have fallen to my death, but I fell into the Koo and that broke my fall.

Bosco told me to slope down more slowly. I told him, "Bosco, I have run out energy." My whole body started shaking; my heart was beating fast. I thought I was going to die. I could not even lift myself; I lost energy and just sat there. I started sweating like nothing, and I began to wonder if I was about to die. I sweat so much. I was so afraid to fall off the narrow path.

If you fell, there was no one who was going to scramble down the mountainside to rescue you. There were children who fell to their death, their bodies to remain at the bottom forever. I was so worried. I prayed to God to help my children. I asked, "If I am to return home, let me return with my two daughters, but if one child is to fall and die, then let us all die together." These were my prayers to God.

Ladit passed me where I had fallen in the trees. I was holding Winnie. He yelled, "You are so weak! Every time you see someone falling behind, it is Betty." I told him, "*Afande*, you will one day get what you deserve. At least I have paid for my sins." People were passing us and continuing their descent, but I could not do anything. I just lay there talking.

When I finally regained my strength, I managed to slowly reach the position with a piece of wood someone had cut for me to use as a crutch. My energy was finished. I did not even have the strength to eat. My arms were without energy. When I arrived in the position, *Ladit* started laughing at me and told me that I resembled someone who was very old. I was in shock.

Ladit told me to bring him hot water so that he could bathe. I told him, "*Afande*, I am not able to do anything. I have no strength." So I went and lay down. I unwrapped the baby from my back and made her sleep on my stomach as I lay on my back. Bakita lay next to me.

Kony again came and told me to prepare bathing water for him. I asked him, "Can you not see the condition I am in?" I had no strength to do anything at the time. Then he said, "Sometimes you are stubborn, and maybe you just do not want to take for me bathing water. It is okay; leave it if you do not feel like it." Then I asked him, "How can you ask for water for bathing when I am sick?"

We rested there for three days and began to move toward Torit. We moved from homestead to homestead, picking up foodstuffs. We had no food. We walked and walked and walked. I worried for my children. I worried about Bakita and Winnie. I worried that they were suffering for nothing and that they would never reach home. I cannot predict the future, but I pray to God that I will never have to climb a mountain again.

Winnie Disappears

My second-born daughter was four years old when she disappeared. We looked for her body after the battle in vain. Up to this day, I do not know if my daughter Winnie is alive or dead. She would be about ten years old by now. Her Acholi name is Angeyo Can, which means "I have known suffering."

There was a temporary ceasefire, and we had settled in a place called Birinyang. We had constructed huts and planted seeds. By the time the UPDF attacked us, the gardens were ready to be harvested. In Kony's home we were seven wives and children. The soldiers first monitored and mastered our base before they attacked us. They would even come and find LRA at the garden harvesting their food, but, when shot at, they just ran away and did not fire back. All along they were trying to master the place. They combined with the Arabs and other soldiers who were from Uganda, and they surrounded Birinyang. They cut off all routes leading to and from Birinyang.

The morning of the attack, I was washing clothes. *Ladit* told me to stop washing and go take other women to the garden to harvest. Binany was our escort. Winnie was crying. I asked *Ladit* to allow me to take Winnie with me to the garden, but he refused. He told me that he would take care of Winnie. We left for the gardens, unaware that soldiers had already surrounded Birinyang.

As soon as we reached a certain place, I smelled cigarette smoke. I told my co-wife that I could smell cigarettes, but she asked, "Who smokes from the bush? LRA doesn't smoke." I looked around a bit and saw footprints from gumboots. All along we had been moving among soldiers ready to ambush us. They did not shoot us or it would have spoiled their ambush. I told Binany, "It seems there are soldiers in this place." Suddenly we heard gunshots not far from us. The LRA had found soldiers in the garden and shot them.

When we reached the garden, we started to harvest maize and sorghum and pick tomatoes to take to the compound. Three aircraft flew overhead toward our compound where Kony had remained with the children. They started shooting right away, and at once UPDF soldiers were everywhere. In each direction we took, there were soldiers. We tried to retreat to the garden, but soldiers were already there. We decided to run toward the children we had left behind at the compound. The plane would drop bombs on the compound and then circle around above us.

I told Binany that I was going to run to save my children. He cautioned me to remain where I was. I told him that even if it meant I would die, he should let me go. He held me down and started begging me, "Mother, please don't run. We shall find the children, do not worry, these planes are just scaring us for nothing. Not everyone will die."

I worried and prayed that God would save my children. I kept thinking about how small Winnie was. That she could not run yet. That she would surely die. In my stomach, I knew I would find only one child alive. I wanted to chase the planes so that they would kill me along with my children. I felt that if one were to die, I should die too. Binany would not allow me to leave his side.

At last the planes left. The soldiers on the ground also stopped shooting. Everywhere was quiet. We started moving toward the base. We had not moved for long before we found an injured person who told us that Kony's compound was not well, that the children had scattered anyhow. He told me he doubted I would find my children and that he had overhead Kony say, "Ha, Betty will kill me today when she comes and finds her child missing. She told me that she wanted to go with her to the garden, but I refused."

We continued toward the compound when we found another group of people and begged them to tell us what was ahead. They were also looking for *Ladit*. We were moving any which way and found ourselves somewhere near a hidden well, where *Ladit* sat alone.

Binany went first and spoke to him. He asked Binany if I was around, and Binany said yes. He told Binany to call me, and I went to him. When I reached him, I started to cry and asked him what he had done. I told him he should have allowed Winnie to go with me to the gardens, but he had refused. He told me that if God planned for something to happen, then it happened. He told me many other children were missing, not only mine. He then told me that Bakita had been found and that I should go to her.

When I saw her, she was naked. She had been wearing a pink dress, and someone had torn it from her body so that the planes did not see her below. I took off the blouse I was wearing and covered my child. There were no other children around.

When I learned that my other co-wives' children were also missing, I became stronghearted. We had found no bodies and believed they had been captured. That same evening, I heard over BBC radio that four of Kony's wives and many of his children had been captured by the UPDF.[1] I began to believe that Winnie was alive and had been taken by UPDF soldiers.

We moved back to the mountains, and, when the LRA intelligence confirmed it was safe, we went back to Birinyang to see if we could find any of the children or their bodies. We did not find a single child. We found only the bodies of a woman and her baby lying together. They pulled the bodies into the bush.

After two days, two children who had run into the forest to hide were found alive. It was decided that we would stay near Birinyang until it was determined who had died and who was missing. We hoped we

1. Around the end of July 2004, it was reported in the Ugandan national newspaper that twenty-eight people had been captured by the Ugandan military and transported to Uganda, including four of Kony's wives and twenty-four of his children.

still might find any other children who had run into the bush and become lost. The LRA returned to Birinyang frequently, but no other child was ever found. After a while, *Ladit* told me that it was no longer safe in Sudan and that it was time to leave.

My co-wife Margaret said that she was not willing to leave yet, as she still did not know the fate of her children. She first wanted to be sure of what happened to them before she moved anywhere. If they had died, she wanted to find their bodies.

I remember it was so cold, and we had no spare clothes. The only thing we could do to stay warm was to light a fire every evening. Rain beat down on us, and there were so many mosquitoes. We had only the clothing on our backs, no other. Those with clothes gave what they could to those who had nothing and who were doing badly. I continued to move bare-chested. I just carried Bakita in my arms, and I cried, as I had no way to help my daughter.

The Concerned Parent's Association advocated for the peaceful release of all abducted children. Gulu, Uganda, 2003. Photo by Erin Baines.

Evelyn Amony among civil society delegates to the Juba peace talks. Place unknown, date unknown. Photographer anonymous.

Evelyn Amony meeting with civil society delegates during Juba peace talks. Garamba, Democratic Republic of Congo, 2006. Photo by Erin Baines.

Vincent Otti, then second in command, at the confidence-building meeting between the Lord's Resistance Army and Acholi civil society members. Garamba, Democratic Republic of Congo, 2006. Photo by Erin Baines.

Joseph Kony (*left*), General and Commander of the LRA, and Vincent Otti (*right*), second in command, meeting with civil society delegates during confidence-building talks. Garamba, Democratic Republic of Congo, 2006. Photo by Erin Baines.

The LRA high command at the confidence-building meeting between the Lord's Resistance Army and Acholi civil society members. Garamba, Democratic Republic of Congo, 2006. Photo by Erin Baines.

Nixman Oryang "Opuk" (*left*) and Vincent Otti (*right*) at the confidence-building meeting between the Lord's Resistance Army and Acholi civil society members. Garamba, Democratic Republic of Congo, 2006. Photo by Erin Baines.

Evelyn Amony holding her daughter and standing beside two male relatives in the LRA during the first confidence-building meeting between the Lord's Resistance Army and Acholi civil society members. Garamba, Democratic Republic of Congo, 2006. Photo by Erin Baines.

Evelyn with friend. Garamba, Democratic Republic of Congo, 2007. Photo by Michael Otim.

Evelyn Amony. Gulu, Uganda, 2009. Photo by Erin Baines.

Evelyn Amony. Gulu, Uganda, 2011. Photo by Lara Rosenoff-Gauvin.

Evelyn Amony. Gulu, Uganda, 2012. Photo by Jodie Martinson.

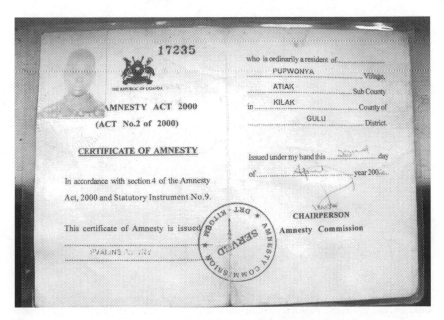

Amnesty card for Evelyn Amony. Gulu, Uganda, 2013. Photo by Erin Baines.

Evelyn Amony. Gulu, Uganda, 2013. Photo by Erin Baines.

Evelyn Amony with *(left to right)* Grace Acan, Kassiva Mulli, Claire Kahunde, and Nancy Apiyo, the Gender Justice Unit of the Justice and Reconciliation Project, which supports the Women's Advocacy Network. Gulu, Uganda, 2013. Photo by Erin Baines.

Evelyn Amony holding a draft copy of her book. Gulu, Uganda, 2013. Photo by Erin Baines.

Evelyn Amony holding the Women for Peace Award. Gulu, Uganda, 2014. Photo by
Erin Baines.

5

Home

Palabek

After we left the place from where my daughter Winnie had disappeared,
Kony announced that we would split into groups; some would move
into Uganda and the rest would remain in Sudan. I was pregnant. I told
him that I would be among those who returned to Uganda. He told me
I could go but that I should not think of trying to escape. He said that if
the UPDF found me, they would kill me. He reminded me that even if
they did not kill me, life would not be fine. He told me that other
women who returned had become drunkards living in poverty. Then he
told me that he was going to keep Bakita with him so that I would not
think of escape.

I began to cry in front of him and all his officers and told him that if
Bakita were to remain in Sudan, then I too would remain. I had just lost
my baby, Winnie, and I would not lose Bakita. Kony ordered some of
his escorts to come and take Bakita away from me as I cried. One of
Kony's commanders, named Lakati, pleaded with him. He said, "*Ladit*,
please allow Betty to return to Uganda with Bakita. They are suffering
here; the UPDF are always following you." After listening to Lakati,
Kony told us to leave immediately for Uganda with Bakita. We quickly
collected our belongings and left. We had not traveled far when *Ladit*
threw the wire up [made a radio call] to Lakati and told us to stop
walking and to remain where we were. It was just 10:00 A.M. We waited

the whole day for him to contact us again. I lost hope. I thought Kony would insist I remain in Sudan with him. Lakati consoled me. He told me all would be fine.

We spent the night by the river. In the morning, Commander Lakati said he had been given permission to continue to move, but he said that first we should be cleansed. He sent some boys to look for white stones to take with us, to help protect us. When they came back, he did a ritual, and when he was done we sewed the stones to our wrists and began to make our way across the mountainside. The UPDF were close by, but they did not hear us pass.

We walked for a long time until finally we entered Palabek, where we divided into smaller groups and each moved in different directions. I moved with Lakati's group to a hidden base in Pangira [near Palabek]. Lakati had hidden food there, and the boys dug it up. He told us that we were going to stay there in Pangira for some time. We were given fresh clothes to put on and were able to rest, as we were not detected by the UPDF. We left Pangira only to meet other LRA in an RV [rendezvous]; then we would disperse quickly back to our position. Even though no soldiers disturbed us during this time, I knew that my co-wives and their children were still behind me suffering in Sudan. We could hear the aircrafts in the distance, flying to Sudan, and we knew they would shoot at them like nothing.

After our food ran out, Lakati began to order his soldiers to raid villages. He would say, "Go and get for me a goat. I want people to eat meat today."

Lakati tortured those civilians in Palabek. One day he told a group of boys to go kill fifty men and to bring him their penises, as well as five premature babies, cut from the wombs of women. He said the people of Palabek were totally useless, only sleeping with each other and reproducing when they should be in the bush fighting to support the LRA. I was shocked to hear the orders he gave those boys.

Shortly thereafter, Kony called and asked to speak to me over the radio. He asked me how I found life in Uganda. I told him it was safe. He also asked how I was doing; I told him I was fine. He told me that Lakati should teach me how to speak radio code, but I told him I was already learning. He tested my knowledge and asked me, "If someone has swallowed *panadol*, what does it mean?" I told him that it means that person has been shot dead. Then he also asked what "*te battery*" meant, and I told him it means "so-and-so's wife." Then he told me that I am a fast learner and that it seems I was sneaking and learning the things from his books in Juba when he was not around. Kony then told me that he wanted to talk to me every two weeks. I told him that the aircraft disturbs us when we speak on the radio; they bomb people who are around the places where communication is picked up. I told him that I was not able to run all the time since I was pregnant and weak, and if we are to be talking every time on the radio call, soldiers will detect it and keep attacking us. Then he told me that there were tactics they could use to address that. "Don't you see that I have always spoken with those of Lakati without a problem? We can plan to talk at 6:00 A.M., before the military offices have opened, or we could talk at 8:00 P.M., when the plane has finished its work and gone back to town."

At that point I told *Ladit* that I had overheard Lakati give very bad orders to his soldiers. I asked him, "Why should he kill innocent people like that?" When Lakati got on the radio he denied it; he said that he had given the order jokingly and I had taken it seriously. After we finished talking, Lakati told me not to report everything that was happening to *Ladit*. He added that if I want to be a good person and grow up into a good officer, I should not tell *Ladit* what was happening because it was the equivalent of snitching.

Lakati had a dog that he loved so much. If it got lost, he would become enraged. He would refuse to eat when his dog was missing. I used to wonder how Lakati could care so much about an animal but could send his fighters to kill humans. What was wrong with this man? I later learned that he was sick with HIV/AIDS. Lakati was so brutal! He beat his officers in order to instill hatred in them toward civilians. I told Lakati not to be so harsh or his soldiers would escape and report to the UPDF the whereabouts of our defense. I reminded him that if we were attacked, I could not run. Lakati just laughed.

Later on, one of the commanders, Odongo, told me that I should not criticize Lakati as I had in front of his fighters, or they would escape and disappear. He advised me to approach Lakati when he was alone to tell him that what he was doing was not right. I found that moment to approach him, and I feared he would become enraged, but he was calm and told me that he had never intended for his soldiers to really mutilate civilians like that. He said that he was only joking and they took his orders seriously.

Ociju Escapes

One night while we were still in Pangira, one of the boys, called Ociju, came to help me sew my daughter's clothes. He had lost a leg in a battle long ago, and he would use a stick to move around. His hands were always bruised and swollen because of that stick. Despite this, he could sew clothes well. We sat together, and as he began to sew he said to me, "*Mego*, I am going home [planning to escape]. Look at how I am doing. My hands are rough. Look at the wounds on the small of my back." The small of his back was bruised because of his walking stick. I looked at him and said, "Ociju, I wish you the best if you are going. I will pray for you. I will *niciru* [fast] for you and pray that you reach home well." Ociju said, "*Ama*, I do not want you to remain behind." He proposed we escape together. I told him that if we left together, we would not make it, as I was pregnant and unable to move quickly. I knew that Lakati would pursue us, as he would fear that Kony would punish him if I escaped, and that he would follow us until he found us. So I told Ociju to leave and that I would remain behind to pray for his safe return home. Ociju began to beg me to go with him: "*Ama*, I do not want you to remain behind."

We began to argue. Ociju began to cry, and I also cried. He said, "*Ama*, look at how you are. You are pregnant, and you have to care for Bakita. There is no one to help you with her. If the UPDF attack, you will not be able to run in this condition and carry your child alone." I told Ociju, "I am just worried about you. Look here, you know what I am talking about. If you are to reach home safely, it must be without me. You will walk and reach home safely."

That night Ociju escaped together with a young boy. He promised that before they left, they would come and knock on our tent in case I had changed my mind. He tapped the tent I was in, but I knew it was impossible, so I remained quiet, and they left. I prayed for them all night.

"God, if you are the one to protect those in need please protect these boys. We do not know the reasons why you wanted us in the bush, but tell me you do not want us to die here to be eaten by animals. Lead us from here so that we die in our homes where we can be buried like human beings. Do not let us die in the bush unburied like animals. God, please carry your child Ociju home to safety, Ociju who cannot walk. Console him as he moves. Tell your angels to protect the weak and the vulnerable. Help him."

As they went to change the guard the next morning, his colleagues realized he was gone. He had written a letter to Lakati that said he had not escaped for any reason other than the fact he was suffering from his injuries. "My hands and the small of my back are rough from bruises. It is as though a gun is shooting the small of my back daily. Won't you feel sorry for me? I know that I can limp and reach home. If you want to kill me, you can follow me or you can come and kill me from my home. Today I will either reach my home or you will kill me, but I am suffering, and I do not know what else to do. That is why today I am going to leave your company. This is the time that I must leave. If God helps me and I escape, then that is it. If you catch me and kill me, then that is it. This is me, Ociju. I have gone."

No one tried to follow Ociju to stop his escape. The next time I turned on the radio, the program *Dwog Cen Paco* ["Come Back Home"] was playing on Mega FM, the local station. The show used to call to us to return home from the bush and feature those who had escaped. Ociju was speaking on the radio program—he had reached home! Ociju spoke directly to me, calling my name. He begged me to be strong and to come back home. He said, "*Mego*, think of how big your pregnancy has grown. I know that you cannot walk. When any soldiers attack, you will die." I started to regret my decision not to leave with him. He was now gone. When I heard Ociju talk on radio, I began to cry. I cried a lot, but after a while I realized that crying was not going to help me with anything. Whenever the planes would fly over and shoot at us, I would think of Ociju asking me, "*Mego*, you cannot even run; what will you do?"

My Co-Wives Join Us from Sudan

It was almost Christmas when two of my co-wives—Margaret and Cecile—and their children finally reached us in Palabek, having traveled from Sudan. Oh how they had suffered in Sudan! By the time they reached us, they were pale and thin. On the journey, they had no food to eat and had lost much weight. They had lice, as they were unable to find any source of water to bathe in; soldiers guarded all the water points by then. I shed tears when I first saw them. They did not even look like human beings. Their bodies had no flesh on them. We celebrated Christmas together, and when it was time to separate, Cecile's son refused to go with his mother; he wanted to remain with me.

On the twenty-sixth of December, *Ladit* communicated via radio that I should no longer stay in Pangira, and that I should leave immediately for a new defense. There were peace talks during that period. Betty Bigombe was the peace mediator at that time. She would walk into the bush to meet some of the LRA commanders and would bring foodstuffs and other things for us. *Ladit* told me not to eat a single thing Betty Bigombe brought for us. He told me the food was poisoned. So I sent the young boys to bury the food. *Ladit* said even the gumboots should not be worn by anyone but be buried. So the boys carried all these things and buried them.

Despite the promise of a ceasefire, the aircrafts appeared on December 26. We had barely begun to run when they began to fire at us from the plane. The UPDF soldiers on the ground captured people and took them away. I moved in a small group with my co-wife Margaret, our children, and an escort, Okete. All the boys were sent on standby to fight; only Okete remained behind to help us. The plane shot at our small group for a very long time as we scattered and hid. Cecile's son disappeared from my view. I thought he had been killed, yet I found out later that he survived the attack. We moved and spent the night somewhere. I was by now nine months pregnant and also carrying Bakita with me when we ran.

We were so thirsty. Whenever I tried to approach a well, there were UPDF soldiers surrounding it. I felt so desperate that I just wanted to walk up to them. At one point, in the confusion of running and hiding, Bakita, Okete, and I lost the others. We hid as the soldiers passed in front of us. We heard them speaking Luo [my language]; they said, "Hmm, these people are struggling to run for nothing; they should just come back home. I wonder what Lakati wants." Eventually, when it became cool, we made our way back to the larger group.

If You Care about Us, Kony, Let Us Go

One day we were told to meet the LRA army commander Raska Lukwiya in an RV some distance away. I was heavily pregnant by then, yet the commanders forced me to walk such distances to meet them. I remember thinking that Raska should have been the one to walk to me.

When we reached the position of the RV, Raska said that he wanted to talk to me. We spoke for a long time, and he could see the condition I was in. He said he would talk to *Ladit* to ask for permission to release me and another woman, named Jackie, who had just lost her baby. He said staying in the bush was difficult. Raska had already planned to release several other women who were pregnant at the time. Jackie and I were told to wait with the other pregnant mothers, but as they prepared to release us, we were pulled from the group and told to remain behind.

One of the mothers to be released came to me and told me that *Ladit* had called and refused to grant Raska's request. I begged her to appeal to Raska because he would listen to her. Kony told her that if I were released, the UPDF soldiers would kill me. I was bitter. I said, "Those are foolish words. Was I there when Kony went to the bush? I was not there, and I do not know what brought him to the bush. I am not him! I walk separately from Kony. He walks alone, and so do I. Why should they view us as the same person?" That was what I said, but to no avail.

We began to move together in a group. As we approached a river to catch fish, people panicked, as they mistook a group of baboons for soldiers. People shouted, "Soldiers! Soldiers!" and we ran for a long time before we realized that these were not even people. We regrouped, and I was again in Lakati's company. I appealed to him, "Lakati, I should also be released with the rest of the mothers! I keep getting separated from my daughter whenever we are attacked by soldiers, and I fear she will be killed. Please talk to Kony and ask him to release us."

He said, "I will wire him and you talk to him." When he wired *Ladit*, Lakati told him, "*Mego* wants to speak with you." I got on the wire and asked him, "Do you really care about your child and me? If you care about us, Kony, let us go. I cannot run. I cannot manage anything. We run all the time. I am begging you. Let me go. My going does not mean that I do not want the LRA. My body just cannot manage staying in the bush. I cannot manage anything in this war." He told me to be patient for two more weeks, and then he would release me.

When the other mothers were released, Jackie and I wept. I said, "We have been left behind! Look at how we are suffering! I am tired of being hungry! Kony does not care about us." We stayed, and the other mothers left. Raska came and began to console me. He told me not to miss home. He said I was going to be their mother now. He said I should concentrate on staying with Kony. I thought about it in my heart. I told Raska, "Whether I am going to be an elderly mother or what, it is all the same." I am a mother, but my heart is home in my village, not here in the LRA. The battles had become tough, and things were not easy. We bade Raska farewell and separated.

Later on, we met Vincent Otti's group, and he gave me new gumboots and soap. The soap was called "sunlight." That soap was yellow and big. I was also given TipTop Vaseline and [a container of] cream with the words "Big Love" written on it. Vincent Otti also gave me a baby shawl, towel, and a sheet for carrying the baby when it was born. He said, "My sister, be strong. I will meet you later." I said, "Look, Otti, I am alone. All the boys who once helped carry the children and my belongings have been sent to fight. When a battle starts, there is no one I can rely on." Vincent Otti gave me eleven boys from his group to help my co-wives and me. He gave us two officers and nine boys. He called all of the boys together and instructed them on their new orders. I felt happy because in the bush, if you do not have people, it is a big problem. I was happy when I started staying with those boys, because when a battle started we would run and hide together.

Finding Kony's Child

As we were moving one day, we found one of Kony's children alone in the bush. The boy who had been carrying him had dropped him on the ground during a battle and left him behind. He must have been there for more than a week. The boy had survived by eating raw cassava and drinking water from the jerry can the boy carrying him had also dropped. Somehow, the Ugandan soldiers never found him. I had two children with me now, Bakita and Cecile's son. Because I had boys to help me, I told them to give me the child to carry. After some time, during another attack, we lost him again. I heard that Kony struggled endlessly to find his child again.

By then Kony's group was not far away from us, but each time we tried to reach them, the UPDF would attack us, and so we never met Kony again in Uganda. There were so many UPDF soldiers! At one point the UPDF shot Kony and one of his wives as they crossed the road that goes to Atiak. Kony was not harmed terribly, but his wife died later that day, and her body was left on the banks of the Ayugi River. It was a confusing time. There were rumors that Kony was dead. We waited to hear it announced on Mega FM, the radio station, but we heard nothing. One night we could hear people camped close to us, and the voice of Kony traveled. We knew we were very close to where he was, but in the morning the UPDF were once again on top of us. As we ran, we met the group of Commander Odongo. They had laid an ambush for the UPDF soldiers pursuing us. As they approached Odongo, he launched a mortar and killed so many UPDF soldiers. We went and saw their corpses in the evening but quickly left, as we knew the government would send their troops to recover their bodies. I remained with Odongo until we were captured together.

Giving Birth

One evening Odongo looked at me and knew I was about to give birth. He said there were more battles ahead and asked what we should do if I was to give birth during a battle. He decided we should move toward Atiak, but we failed to cross the Aswa River as the UPDF soldiers were everywhere. We began to retrace our steps to return to the place we had rested the prior evening, but the planes came and began firing all around us. At first, I thought the pain in my back was because of the bombs dropping from the plane. We continued moving the whole day, trying to evade the soldiers, and the pain increased. When the bombs fell, my waist felt like it would split open. By the time the evening came, I was in full labor.

I separated from the rest of the group, including my daughter and the other children. I suffered through the night in labor, but by morning my co-wife Margaret found me. She ordered the escorts to find and boil water for me. I gave birth and used the hot water to bathe the baby and myself, but that was the last time I would use water in the bush. There was no food, and the planes were again in the sky with the UPDF soldiers all around us. So we had to move. I was in so much pain as we walked, and I grew weak from blood loss and exhaustion. One of the boys had found sorghum, and we ate it without grinding or cooking it that night. Another boy had caught an edible rat and prepared it, but just as we were about to eat, the soldiers attacked. I was again separated from the rest of the group and moved through the night with my daughter Bakita beside me and my newborn tied to my chest.

By morning, the planes had already returned. I was so thirsty and weak from having given birth. My body was shaking all over, and I could no longer find the strength to carry the baby. I untied her from my chest and laid her down in the grass. I then told Bakita that we must continue to move without the baby. Bakita begged me to not leave the baby behind, and I tried to drag her away. I told her that I could not carry her any further.

Bakita refused to walk. She was begging and crying. I collapsed by a tree. Bakita picked up the baby and let me rest. She then removed a breast from my shirt and the baby suckled. At that point I knew I could not leave this child behind. After we gained some strength, we continued to walk together.

Capture

We kept on walking and sitting, walking and sitting. By nightfall we had caught up with the rest of Odongo's group, and we spent the night together. In the morning, Bakita spoke excitedly and told us that she had a dream that soldiers had captured us and that she and I were the only ones who were left unharmed. I told her to be quiet and not to talk like that, but my co-wife Margaret insisted that she narrate the dream in detail. Bakita told us that the soldiers would ambush us and everyone would be shot except her and me. I slapped her and told her to stop talking like that.

We received communication to meet Vincent Otti in an RV, but just as we gathered at the meeting point, the planes arrived. There were very many people at the RV, and the Gilva, Sinia, and Stockree Brigades were not far away. The plane just started shooting and then dropping bombs. We went and climbed the hills until we were high up, but as soon as we stopped to rest one of the boys warned us that UPDF soldiers were coming. Wherever we tried to run there was another group of soldiers. They surrounded us.

They shot us with a mortar; we ran, and I decided to separate from the rest of the group. I tried to run away with Bakita and the baby, but Odongo and my co-wife followed me, together with another girl. Odongo turned and started to shoot the soldiers who followed us. Each one fell dead. We continued running and entered into a clearing. When I turned to look behind me, I saw that Margaret had fallen down and that she had been shot. Bakita and Odongo had also fallen down, but I could not see if they had been shot or not. Fear gripped me, and I stood in the clearing as the soldiers approached me, their guns raised. I could see my Bakita crawl over to my co-wife Margaret and struggle to free the child tied to her back.

As I stood in the clearing, one of the soldiers started to shoot at me rapidly. I raised my newborn baby above my head to surrender. The bullets passed on either side of me; one passed straight through my skirt. He continued shooting despite my surrender. Another bullet just missed my neck, burning me. The soldier shooting at me moved closer and closer to me. When I did not fall, he lowered his gun and studied me. He came up to me, and as he inspected me he finally said, "You, woman, you are very lucky, that medicine you have tied on your body must be strong. And for that reason, you will not die." He threw his gun away. Other soldiers arrived and started looking at me, discussing how I had defeated the bullets, how a mere woman had defied them. They told me to come with them, and we walked toward where Bakita lay. She had been able to remove the child from my co-wife's back and had tied him to her back. My co-wife had been shot in the chest but was still alive and conscious. Bakita's whole body was full of blood, and I did not know if she was injured or not.

I untied the child from Bakita's back and tied him onto mine, as I carried the newborn in my arms. At the time, I was sure Bakita had also been shot, but I could see no wounds. The Ugandan soldiers allowed us to fix a *kita* [a makeshift stretcher] for my co-wife Margaret. As we began to move together toward their defense we came across Odongo, who had also been shot but was still alive. One of the Ugandan soldiers just raised his gun and shot him again, cursing him for making people's children suffer in the bush and for raping other people's children. In anger, he again turned as if he was going to shoot Odongo again, but instead he shot the ground. He then turned and shot Margaret in the leg. He shot her even after it was clear we could no longer fight them, after we had surrendered.

The same soldier then turned to me and asked me whose wife I was while in the bush. I told him that I was Odongo's wife. When Odongo heard that, he started to deny it and told me to speak the truth to the UPDF, that we were Kony's wives. I felt so heartbroken when I heard him say this, and Margaret urinated in fear. I thought that was the very moment my life would end. Odongo just kept on talking. He told them many things, including where the LRA had hidden weapons. He just continued talking nonsense.

The soldiers then began to fight among themselves about who had made the arrest, realizing they had captured high-level people and that there would be a reward. They did not care that Ondogo and my co-wife were in pain, so I began to nurse their wounds as they argued. As I cared for Odongo's leg, one soldier began to shout at me, "Don't help that man, let him die, he is the very one responsible for your suffering! After all he has done, why are you still helping him? Don't!" And then, "As for you, Odongo, I should have killed you right away, because as soon as we get back home I know the government will give you a higher rank than mine![1] I should just kill you. Let us see if you arrive home alive!"

At the UPDF Base

The soldiers led us to their base. Their boss was sitting under a mango tree. One of the soldiers came and started asking Margaret what part of her body had been hurt. He reassured her and told her not to worry, that she would return home and soon see her family. Soon other soldiers started to gather around and ask us a lot of questions. One soldier wanted

---

1. A strategy for "reintegrating" high-level LRA officers was to integrate them into the Ugandan military at the same rank they had obtained in the bush.

to know if his sister who had been abducted was still in the bush and alive. I said that she was, but Odongo in his crazed state just started to say that I was lying, that she was dead. I became afraid, and my whole body started trembling. I worried that we would all be killed. Then one of the soldiers started saying, "Lady, be stronghearted, nothing wrong will happen to you, you will reach home."

The boss came and dispersed the soldiers back to their *adaki*, and we remained there with their leaders. He told some of the soldiers to inspect my body, because I might have a wound but not know it, as I seemed to be in shock. I again started shaking as one of the soldiers lifted my skirt. The soldier began to caress my thigh, asking, "Did you not get shot here?" I thought about the day we had seen Raska's wife raped to death by soldiers. Then one of the soldiers discovered a bullet hole in my skirt, and they looked at it together and discussed it. "Lady, it's a miracle you are alive; that medicine Kony gave you must be very strong," one of them said. After that they mostly left me alone. Still, they began to argue over who would get the gumboots I was wearing and began forcing them from my feet. Their boss overheard them and started to shout at them, "Why are you stealing that girl's gumboots; what will she use? Give her back her gumboots." Then they gave me back my new gumboots, but one of the soldiers insisted that I remove my socks and give them to him.

They started telling me that I should go and prepare food for the children, and someone gave me a fish. They also gave me water to bathe the children and wash their clothes. Before their clothes had dried, a long row of vehicles arrived. We were told to get in one of the vehicles with the children. I had my new daughter in one arm and Margaret's son in the other, and I breastfed both as we moved in the vehicle. At one point, a soldier started to complain that Margaret was bleeding all over the place and was going to ruin the vehicle. He insisted we push her out of the car, but we continued driving until we reached a small trading center called Paludar. When we arrived, a crowd of civilians came around the vehicle, staring at us. We were carried into the UPDF defense, where Odongo and Margaret were taken to the medical clinic. I was given more water and continued to wash the children's clothes. When I was done, I went to find Margaret being interrogated by the UPDF. They were asking her a lot of questions. They then took me to a separate room and asked me a lot of questions, and I told them every-thing I knew in detail. At the end, they asked me my name and that of my parents, promising to announce that I had returned on radio Mega FM so that my family would learn that I was alive.

Transport to Gulu

That same day a plane arrived to carry us to Gulu. I was so worried that Margaret would die in the plane because she was so weak. The plane landed in the Fourth Division in Gulu town, and we were all taken to the dispensary and admitted to the military ward. That same night, former LRA Brigadier Mzee Banya and Commander Ray Apire, who had been captured and returned to Uganda some months before me, came and found us there, but I did not speak to them.

I desperately needed water to bathe. There was a UPDF soldier who spoke some Luo, so I begged him to bring me water. He went to the kitchen and took the water being boiled for *posho* [bread] and brought it to me. His colleague was angry and started to yell at him, "Why are you fetching water meant for preparing bread? Why didn't you wait for me to first prepare the *posho* and then you put more water to boil?" The soldier just continued to bring me the water. Since I had given birth, I had not had a proper bath, and the blood had clotted in my womb. I was weak, and one of the women medical workers followed me to the bathroom to help clean it before I bathed. When I started bathing, I became even weaker. The medical woman came and started pressing my tummy with hot water, and pus just started flowing out of me. She brought more hot water and continued to help me. She told me, "My daughter, don't worry, you will survive. Nothing wrong will happen to you." She went and brought for me penicillin V tablets. I was afraid that she was trying to poison me, so I pretended as if I was swallowing the tablets, but instead I threw them away. She told me that we should go back in the house. We walked as she held my hands; I felt so dizzy, and my vision became dark. When we reached the room, I was brought milk and biscuits to eat, but I did not. Margaret also refused to eat anything. We were sure they were trying to poison us.

Shortly after that, Lacambel, the radio announcer of the "Come Back Home" program on Mega FM, came and told me that Vincent

Otti was on the phone and wanted to talk to me. Lacambel gave me his phone, and we started talking. Otti told me that he had heard that we had been arrested but that we should be stronghearted and know that nothing wrong would happen to us, that we would not be killed; we had already reached home and did not need to worry about anything. He asked me if I was hurt. Then I told him that I was not hurt, that it was Margaret who had been injured. He told me that since Margaret was hurt, he would not speak to her, but he wanted to speak to Odongo. Lacambel took the phone to Odongo.

Later on, Lacambel came back and asked me to make a recording of my name, my parents' names, and the name of our village so that he could send a message on Mega FM to my parents that I had returned alive. I recorded a message to my parents and those I love so much. Little did I know that most of the people I called by name were already dead. Later on I heard Lacambel on the radio program calling for my parents: "You people whose names have been read here, your daughter has returned home from the bush. While in the bush she was called Betty Ato, but her real name is Evelyn Amony. She returned with two children. If you want to know more details, go to GUSCO [Gulu Support the Children Organization, a rehabilitation center] or World Vision tomorrow morning or come to me at Mega FM, and we will reunite you with the children." I found it strange that he and everyone else kept calling us children, yet Margaret and I were no longer children. The next day I was taken to the GUSCO rehabilitation center in Gulu town, where I would remain for nearly eight months as I recovered.

Reunion with My Parents

As I was resting in the sleeping quarters of GUSCO, a staff member entered the room and asked, "Who here is called Evelyn Amony?" I said, "From home I am called Evelyn Amony, but from the bush they called me Betty Ato." I was informed that I had a visitor. I asked them where the visitor was from. They told me my family had come. I followed the staff person to the visitor's room to find my father and my younger brothers had come. To be honest, I did not recognize any of them. I greeted them, and then just looked at them. My father also stared at me. He asked me if I knew him, and I told him that I did not. He asked me where my home was, and I told him it was in Atiak. My father asked me again, "What is your father's name?" I told him, "My father's name is L. Marcellino." He asked me, "What was your father doing at the time you were abducted?" I replied that my father was a veterinary doctor. He then said, "I am your father. The person you are talking about is me." I began to cry. My father also started crying. I was confused; I did not know for sure if this was my real father. We cried for almost an hour before my brothers told him, "Dad, if you continue to cry, Evelyn will not stop crying."

When we were calm, I sat at his feet and just looked up at my father. Before long, my mother also came to the visitor's center, and immediately she too started to cry. I held her to console her, telling her to keep quiet. When she calmed down, I started crying. We just kept going on like that, consoling one another, crying. When my parents left the rehabilitation center, they promised to return in a few short days to see me again. I did not tell them I was sick because I did not want them to start crying again.

My strength deteriorated after they left. I could no longer stand or walk. My stomach pained. It was as if I had been shot in the stomach. I had developed an infection after giving birth in the bush. I could not even hold the baby, and if I went to the bathroom, I had to crawl. In the middle of the night, I fell unconscious from the bed and could not move; the staff sent for a driver to bring me to the hospital. When I woke up, I found bottles of drip [IV] had been inserted into each hand. I did not remember how I had reached the hospital. My co-wife Margaret was beside me, taking care of the baby. GUSCO sent news to my family to hurry back to Gulu.

I was so fearful in the hospital. I thought someone was going to poison me, so I refused to eat any food that had been brought to me. When I awoke next, my mother was by my side, soothing me. She had bought fresh fish and prepared it. I just looked at the food but refused to eat it. Finally, my mother said, "My daughter, I am the one who gave birth to you. Why don't you eat what I have prepared? Try eating it." I looked at my mother and thought, "Yes, it is true. This is the woman who gave birth to me. I did not separate from her to go to the bush by choice. God, if you want my mother to be the one to kill me let her do so." So I started eating my mother's food.

6

Peace Talks

Busia

I recovered at GUSCO before I began a tailoring course at St. Monika's Secondary School in Gulu town as part of my rehabilitation. After I had had a few months of training, a man named Odoch came to the school and asked to speak to me. I knew him from the bush. Odoch told me that a local leader in Busia had recently contacted him because they had found a group of children who claimed to be those of Kony and who had fled the attack in Birinyang. He said Winnie was among this group of children. I believed him.

Odoch let me speak to a man who claimed to be the local councilor [LC, government representative elected at the village level] from Busia. He said that Odoch would bring me to him in Busia and that he would take me to the children. Busia is a town on the border between Uganda and Kenya.

Odoch returned a few days later with a vehicle. He drove me, along with another co-wife whose child had also been found, to Busia. We both brought our youngest children with us. My daughter Grace was just over a year old at the time. It was a very long drive before we finally arrived in Busia. When we arrived, Odoch went and met the LC, and they began to argue about how to proceed.

While they were arguing, Odoch received a phone call, and I could hear Kony's voice on the other end of the line. I could hear Kony say that he was so happy my co-wife and I had been found. I heard him say that we should be taken across the border and into Kenya so that they could arrange to bring me to him. Immediately I felt so bad. I told my co-wife that I had overheard Odoch speaking to Kony on the phone, but she found it hard to believe me. Then Odoch and the LC told us we were going to cross the border immediately. We both still hoped that our children were alive and waiting for us in Busia, so we accepted to go with them.

When we got to the border, the border guard insisted on seeing our passports, yet we had none. Odoch tried to convince the border guards to let us pass. He said we were going to attend a funeral. The border guard called the police and asked them to come and advise him on the matter. The policeman came, but when he saw the children, he immediately asked if these were the children of Joseph Kony. They must have recognized Odoch and suspected what was happening. Immediately things became tense, and the police arrested Odoch, removing his shirt.

We left the border with the LC and returned to his home. The LC told us to relax, that there was nothing to fear. I asked the LC where our missing children were, and he told me not to worry, that he would take me to my child. He said we had to stay in his house for the night, and in the morning we would sneak across the border. At that point the truth began to sink in; I realized that Winnie might not be alive and that this was only a plan to take us back to Kony.

My co-wife and I eventually fell asleep on a mattress the LC had placed on the floor in his home. In the middle of the night, he woke us up and said, "We have to leave now. We are taking a *shortcut* [illegal way] to Kenya, and we will go to Nairobi and you will be safe." I refused to go. I told him it was about to rain. The LC said, "How can you say that you fear rain when you've moved in worse rain when you were in the bush?" But I just continued to refuse to go. The LC said it was fine, that we would wait until the morning and find another route.

The next day, the LC brought a photographer to his home to take our photos. He told us he was going to use them for a visa and a pass-port. My co-wife and I began to talk quietly about what we should do. She was afraid of returning to Gulu in case we were arrested, but I was afraid of going to Nairobi. More than that, I wanted to be with my family in Gulu, to be with Bakita, whom I had left behind. I told my co-wife that I was going to go to the police, but out of fear she told the LC of my plan and he confronted me: "What kind of an Acholi woman are you? Where are you going to get the money to go back to Gulu?" I said that I would get a driver to take me all the way to GUSCO and that GUSCO would pay for it.

I again began to demand to see my child Winnie. The LC said that the children were waiting for us in Nairobi. I warned him not to play around with the memory of a dead child. The next day, a truck came to take us away. I did not know where that truck would take us, so I refused to get into it. The LC and his wife tried to convince me to get in that truck. I finally agreed when they said we would move only to Busia on the Kenyan side and then return and that we could leave our two children behind. My hope was that I would see Winnie across the border, as they promised. We took a shortcut across the border and ended up meeting with Alice Lakwena [former spiritual leader of the Holy Spirit Movement] and a large group of other exiled Acholi. My co-wife stayed in the truck while they sat me down in a hotel room and tried to coax me to continue on to Nairobi. They told me that a house had been prepared for my co-wife and me to live in. I kept insisting I had to return to Gulu to care for my family. They said that Kony still wanted me as his wife and that I didn't need to worry about my family in Gulu because they would send money to take care of them and my mother, who had fallen sick. Alice Lakwena gave me 100,000 Kenyan shillings, and we were taken back across the border.

We spent a second night in the LC's home, but in the morning I asked his wife to help me find a female police officer. She also didn't like what was happening and agreed to help us. She left and then returned sometime later with an Acholi female police officer. We sat together as I told them everything that was happening. The LC in the meantime had fled the house, and his wife was furious! Her husband had abandoned all of us. The female officer called for a car to bring us to the police station. As we reached the station, a UPDF commander was waiting for us. We were immediately brought to a room for questioning, where my co-wife and I repeated what had happened in full detail. After the interview we were brought to the central reception area, and suddenly there were so many journalists around asking us questions. They took many photos, and the next day they published headline stories about us.

We went to Busia to find our children, and it was only when we were there that we learned of Kony's plan. The newspapers wrote about us as if we were trying to rejoin Kony. It was never our wish to rejoin Kony! The UPDF transported us by vehicle to the barracks in Gulu. As we arrived, so many soldiers came to abuse us, saying that we were stupid for wanting to go back to Kony after all the suffering we had gone through in the bush. They would shout, "If you want a man, there are many here in Uganda!" I was in shock by that point and could no longer speak.

We were locked in a house in the military barracks in Gulu for several weeks. We did not know what was happening. If people came to see us, they had to speak to us through the window. No one was permitted to enter the house, and we were not permitted to leave it. UPDF commanders would come and peer through the window. They accused us of trying to rejoin the rebels. We were treated very badly. The children would cry and bang on the door, but no one came to rescue us. The children lost weight.

The soldiers would take us from the house only to ask us questions and beat us on the knees. We were given beans and *posho* that was very hot, but before we could finish eating they would take it away again. *Haa*, we were beaten too much. Our knees would be hit with heavy sticks to the extent that I was no longer able to squat. We were forced to eat very hot food. They kept asking me things that I did not know. They kept asking me to admit that it had always been my plan to rejoin Kony, that I was not actually looking for my lost child. When I would try to explain what had happened, they would beat me again. They interrogated my co-wife separately, but later she told me she experienced the same thing. She said that they would slap her and ask her to tell them the reason she was trying to join Kony.

There was a white man from the Red Cross who used to visit the prisoners. He found soldiers beating us and told them to stop. The soldiers began to treat us fairly from that day on. The man from the Red Cross insisted that we were innocent and that we should be released immediately. The UPDF commanders in charge agreed, and we were transferred to the Child Protection Unit [CPU, a division of the military where child soldiers were brought before being transferred to a rehabilitation center]. The Red Cross contacted the rehabilitation center in Lira and explained the situation. The chairperson of the center rushed to the

CPU to negotiate our release into the center's care. He insisted we be transferred to Lira in the next district because if we remained in Gulu, we wouldn't be treated well by the community. The media had spread the story that we wanted to return to Kony, and our photographs were everywhere. My father had also come to the CPU, but he refused to give permission to the rehabilitation center's chairperson to transfer me to Lira. My dad was told to sign a piece of paper to swear he would be responsible for me. He was told that if I should ever disappear again, he would be the one to be arrested. So my dad insisted I remain in Gulu. I was allowed to return to my home and children in Gulu, but I had to report to the division commander every day.

My mother refused to come to see me while I was in prison. She was bitter, having read the newspaper reports. When I saw her again, she expressed her anger: "My child, I wish you had not returned. You should have died while still in the bush. Now you still want to go back to the bush?" I begged her to listen to me. I said, "Mum, why do you talk like that? Why don't you first ask me what happened before talking like that?" She was so hurt by what had happened. She is usually not the type of person who just blurts out accusations like that. She listened to what I had to say, and she said she understood.

July 2006:
First Meeting

Sometime following my release from military prison, government officials informed me that the vice president of South Sudan, Riek Machar, had met with Kony and the other leaders in the Congo. The LRA had left Uganda and was now based in Garamba National Park.

Kony agreed to participate in peace talks chaired by Machar, but first he wanted to meet with my co-wives and me, as well as his mother and his sister Lakot. I was given a few hours to pack my bags and prepare for the journey to meet Kony where he was based in the Congo. The government representative told me to be brave, that I was doing something great for Uganda. The next day, three of my co-wives and I left for the Congo with the peace team. We linked up with Riek Machar in Juba, South Sudan, and then flew to Maridi. Thereafter it was a twelve-hour drive to Nabanga, where we slept in a SPLA military outpost until

Kony sent his soldiers to pick up his family and bring them to his bases across the border inside Garamba National Park. It was a long journey.

When we finally arrived at the LRA base camp in Garamba, we were taken to see Kony, Vincent Otti, and another commander, Okot Odhiambo. They were very happy to see us. They immediately admitted that they were the ones who had concocted the story that our children had been found in Busia. Vincent Otti told us that they knew we were suffering at home in Uganda and that they wanted us to live a good life with them. I told Vincent Otti that he was lying because if he wanted us to live in peace, then he would not have taken actions that landed us in prison in the hands of military men. I told him how the children suffered like hell in prison, all because of Kony. Otti just laughed at me. Odhiambo encouraged us to be stronghearted. He said that he too had once been in military prison. He had been a Ugandan military soldier and had committed a crime. He was waiting in prison for his sentence when the LRA attacked the prison and freed him, and that is why he remained in the bush up to this day.

We spent several nights at the base camp socializing and meeting with others we had not seen in several years. I did not speak to Kony about the talks until the last night, when he asked me to go to his home around nine o'clock at night. He asked me very many things, like if I was sure that the government would commit to peace talks and didn't I think that the government had agreed to the talks with the intention of arresting him and bringing him to the International Criminal Court? We argued up to three in the morning.

I was supposed to return to Uganda the next morning with the rest of the peace team. Kony insisted I remain with him in Garamba as his wife. I told him that it was not that I did not want to be with him but that I had met a man at home and I had heard rumors that he had AIDS, which meant I had acquired AIDS. I told him that I did not want to infect him because he is the father of my children.

Ladit was very upset. He said that he would heal me of the disease using traditional medicine. He said there is no way he could live without me. He said that among his wives I was the one who listened to him and that I never caused chaos among his soldiers. He said I was the only one who treated all of his children equally. He said so many things to try to lure me into remaining with him, but I told him, "*Ladit*, you have taken care of me for a long time now, from the time I was eleven to twenty-two. You took care of me most of my life, for longer than my own parents did. I will never forget that it was you who saved my life when I was drowning in the river . . . I was drowning but you rescued me. So I cannot think of infecting you with my AIDS." At some point, Kony became very quiet. Then he concluded out loud that I had been infected purposely by the Ugandan military so that I would infect him, and that meant that the government was trying to kill him. He was annoyed, and he said that he was going to kill everyone who had assembled for the peace negotiation in Nabanga.

I told him not to be annoyed. I told him that if the talks were to continue, he would be able to see family members for the first time since he had gone to the bush. He would see his mother and also our daughter Bakita, whom he said he missed so much. Kony asked me what I would do if I were him. What would I do if he had told me that he had AIDS? He told me to go back to Gulu and get an HIV test and bring him the results. He said he would prepare medicine to cure me. I accepted. He again asked if I would stay for longer, but I refused. I told him that my mother was sick. I told him that I had to go back and take care of my family even if I was poor and weak. I told him that there was no one else to care for them. He said that what I was saying was right, but he felt that I should stay behind so that he could treat me.

Finally I left Kony's house, and I went and slept with his sister Lakot in her tent. Sometime later he sent an escort to bring me back to his house. You know, in the LRA, once you are in your monthly periods, you are respected. So I told the escort to leave me alone, that I was having my period and couldn't return to Kony's home. The escort left but returned shortly after. Kony told the escort that I was pretending to be menstruating and to insist that I go to him. I again argued that my period had just begun and sent the escort away. He did not return again.

In the morning, as I prepared to return to Gulu, Kony once more sent an escort to bring me to his home. I accepted to go and found Vincent Otti and Okot Odhiambo waiting for me at Kony's home. Kony had informed Vincent Otti of my HIV status. Otti was counseling Kony. He said he knew *Ladit* wanted me to return to the bush because he misses me and because he did not want anyone else to become my husband. But he told Kony to let me return to Gulu to care for the children. Odhiambo began to take Kony's side and said the children would be fine and that I should join *Ladit* in the bush. I told them that people in Acholi were insulting them, because they had given birth to children whom they are not taking care of. It was just like bearing a child and then throwing the child away. So it was better to care for the future of the children we already had, instead of thinking of having more. Vincent Otti continued to support me. He told them that I was the only mother who cares for all of Kony's children, that there was no one else.

It was actually Vincent Otti who had told me to tell Kony that I had HIV and to refuse to sleep with him. Earlier on, Vincent Otti had confided to me that life in the Congo was very difficult and that I would just end up struggling if I remained there. Otti had told me it would be better if I returned to Gulu to care for the children I have, rather than remain in the Congo and bear Kony more children he could not care for. Vincent Otti confessed that he used to feel bad when he saw me suffer with the children but that there was no way he could have helped me to escape. He wanted me to go back home this time. He said he was worried that if I remained in the Congo I would die, as many other mothers already had.

Eventually Kony agreed to let me return to Gulu on the condition that I would return to him at any time during the peace talks. He told me he missed me more than anyone else in this world. We then prepared to go to meet the delegates across the border in Nabanga, from where I would travel back to Maridi and catch the plane home to Gulu.

As we moved along the path toward Nabanga, the child soldiers kept saying, "Father [Kony], why are you letting *Mego* [referring to Evelyn] go back? *Mego*, don't go!" I was so angry. The child soldiers wanted me to remain behind with them. Fatima's eldest son, whom I had once raised, also wanted me to remain behind to take care of him. He asked me, "Mum, if you go back, who will take care of me?" I told him that he was old enough to take care of himself but that if his father accepted, then I could take him back to Gulu with me and care for him. Kony refused to release the child.

As we walked down the path, Kony said many things to me. He said that the next time I returned I should bring his mum. He insisted that I go to her home and visit his mum. He told me to be careful in Uganda, because everyone knew that I was his favorite wife and would want to kill me. He said that people would think that everything in my house was given to me by him. He said that his name would sound in everything I did, including the sound made by my saucepans. Everything I did, people would think it was Kony who did it for me and that I wouldn't be at peace. At times I think what he said is true.

September 2006:
Second Meeting

I returned to Gulu for a month or so before we were informed that we must return to the Congo again. I could not believe it. In my heart, I never wanted to be with the LRA again, but I did not have a choice; I worried I might be again put into prison. We left together as a delegation: Acholi elders, religious and cultural leaders. Big men were to join us at the talks, including the leader of the government delegation and UN officials. When we arrived in Nabanga, though, Kony forbade anyone to meet with him until he had first spoken to me. I was terrified. As soon as I entered the bush to move along the path to Garamba, I felt my spirit run out of me. I was together with only three child soldiers from the bush. I was all alone; even Kony's sister Lakot had remained behind.

As soon as we reached the base camp, I was informed that Kony wanted to speak to me. He asked me all sorts of questions. He asked, "How many people came, who came, were there any whites? Were there any soldiers?" He said that there were people who wanted to undermine the peace talks and were spreading lies that there were soldiers there to arrest him. He told me that the reason he asked me to come ahead of everyone else was that I had lived there with them and knew all the struggles they had been through and that I would tell him the truth. He was worried that they wanted to kill him despite his good intentions to participate in the peace talks. He said he was ready to kill everyone who had assembled to talk peace, because some came with bad intentions.

I told him, "*Ladit*, there is no one here that is going to try to kill you. Do not attack these people assembled here; innocent lives will be lost, including children." The next day, Kony agreed to meet with those assembled. He told me I should attend the meetings as a delegate for peace representing the women. He told me that I was no longer part of the LRA but a soldier for peace.

I quickly changed my clothing and accompanied them to the meeting point for the peace talks in Ri-Kwamba; Riek Machar had already arrived with former Mozambique president Joaquim Chissanno, who was also the UN special envoy to the conflict. As soon as they arrived, negotiations started. *Ladit* wanted Uganda to be divided into two and to be given Kitgum or Gulu to live in. He said the LRA soldiers missed their people. He said so many children in the LRA believed their parents were still alive and wanted to see them. Only by returning to Uganda could they see them, and only in Uganda could peace negotiations be successful.

The leader of the government peace team, Ruhakana Rugunda, responded to Kony. He said that in order to proceed with peace talks, the LRA should split its troops in two and relocate them to Owiny-ki-Bul and Maridi. Once there, they would receive food and medical help. We spent a long time discussing this topic. Eventually we began talking about mothers and children, and I was asked to speak on their behalf. I said that mothers should be compensated when they returned to Uganda, because the government was helping former commanders to live good lives in the army but doing nothing for mothers.

We spoke the whole day and never reached a compromise. Sometimes Kony would talk until he would have to be held down by Otti, while Chissanno would also talk very strongly. It was a hot debate. Kony accused the government of not having good will in the talks and said that the LRA was surrounded by government soldiers. We spent up to five days talking. We would talk throughout the day, rest, and then resume the next day. When it was time to leave, I returned to Uganda, and Kony did not protest.

November 2006:
Third Meeting

The next time I returned to the Congo, it was to accompany Kony's mother, Nora, and his eldest son, who had been raised in Kampala. When we left Uganda for the Congo, my own mother was very sick.

As we traveled to Juba, Kony's mother said to me, "Min Bakita, am I really going to see my son Kony, to whom I gave birth?" I told her, "What will stop you from seeing your child?" When we reached Garamba and she first saw Kony, she was shocked. I began to fan her, but she became weak, and we had to carry her to a bed, where she lay with her head in my lap until she regained strength.

When she recovered, Nora was very happy to see her son. Kony was also very happy to see his mum. Kony made everyone dance to celebrate his mother's arrival—people danced until 3:00 A.M. Nora danced until she could no longer even walk.

Over the next few days, meetings were held with government officials, but I did not take part in them because Nora wanted me to stay with her. She wouldn't even eat food unless I was next to her. She said that I was the one who helped her see her son once again, and so I shouldn't leave her side. If I had to leave her to do something, she would ask Kony, "Kony, Kony, where is Min Bakita? Where is my daughter?" So *Ladit* insisted I stay with his mum.

That evening after the talks had concluded, Nora spoke to Kony at length. She said, "Kony, my son, I am the one who bore you, so you should listen to what I have to tell you. You have fought enough battles, my son; please come back home. People's sons have returned home; why can't you?" Kony would just laugh at his mum. He told her, "*Maa,* you don't know what you are talking about." She would sometimes talk and even refuse to eat until he answered her questions. Kony told his mother that he would not return because he would be arrested. She called him by his Christian name, Joseph. The soldiers wanted her to refer to him as a general and they would look at her badly when she called Kony by his first name, but she said, "He is my son, and I can call him the name I gave him. Have you heard?" Then she continued to talk to her son: "Joseph, my son, listen to me. My future is short. It is you who has a long future. It is painful to hear that it is you who is killing people. It is because of you I no longer have a home. If am the one who gave birth to you with my womb, then listen to me, my son." At one point Madam Nora broke down and cried. Kony also broke down and cried.

There is nothing more important than a mother. Nora's words hurt him so much. Even if Kony's mother was old, she still offered him the comfort of a young mother to her child. Nora kept begging Kony to come back home, but he refused her request. She asked him very many difficult questions. She even asked him, "Why do you live with many women like this? How do you marry more than twenty wives?" *Ladit* lied to her and responded, "These are not my wives; the ones captured were my wives, but these are my servants who work in my home." Some nights while we were there, Kony's mum would just get up in the middle of the night and start calling her son, "Kony! Kony!," and his escorts would go and call him to come and chat with his mum. She would say, "When you went to the bush, how could you just leave me like that?" She told him how his father died and where he had been buried and by whom. They spoke endlessly until it was time to leave again for Uganda.

December 2006:
Fourth Meeting

In December, we were again called to return to the Congo. I was very worried about my mother's health, as she was very sick when I left. When we were in Garamba I borrowed a phone and called my brother, who informed me that my mother's condition had become serious and that I should at all cost return home. I told *Ladit* Kony. He said he would give me some money to pay for her to be taken to the hospital. I said, "*Afande*, you cannot help us from here. There is nothing you can do." He began to laugh at me. He said, "Do you not know that I have wide branches? I can help you anywhere, but it is just that if the government or anyone learns that Kony is sending money to his wife or to his women at home, you will be killed. So it is better if you suffer without my help." I then asked him, "Since my mother's health is failing, please let me return to Uganda on the next plane." He agreed that I should return.

Ladit dug up a lot of herbs and gave them to me to take home to treat my mother. A plane came, and we landed in Juba to connect with another plane on to Uganda. I arrived in Gulu the very next day. I went straight to my mother in Lacor Hospital. I had bought *bala* [dates], *tania* [a sweet made of *sim sim*], and milk in big tins. My mother ate the *bala*.

My mother kept repeating the question, "Amonya, have you arrived? Eva, have you arrived?" I reassured her I was there to care for her. She said, "My child, thank you for coming." Those are the words my mother told me. My mother ate the *bala* and said I should mix for her the milk that I brought. I boiled it and gave it to her. That day my mother ate well. It was also the last time she would eat. The next day her strength deteriorated. We spent another night together, and the next day a doctor came and put a tube in her nose that went directly to her stomach. Milk was given to her through the tube in her nose. I also gave her medicine through the tube. I had to give her everything through that tube.

I was so worried and confused. I prayed and asked, "God, why do you torture my mother like this? You separated my mother and me when I was abducted; why do you now want my mother to die after we have just been reunited?" I did not eat a single thing. I just sat next to my mother and stared. People on the ward kept dying all around us. Soon my mother's sickness intensified. I kept on praying. I had no appetite. I kept on worrying about my mother.

My mother began to suffer convulsions. My mother was tortured in life. My mother suffered in this world. My mother gave birth to me. I was her firstborn. My father took a second wife. My mother's co-wife mistreated her, so my mother took her children and left my father. It was after she separated from my father that my mother became sick. She began to live with a man who had the HIV virus. My mother had convulsions, and if you saw it you lost your breath. My mother lost her life that night. When she died, I called my brothers and sisters. I called everyone, everywhere. I called all of my mother's brothers and her father's brother. I then wrapped my mother's body in sheets.

When my mother died, I was sleeping. I never slept once; the whole time I was in the hospital with her I did not sleep. Yet the moment when I drifted off, my mother died. It was my grandmother who came and woke me. She said, "Evelyn, Evelyn, wake up." I got up and asked her, "Should I change Mummy's position?" She held me and said, "Evelyn, your mother's life is over. You be strong." I turned to my grandmother and asked her, "Is my mother really dead? Is my mother really dead? Let me carry her!" I began to pull my mother on my lap.

My grandmother begged me to stop. The doctors came and shielded me from my mother's body. I thought I was going to scream, but I made no sound. I had no tears. When a stretcher was brought to carry her body to the morgue, I carried my mother together with the doctor.

They asked me if I had money to pay for a refrigerator, and I told them that I had it. When we reached the morgue, we put my mother in the refrigerator. When we put her there, something overcame me and made me want to stay in the morgue with her. Whether it was her spirit or what I do not know. The doctor told me to come out, and I sat down in the morgue, where there were so many corpses. The doctor coaxed me out when I wanted them to close the morgue door with me still inside. I wanted to care for my mother's dead body. She told me, "This dead body is no longer your mother. You are left without a mother. You be strong." The doctor then held me. She held me and brought me outside.

As soon as they closed the door to the morgue, my tears began to flow. Something gripped my chest very painfully. I could only stare. The doctor held me. I could hear people comment that the doctor was kind; they thought she was a relative the way she cared for me. In the morning we bought a coffin and then set off in cars for Atiak. I sat beside my mother's coffin the whole journey home. When we reached home, I was taken over by my mother's spirit. Always when I reached home from a journey, my mother ran and welcomed me. She would say, "My daughter has come! My daughter has come!" Since she died, I have been left in darkness. There is no one who welcomes me when I am back home like my mother did.

As we buried my mother, I began to ask God why he mistreats me. I had to grow up without a mother in the bush, and again now she was lost. I was with her for only a year and a half after I escaped and then she died. I told God, "You should have let me stay together with her. Now you have killed my mother!" I began to feel angry and started crying. I cried until I no longer even knew who I was.

I stopped eating and lost strength. I could not even stand up. Some of my co-wives from the bush came to stay with me, and I felt stronger when I saw them. They sat next to me to comfort me. I never even cooked for my mother's funeral, for when I went to start cooking my co-wives told me to go and sit. Sometimes, when I found it hard to sit, I began to wash utensils, but my co-wives took away what I was washing. My co-wives helped me.

My sisters who came back home with me, those who shared with me the pain of abduction, showed me love. The bad thing was, as soon as mother died, the government officials announced it on Mega FM. Even the BBC reported that Kony's mother-in-law had died and the burial was at two o'clock. No one at home had known who I was. Even my mother's neighbors did not know that I was Kony's wife. They began to ask, "Who is Kony's wife?" Someone pointed at me and said, "That is the one. She is Kony's wife!" Two days after my mother was in the grave, I overheard a neighbor say, "I used to stay freely with Margaret, yet her daughter is Kony's wife! If I knew then what I do now, I would have hated Margaret. I will not attend prayers for Margaret because her daughter is Kony's wife."

I got so angry. I thought that I should die, and if I was to die I should bring this woman to the dead with me. It was not my wish to be Kony's wife. Immediately my younger sister came. She held me. I began to quiver. What hurt me was that many people were talking about me. They said I was going to Juba [the peace talks] to get money from Kony, and that was why my mother's life had changed for the better as of late. Indeed, when I came back from the bush, my mother was selling things at the market. I told my mother to stop working and stay home because she was sick. I had begun to take care of my mother. The neighbors looked at that badly, as if Kony were assisting her. I had given all the things that were distributed to us from GUSCO to my mother. It was my rule to live by, to try my best to buy things that my mother liked and would enjoy. When she wanted something, I looked for it and brought it. I bought juice and put it in the house. My mother died when there were many tins of milk still in the house.

She was the one who gave birth to me. So I felt that I should care for my mother more than my own child. My mother gave birth to me. She was just unlucky. We should have given her a good life. When I just came back from the bush, all my strength was embodied in my mother; even if my mother was crippled and vulnerable, even if she had no legs, even if she was blind, when I smelled her scent, it gave me strength.

Now I am left *adato* [widowed]. I am on my own. I cannot remarry, because any man that might be interested in me is soon chased away by the fear that if Kony comes out of the bush he will kill him for staying together with his wife. Even if I am to cry, it will have no end. God should help me, and I should help my children. That is my prayer to God: that I am able to support my children. God should let them study. Maybe tomorrow one of them will help me or one of them will cover me with soil.

Everything that I do, people say that I am Kony's wife, Kony's wife, Kony's wife. Why do they look at me? Why do they talk so much about me? Who am I? I think of it, yet I know such thoughts will not take me anywhere. Even if I take my own life, I will not have done a good thing because I will have left my children orphaned. I should wait for God to decide when I die. Console me. Staying without a mother is harder than staying without a father. One day when my mother had died, my tongue slipped, and I said, "Instead of losing my mother, God should have killed my father." Yet I did not realize that my father was next to me. Immediately my father started crying. But, in truth, I find that it is more important for a mother to be there than a father. *Mego ber* [a mother is good].

March and April 2007:
Fifth and Sixth Meetings

After I had buried and mourned my mother, we once more returned to the Congo. It was the last time I would see Kony. During this trip the LRA's mood had changed; the delegates were separated from one another and forced to sleep in individual places. I was not allowed to sleep with my former co-wives. It was an unusual trip. We returned to the Congo in April to try to meet Kony again, but he switched off his phone, so no one was able to communicate with him. I felt sorry for the Acholi leaders who had traveled so far. Many were elderly and not used to the kind of conditions we found ourselves in. At least for us, the young ones, we were used to the kind of suffering we faced in Garamba, such as walking long distances and staying for long without drinking water, but they, the elders, were really suffering.

Finally Kony called. He spoke to the paramount chief and then asked to speak to me. He asked me, "How do you see this situation? I heard a rumor that you people have come with some Americans who want to kill me." I told him that he shouldn't believe in rumors. He shouldn't be listening to what people told him from out there, because he was the one feeling the pinch, he was the one lying there in the cold in the bush. Then I also told him that it was bad to make all these elderly leaders come here just to suffer. I told him that these were leaders who were really respected back home. I asked why he just switched off his phone like that and told him that he had to think wisely. He said that he also felt the same way I did; he also knew that these were people we respected back home, and he really had to listen to them. He even knew that he was the one who called these people to come and meet him, but, because he heard that rumor, he had to protect himself. He said he was not sure whether these people had really come to meet him or if they had come with other intentions, like to kill him.

Then he told me that we shouldn't give up, even if it meant going to Garamba ten or fifty times or more than that. He said one day peace would return to this region, so we should not tire in our efforts. Then I told him that if he didn't sign the peace agreement and return home, I would not wait for him. He then asked me, "If I am to return home tomorrow, where will I go? Do I have land? Are they going to give us land? Where is the land for the Acholi people? We need to know where we are going to stay when we return home!" We spoke for hours on the phone. When we finished talking, I handed back the phone to the paramount chief, and he told me that I'm really a brave person. We returned to Uganda without seeing Kony.

October 2007:
Kony Kills Otti

The next time I was contacted by the peace team to travel to Garamba, I refused to go. My daughter Bakita begged me not to go again. I also saw no use in returning to Garamba. I knew that Kony was just lying to people, that he was not interested in talks. He just lied to everyone. The peace team tried to convince me to go, but I refused. Later on, *Ladit* called me and told me that Vincent Otti was sick and that I should come to be by his side.

I knew better. Vincent Otti had called me a few days before Kony to say that he had been accused of betraying Kony. He had been arrested and told me to pray that God help him. An escort to Vincent Otti called a few days later to say that Kony had executed Vincent Otti for double-dealing during the peace talks. The escort hid in a well to call me and let me know Vincent Otti was dead. He told me to tell others what had happened. You see, the LRA commanders began to turn on one another because of the distrust purposely sown by other parties conspiring against them during the talks. It was very difficult to bring out the truth during that time; it was so confusing. When Kony next called me, I asked him what had happened to Vincent Otti; he said he now saw they had gotten to me too and hung up the phone. It was the last time I ever spoke to Kony.

7

Daily Life

Editor's note: This chapter presents a selection of diary entries recorded by Evelyn between October 2009 and July 2010. It was during this time she recorded the bulk of the stories in this book. This section was edited in consultation with Evelyn to provide the reader a glimpse into day-to-day life for Evelyn, highlighting the struggle of all women who returned with children to create a new life after so many years in the LRA. I have provided notes to contextualize some of the events where necessary.

October 29, 2009

I am Evelyn Amony. This morning I took my daughter Grace to the hospital to check her ears, and they told me to return in the evening for medicine. Grace's ears have been infected since she was a baby. Pus constantly flows from her ears. I apply medicine, but it always returns. I returned to the hospital at six o'clock for her medicine. The doctor told me that I must bring her each day for one week and then the dose will be finished. When she is injected with this medicine, it is very painful. She cries a lot. I hope that she recovers. I am going through a great difficulty; Grace is constantly sick. Her ears hurt a lot. She is always in pain.

That night, I attended a meeting for parents of students at my children's school. They informed us that gowns are required for graduation and that this cost 18,000 shillings. Every child must also wear stockings and shoes. I cannot afford to get these things. I have to pay rent and take care of other things using the money I earn from tailoring,[1] but it is not enough. That is the bad thing. The good thing that happened today is that I did what I could. I took my child to the hospital. The most important thing to me is good health. Even if Grace is in great pain, I have to do my best as a parent to see that she recovers.

November 2, 2009

I am Evelyn Amony. In the morning, I bathed Grace and took her and Margaret's son who was also sick to the hospital. A friend called and told me that there was a free medical clinic in Layibi and suggested I take the children there. I did not have any money with me so we walked until I saw a neighbor who owed me money. I asked him if he could repay me. He said that he did not have any money but offered to help pay for our transport to the clinic. I thanked God because at that time the children were already tired. When we reached the clinic we were told to go to the end of the queue to get a medical form. By one o'clock, I still did not have the medical form needed to see the doctor.

It was three o'clock before we finally got to the waiting room. Many people were ahead of us, also waiting to see the doctor. I started to wonder if I would see the doctor before six o'clock. I asked the people there, and they told me to be prepared to wait until eight o'clock, when the clinic closed. I started to think about my young child that I had left at home, Cynthia.[2] The other kids were also soon going to come home from school. They would all be hungry. So I decided to leave the queue and go back home. I arrived home at four o'clock, worried Cynthia would be crying due to hunger, but I found that Bakita had bathed and fed her and she was playing. That night, I took Grace to the hospital for her final treatment. This time I want to follow the doctor's instructions exactly.

1. Evelyn was employed in different international nongovernmental organizations with programs designed to assist women who returned from the LRA with children in finding employment. She worked as a tailor and jewelry maker, producing goods for international sale, for two different NGOs.

2. Evelyn had a fourth daughter in March 2009. She also adopted an orphaned child around the age of Winnie in her memory.

November 16, 2009

I am Evelyn Amony. Kony's mother, Nora, died on the tenth of November. I went and buried her. It was the first time I was able to go to Odek, Kony's village. Kony used to talk about Odek a lot. It is far.

There are some people whose children had not come back from the bush, and they are still bitter. But at the funeral, people were united. When help was needed, the Acholi pitched in. Government ministers and representatives came. Many people came for the burial that day. Some went with a bad motive. I did hear some say, "Her son has finished people." Some people went with a good motive. Others went to see who Kony's mother was.

I began to wonder if Kony could be forgiven. He killed a great many people in Sudan and in the Congo, but at this moment, as they buried his mother, people seemed to forgive him. If Kony came back, he might be forgiven. He might be given a chance to justify himself. He will not be hanged immediately. I wondered about this as I saw how people buried his mother.

I had never visited Kony's home in Odek before. I am now able to say that I have been to my children's real home. I went to their real home, and I was shown where their ancestors are buried. I know now where Kony was born.

When I left there were still so many visitors at that place. Some of Kony's family members said that I should bring Kony's children home so that they know where it is. They said that if I have no place to farm, I can always go there and dig their land. When I think about it, it could help us. The good thing is that I have girls. It is bad for those who have boys. Boys disturb their mothers about the whereabouts of their fathers.

November 21, 2009

I am Evelyn Amony. Cynthia was very ill this morning, so I took her to the hospital, where she was given medication. I came back and packed my things to go to Lacor Hospital to visit my sister's and my brother's sons who had both been admitted there. It was a bad day. It was drizzling. Each morning I have to budget for a hospital visit, for food to bring my nephews, and for transport to and from the hospital. I also went and visited my daughter Bakita in school, and her teacher said she is a very bright and obedient child. This made me so happy because I had thought my child was so stubborn in school.

November 23, 2009

I am Evelyn Amony. On reaching the hospital today, I found my father visiting the patients. When I found him there, I was so happy. All this time, if any of us had fallen sick he would never come from Atiak to visit us, even if we relayed the information to him. I was so happy when I saw my Dad. Even if you have lost one parent, the other should always be there for you and act as though both parents are alive. When our mother was alive, she loved us very much. If we were sick, she would always be there for us. After her death, we were left in our grandmother's hands, yet she is so old. So my Dad's visit made me happy. I talked to him and told him how we were planning to go and visit them. He promised to wait for us.

November 25, 2009

I am Evelyn Amony. I woke up in the morning not feeling so fine. I was feeling sickly. I had a dream in the night; it was as though I were once again living with Joseph Kony. In the dream, Kony told me to bring his mother to him, and yet I didn't know where she was. He gathered all of the co-wives in his home together and told us to take care of his mother. I even dreamed that Fatima was there. In the dream, I also saw his escorts carrying guns, and so I was worried when I awoke. I felt that the dream might mean that war will break out again. I told a friend about the dream. She told me it is the past, and, as much as this encouraged me, I still had some fear. I was so relieved when I woke up and found that I wasn't in the bush.

November 27, 2009

I am Evelyn Amony. Today I traveled to Kampala at the invitation of a religious humanitarian organization. They invited some of us who came from the bush to speak to their congregation in Kampala. Some of the women we traveled with had never boarded a bus in their lives. As we reached the outskirts of the city, one of my friends started saying, "Ehh! How come there are so many houses here?" When we reached Kampala she said, "Evelyn, look, houses are climbing each other! We won't step on the ground, there are houses everywhere!" She amused me so much, despite the fact that it was also sad that our abduction had left us so ignorant that we did not even know what a city looked like. Somehow, I was comforted by the fact that there were people even more ignorant than me.

November 29, 2009

I am Evelyn Amony. Praise God! We were woken up at 5:00 A.M. to prepare for church. We presented our stories at the first, second, and third services. We prayed for our friends who are still in captivity to come back home because we know they are still under very harsh conditions. I urged my fellow born-agains to pray for those who are still in the Congo because things are not easy there. It is a fact that a lot of children are still in captivity; they are still suffering, traveling long distances and going through a lot. We were slightly more fortunate, because during our time we mainly camped in Sudan. It was less forested in comparison to the Congo. The Congo is a jungle, bushy, and it is very hard to escape from there. I told the congregation to put such children in their prayers so that they can also come back home. I know that nothing is impossible with God. It was by God's grace that I also managed to come back home, and those people still need our prayers.

We truly danced in Kampala. I was happy, and the congregation got so excited because they saw that, despite our bush experience, we still had a lot more to offer. In that service, I told Christians that my troubles did not start with my abduction. I said that I, together with my family, suffered a lot at the hands of NRA soldiers, describing how they set our hut ablaze and how it was one of them that set us free. My story drew a lot of sympathy from them—many shed tears. I also told them how it was only by God's grace that I am still alive, that I survived. I asked them to pray for a change in my life and in my children's lives. I asked them to also pray for Joseph Kony and forgive him, despite all the mayhem he caused, because he is just a human being like the rest of us. I asked them to pray for children from northern Uganda, as many went through the adverse impact of war and were enslaved in camps, and now the very northern populations are the ones dying from poisonous alcohol.

I told them so many things. I told them how my own child Winnie was lost in the bush and that I am not certain whether or not she is still alive. In the afternoon we had lunch, and I met one of the girls, Jennifer, that we stayed with in the bush. She was one of the Aboke girls. She told me that when she heard me mention Winnie's name, she burst into tears because she remembers Winnie's disappearance well. After I had left the stage, she came and hugged me. I had forgotten what she looked like. She said, "Betty, do you no longer remember me?" I looked at her critically and then recalled her. The Aboke girls have very few problems compared to the rest of us; they returned to a nice boarding school in Kampala while their children remain at home and are taken good care of. For us, it is a different story. You are both the mother and the father to the child. I was happy meeting her after such a long time.

December 1, 2009

I am Evelyn Amony. This morning I dreamed that we were there again at the peace talks. As I had always done, I was told to lead the way into the bush, and in my dream Vincent Otti was still alive. He was wearing a brownish suit and said he knew politics these days were complicated so they had to fake his death to make things easier. Vincent Otti was alive! When I saw him in the dream, I started weeping. Kony came and asked me, "How are the children? How is your new baby? I thank God for having given you a child." He then said that he didn't have much money but pulled out some notes from his pocket and gave them to me. I didn't check how much it was. He told me to not check the amount and to open it later. I left with the money, and when I opened it I discovered there were eighty thousand shillings. I started quarreling with him: "Do you think this money is enough to cater for all the children's needs during the festive season? Prices are rising!" I had in fact overslept, and when I woke up it was already 8:00 A.M.

December 10, 2009

I am Evelyn Amony. I woke up and organized myself to go for prayers. I made the fire. I bathed Grace and Cynthia, and then we attended the first mass. We finished the first mass and then began the second one. The prayers stopped at midday. On our way back we stopped at the World Vision reception center to greet some women who had just come back from the bush. If you are to listen to their stories, you will learn that they went through a very hard time. They said the Congolese were suffering. I have always been sad because of the children who remain in the bush. At least now some of the children are coming back home. God is helping them, and many more will continue to come back home.

December 20, 2009

I am Evelyn Amony. Today we were summoned to go to St Monika's as the parents of children sponsored by the school. They were going to distribute clothes to the children. When I arrived, the sponsor was angry that his sponsor-child Grace was not with me and said that he was not going to give me Grace's clothes. I told him that if he had brought something for Grace, I could still receive it for her even if she was not there. I asked him if I could wear Grace's clothing. How could I steal my own children's clothes? He said that he did not mean anything bad but that he wanted to take Grace's photo with the clothes to show that she got them. With anger I left the place and went back home empty-handed.

December 22, 2009

I am Evelyn Amony. Today I spent a long time talking to my child Bakita. We talked about the past. She said that she recalls the long journeys we took across the Imatong Mountains and how we walked on the rocks. I realized then that she had not forgotten what we went through. These things happened sometime back, and yet Bakita remembers them clearly.

December 24, 2009

I am Evelyn Amony. I began the day doing my usual work, and I ironed clothes. I went to the market and bought pork. We ate dried fish and pork. In the morning, we made tea. When I came back from the market, I began to wash the plates. After this, I prepared the house for Christmas. My friend whom I had stayed with at the rehabilitation center GUSCO came to visit me. We talked about things that happened in the past. When he left, I went to my other friend's place. I found out her mother had come. Her mother was happy with me because I had registered the name of her grandchildren for sponsorship. Her daughter had died in the bush. We find that we should help those we suffered with in the bush and find ways of getting access to education for them. These people were very happy when I went to their home. I spent a long time with them. I was watching Acholi songs on video. She has many videotapes. I got back home at eight. I decided to wait for prayers, but I fell asleep on the chair. I woke up at midnight. Mosquitoes had bitten me. I woke up and went to bed.

December 25, 2009

I am Evelyn Amony. I woke up early to go for prayers. I left Bakita in charge of preparing the food and other things at home. I spent a long time praying: I went for prayers at nine and the mass ended only at one. On the way home, I met a boy I had stayed with in the bush. When I met him, he said, "Evelyn, it has been many years since you let me buy you something." We entered a guest house. He bought me three sodas. I took the sodas, and I walked back home. I reached home, and I found the food had been prepared. They were waiting for me. We started eating the hen that had been prepared, and it was delicious. I ate together with Margaret as our children played together.

This Christmas was good. The first Christmas that I was home, I was in Lacor Hospital. Another Christmas, one of my children was sick. Last year, I took care of my mum in the hospital. I prayed that God would help me celebrate this Christmas in a good way. I asked him that there be no sickness. I think the only truly good Christmases I had were when I was young. In Sudan, I always had a wound in my heart at Christmas thinking about my parents. I kept on thinking, "Even if am celebrating Christmas here, I am abducted. Even if am staying with this man, he abducted me." I had these thoughts.

December 29, 2009

I am Evelyn Amony. In the night I learned that my mother's sister had died in Atiak. I do not know if it is because of her death that I am sick, but I feel so cold, and I am weak. I am trying to find transport to Atiak so that I can see her and attend the burial. Death is a thief. Today death has stolen my aunt from us.

January 3, 2010

I am Evelyn Amony. What I did today is wake up and make fire. After making fire I boiled water. I got water and bathed the child. I also bathed. I then went for prayers. When I returned, Margaret was waiting for me at home with another co-wife. They wanted to consult me about her child. One of my co-wives told me, "I have come to you because I am finding it hard to live in the village with my family. No one wants my child. My sons do not want to go to school. They do not want anything. They fight with others all the time. They even fight with me. I have come to you to help me with advice. I am thinking that you should go to Kony's home in Odek. What are his clan members thinking? We are not pretending that we gave birth to children with Kony. We really gave birth to these children. The family should support our children. They should help us to take care of them. If the clan fails to help them, then the government should help the children. I still want to study and to go back to school." She was crying, saying that her mother does not want her children. She gave us something difficult to talk about.

We agreed to approach the elders in Kony's clan together and find a way forward. I am noticing that those who gave birth to sons with Kony are having a difficult time. The boys are giving them headache.[3] Girls

---

3. There was a general consensus in the research project that male children born of forced marriage are more difficult to handle because of their lack of paternal clan identity and ties. To be an orphan or a child without a paternal clan is considered deeply shameful. A boy's economic and cultural future is tied to the paternal clan and land inheritance, whereas a girl will grow up and marry into her husband's clan, her future tied to his.

are better. They are respectful and are in school. For example, Margaret's son is a thief. He will not be of value to her. Florence's son is also a thief. He does not want to go to school and has no respect. As a parent to such a child, you are always sad. This is what we discussed. We took a long time talking about this. Before we left, Bakita brought for us food and we ate.

January 13, 2010

I am Evelyn Amony. As usual, as a woman, I woke up and did what I was supposed to do. As I swept the house, Cynthia began to cry. I carried her, and she breastfed. After breastfeeding, I bathed her. After bathing her, I told Bakita to let me help her chop the meat I had bought from the market as I lit the fire. I fried the food. Bakita then told me, "Mum, let me cook because Cynthia is disturbing you." When it comes to house chores, Bakita does it all. I carried Cynthia and took her to the neighbor. I left her with a lady in the neighborhood. She remained with Cynthia, and I continued to do other things. I winnowed my millet, and it was very good. I put my millet in a big saucepan, and I took it to the grinding mill. Today I am left with only five hundred shillings in my house.

That night, my neighbor knocked on the door of my house and asked if she could enter. Her husband was imprisoned because of mistreating their children. Before she sat down, she asked for food. I said, "You sit down; there is food." She sat down, and I gave her food. She said, "I thought I was going to die of hunger today. I was feeling really hungry. This is the kind of hunger that takes people to their graves." I felt sorry for her. She said, "My husband's kids hate me. They blame me for their father's imprisonment. When I cook food, they take all of it and eat it themselves. Life is so hard."

January 15, 2010

I am Evelyn Amony. This evening, I came across a man I knew from primary school named Saki. We both looked at each other for a bit, and then he said to me, "Evelyn, is it you?" I said, "I am she." He came and hugged me, saying, "I haven't seen you for more than twenty years, but I heard you came back." He insisted I sit down, and we talked for a long time. I never thought I would see Saki again. He was a very good child, and I liked him so much. We were happy to see each other. He reminded me of those days when we were growing up and of the names of all the different children we went to school with. He said he cried every time he saw my mother and that I resembled her and one of my sisters. He worried about what I was going through in the bush, saying he would imagine me walking in the hot sun and carrying heavy loads in the rain. I realized as he spoke that after I was abducted, my friends missed me. He asked me so many questions! Like how I lived in the bush and what that long journey by foot to Sudan was like. I laughed at some of his questions. He said, "I heard that you were Kony's wife; is it true?" I told him, "What you heard is what happened." He asked, "Evelyn, how were you able to stay with him?" I answered, "Whether you wanted to stay with him or not, you had to. I had no ability to refuse." I began to realize that there are people not related to me who care more about me than my very own brothers and sisters.

January 19, 2010

I am Evelyn Amony. When I reached home this evening, there was a lady there who was also Kony's wife. She had brought her daughter. She said, "Evelyn, I have brought your daughter. Even if I have not come with her here before, she is your child. You helped me with this child in the bush. I thought that it was important to bring her to see you." I was happy. I called Bakita to come see her sister. Bakita came, and they greeted each other. I think it is good to create a relationship with the children. Otherwise, they would grow up without knowing each other. When she was born, the child had a low birth weight, so her mother did not want to carry her. They had brought the baby to the hospital in Juba. The doctors thought she was premature, but it was only that she was small and unable to breastfeed properly or gain weight. I would bathe her and breastfeed her for the mother. I breastfed the baby until she gained weight, and then her mother realized her child would be a normal human being. I was happy to see the child and that she was able to meet her sister. This is the good thing that happened today.

January 20, 2010

I am Evelyn Amony. Tonight as I walked home I passed by the prison barracks. One of my uncles stays at the prison. His wife saw me and told me to stop and visit him. I fear this uncle of mine because when he finds you, he talks a lot. I fear him because one day he said that he was sad because we are giving birth recklessly. That is why I fear him. His wife asked me where the father to my child was. She asked me whether he was supporting me. I told her that he was not. She said that my uncle, the old man, wanted to speak to me and that was why she told me to stop. She told me that he had a lot to talk to me about. He has a bitter tongue. When he talks to you, he adds to your sorrow. I fear him. He is my father's brother. What he says is not bad, but when you think over what he says, you can feel bad. After his wife talked to me, I told her that I was leaving. She sent one of the girls to bring a photo album, and I looked at the pictures. I stayed for a short time and walked back home.

January 21, 2010

I am Evelyn Amony. Today I was listening to the radio program for returnees. When I heard the program, I was very sad. I was reminded of the past. A returnee was talking about the war. I recalled the people we used to stay with. During this time, battles were very tough. There was no water. When I listened to this boy, I found myself crying. The boy who was speaking said that there were only twenty LRA rebels left right now. When I went for the peace talks, people used to say that the LRA numbered only one hundred. When we reached the place for the peace talks there were many LRA soldiers there. I think that some people misguide others on the radio.

Some say that Kony has lost power. I recall in 1993, there was a group of LRA rebels that had absolutely no clothes, so they had tied polythene bags on themselves. Later on the LRA gained power and we were abducted. I worry for the children still in captivity because the war does not discriminate between a mother and a child. Everyone is affected.

There was a mother on the radio program who was calling for her daughter to return home. I felt bad for the girl because she is going to be in hot soup when the rebels hear about it. The mother might be feeling good about what she did, but she has put her daughter in trouble. The rebels will say that it was the girl who started it all and found ways of talking to her mother. Her daughter might not come back home ever now. If you have never been abducted, you cannot know what the LRA hates. It makes me think of the time the white nun called Rakelle searched for the Aboke girls and those girls were killed immediately. At times such things cause trouble for those in the bush. This is what I have to say about the program on returnees. I feel bad about this program sometimes. It is good, but at times some things said in this program are very painful.

When I reached home, a childhood friend was waiting for me. I had been looking for him since I came back home. Before I was abducted, I liked him so much. His character was good. He took my mother's little sister as a wife. I heard that when I was abducted, he cried so much that he almost ran mad. He mentioned my name every time he cried. When I was told about it, I told them to look for him wherever he was. But many years passed without me seeing him. My friend told me, "When you had just been abducted, I decided to join the army in order to get you back. I tried and failed. I thought that I would get you every time I went for battles. I realized that I was not going to be able to bring you back. I then went to stay in the military barracks in the south. Later on I heard that you did come back home. I never imagined that things would happen in such a way." I did not know what to tell him because he tried to do something he could not manage to do. It was hard to get back your loved ones when they were abducted. You can think of many ways of doing so but get defeated each time.

January 22, 2010

I am Evelyn Amony. This morning when I was going to work, I met soldiers on the way. They were all holding guns. My heart beat fast, and I got scared. I was terrified to the point that I felt as though I was still in the bush. They were walking very fast. When I met them, I stood for some time watching them before I continued walking. They were going to a parade in Kaunda grounds. I continued walking. I walked on, and when I reached near the playground, I stood. I saw the soldiers go in.

Some of them had their guns on the back, while others carried them on their shoulders. After work I asked my uncle why the soldiers were parading. He said that Museveni's Day[4] was going to be on the twenty-sixth. When I reached home, I started thinking about how we would march in parade for hours in the LRA. I was once given an award after competing in a parade with the Sudanese soldiers! When I saw the soldiers parading today, I felt like joining them. I promised myself not to think of anything related to the army again.

January 23, 2010

I am Evelyn Amony. What happened that scared me today is that I saw a woman who had been injured by a vehicle. The doctor tried to patch up her wound. It reminded me of wounds caused by bombs. When a bomb hits someone, at times it is the skin that is removed and it falls aside. At times it breaks the bones. The injury was very bad. I realized that injuries from bullets were actually better because when a car hits you, the blood clots do not clot until later. The blood on the woman's head had darkened. I felt pity for her. I was reminded of the bush; nursing wounds for the injured was one of my roles. Kony used to say that I had to be taught how to clean wounds and stitch them. I saw this lady and was reminded of the past. Things were fine when there were no battles, but at times, when there were battles, we saw newly wounded people every day. During battle, you often had to see a wounded or dead person. This happened to both the LRA and the government soldiers. This happened in Uganda and in Sudan each time there was a battle.

January 24, 2010

I am Evelyn Amony. This morning I woke up and swept the compound and the house. I brought out the utensils, and I washed them. After washing the utensils, I felt very cold. I had also felt cold in the night. I covered myself with a bed sheet and added a blanket on top. I am still

---

4. Museveni Day celebrates the fall of Kampala to the NRA and Yoweri Museveni's taking over the presidency.

feeling cold. I told Bakita to boil me some water. She exclaimed, "But it is hot!" I told her that I was feeling very cold. Bakita boiled water and I went to bathe. I dressed and went to the church for prayers. When I reached the church, I entered inside, and I was received with a very cold breeze. I shivered and sat down, and people began to praise God's name. I felt nauseated and went outside. I tried to vomit, but there was nothing. I went to sleep in one of the rooms where children usually pray. I went and slept among the children for a long time. I came out and sat under the sun. One of the ladies came and told me that she wanted to pray for me. After she prayed, I went back inside the church. I sat and continued to feel very cold, so I got a cloth from a lady and covered myself with it. I went back to the room where the children prayed from and slept. My body was shaking. I decided to listen to the preaching as I lay there. I listened to the preaching, but I was still shivering. I got up and walked back to the main part of the church. I gave in my offering, and prayers finished. I left the church and gave back the lady's cloth. I began to walk home.

My temperature was high like that of a child. I asked a neighbor to send someone to Bakita so that she could bring me money to go to the hospital because I was not feeling fine. She said that she would take me to the hospital instead of asking Bakita to bring me money.

When I reached the hospital, the doctor said, "Eh! You are so hot." She put a towel in water and wiped my body with it. After wiping me with the cloth, the lady told me to lie down, and my blood was tested. The results showed that I had malaria. I began to sweat; my whole body was covered in sweat, which was a good sign. I told the doctor that I could leave. She said that I should stay for some time and rest. I stayed in the clinic until the heat cooled down. My head was aching. When the doctor checked my temperature and it had cooled down, she told me that I could leave because I wanted to go. She told me to come back the next day if I was not feeling better. I began to feel better and went back home.

January 28, 2010

I am Evelyn Amony. This morning, I woke up and made fire. As the fire was lighting, I swept the compound. When the fire was lit, I made tea and then sent Bakita to buy cassava because Grace likes it a lot. That is what they took tea with. I bathed and prepared myself to go where I always go for work. I met my aunt's husband on the way. I greeted him and continued walking to work. Today I am not feeling fine. My stomach is aching. It is burning. Life is hard today. I thought that if am to go back home, the baby would be disturbing me and I would not sleep. I decided to stay at work. I slept when the pain intensified.

I met the staff from GUSCO. They were happy to see me. I met one of the managers of GUSCO; she is a very good woman. She liked me a lot. She did not like only me; she liked most of the people who came back from the bush. I was happy when I saw her, and she was also happy to see me. When she first saw me, she almost lifted me up when she hugged me. She said, "My daughter, you are a good person. I pray for blessings for you wherever you go. Whatever you are to do in life, do it properly."

When we reached home, I sat for some time, and my grandmother came by. She had come from Atiak. When she arrived, we sat for some time, and Bakita brought for us food. After eating, we began to tell stories with my grandmother. I was happy because she was back. After telling stories, Grandma began to feel sleepy, and I made up her bed for her. I told her to go inside and sleep.

January 29, 2010

I am Evelyn Amony. When I was on my way back home this evening, I met a man who asked me if I had seen many people at the bank or whether I knew if there was money deposited there. I told him I did not know anything about any bank or whether money has been deposited because I do not have a bank account. He said, "My sister, the issue of school fees has strained me." He talked to me as though he was running mad. He told me he had a child who had passed to Senior One, but he has no money for school fees. I asked him what his occupation was. He told me he is a teacher but he has failed to pay for his children to go to school. I told him, "You wait for school to start. By the tenth most people's salaries will have been deposited." He thanked me for giving him advice and went. I thought about how money makes people behave like children.

January 31, 2010

I am Evelyn Amony. Today I lingered in bed. I was taken over by sleep. Today Cynthia is ten months old. I organized myself this Sunday to go to Lacor Hospital. There is a lot of wind and dust. As I walked and reached Lacor Hospital, I was almost knocked down by a car because my mind was far away. The driver stopped just in front of me. I did not hear the car hoot or make any sound. Today I almost died because if the man had not controlled the vehicle, then he would have knocked me down. People asked me what was wrong with me because I was not looking at what was on the road. When you are thinking a lot, your eyes will stop seeing. You will not know what to do.

There were three things that made me sad today. One of them is that I learned Cecelia's son has died in the Congo. His mother went back to the bush during the peace talks because he had remained with Kony after she was captured. She wanted to escape back home with him. God did not allow that to happen. On top of that I am worried about my sister's child, who is very sick and was admitted to the hospital. Finally, today is the day I almost died. I was worried about very many things, and that is why the car almost knocked me down. Today I have decided to spend the night in the hospital so that I can help my sister, but staying in the hospital is not easy. There are very many children who are sick. There are also very many deaths. Some children die as soon as they are brought to the hospital.

February 1, 2010

I am Evelyn Amony. Today Kony's sister Lakot came to visit us from Odek. She said that she did not have any clothes and asked if I could give her some. You know, when you have children in a family you will have that bond with their father's relatives. This lady said that her husband had sent her to me, so I had to help her with the clothes. Indeed, I selected some clothes for her among the items that my sister sells. I told her, "I do not have any clothes apart from these ones. You take them."

Back at home, my brothers Mark and Charles came over and said that they had come to talk to me. Mark began to talk about school fees for their elder children. He said I had to get 16,000 shillings so that they could go to interviews. I told him there was no money. When I said that, his mood changed as though he thought I had money but was just refusing him. I told him, "Look, I have no money to spare. Maybe if I get more money somehow I will give you some. My children are staying at home because of our lack of money. They are supposed to be in school today. If I get money, I will give it to you. I am not refusing you, I just do not have any money." I told him that my chest was also paining. As soon as they left, I closed the door, lay down, and quickly fell asleep.

February 4, 2010

I am Evelyn Amony. This evening I met a woman I stayed with in the hospital when Grace had tuberculosis. This lady was very good. Grace's cough was very bad, and this lady helped me as though she were my sister. She was by my side and helped me. When we saw each other we ran toward each other and hugged at the market. People looked at us, and they thought that she was my sister. She used to buy things and bring them to me. She is a good person. She got a husband, and they stay very well together. She has few problems. We chatted, and she said that she would come and visit me on Saturday or Sunday. She said that she would come over on one of those days.

February 5, 2010

I am Evelyn Amony. This morning I sent Grace off to school and prepared myself for work. When I got there, I completed my normal tasks. What made me stranded today was that there were people there fixing the electricity who spoke only in English and Lugbara. I was worried. When it was time to go for lunch, there was no way to tell these people that I wanted to go for lunch. I could not tell them because I worried I would not say it correctly. I sat there until a man asked me in English, "Are you not going for lunch?" I replied, "I am going. I am waiting for you." I sat for some time, and the man told the boy to work on a small part and then stop. The man asked me which hotel I was going to eat from. I replied in English, "That hotel near the hospital." I could not go to eat from Min Naomi's place because I told them that I was going to eat near the hospital. We walked and reached the place, but I had never been there before and didn't realize that it only sold milk. The man asked me why I told him that I always eat from that place. You know what I did? I got up to see if there was any place that sold food behind the shop. I met a girl, but she told me that she did not know. She was cooking, and behind her was a hotel. I went and asked them what they had. What helped me was that when I came back, the men were not around. I ate and went back to the office. I walked very fast on my way back. The men returned and found me. They asked me why I did not wait for them and why we did not eat from the same hotel. The English-speaking man had told me on the way there that he was a Moslem. I told him that I loved pork. I told him I had gone to buy pork. I said in English, "I love pork. I was eating pork." The man began to ask me why I eat pork. He said that I had to convert and become a Moslem. I told him that I could not stop eating pork. They continued working, and I continued with my reading. Whenever he said something that I could not answer, I said only "yes." He told me that I do not disagree with anything, and I said that everything was okay all the time. In my heart I thought, "I should not have spoken any English."

February 7, 2010

I am Evelyn Amony. While I was ironing clothes this evening around six o'clock, some ladies came to visit me. They had stayed in the bush with me. One of them was Mary, who came together with Joyce. I used to think that I was the worst off among the women who came back from the bush. In our clan our relatives do not help us with anything, but today, when Mary told me her story, I became sad. Even if my relatives do not support me, they come and visit. No one visits Mary; she is alone. The most painful thing is that she does not have the capacity to take care of the children because she has to look for money all the time. Now she has taken the children to the village. This issue makes me think a lot.

What are we supposed to do in the future? Mary said to me, "Evelyn, I do not know why God made me come back home. I should have died in the bush. God has made me come back home, but there is nothing that I can do. I came back and found my mother and father had died. Only my brothers are there. But, Evelyn, I am very stressed. I reunited with my bush-husband when he returned home some time after me, as he is the father of my children. The inconceivable has happened. The father of my children has now rejected all of us."

She asked me to give her advice, and I reminded her that she was not the only person to suffer on this earth. I reminded her it was not just because she was abducted that men acted this way but that women who were not abducted were also abandoned. I told her, "Men are all the same—even the ones who are educated. If he wants to disturb you, he will." I gave her advice on how she could live, saying, "It is painful when you think about it, but you need to be strong. You have to be strong although it is not easy. It is hard to get a good man in northern Uganda. It is very hard." This is what I tried to tell her. I know that if she has hope and love, she will be consoled. This is what I decided to say because it is painful to hear those with problems similar to mine. It is very painful and very hard. These things happen in people's lives. You pass through them. Whether you were abducted or not, you pass through them. You will go through what you are supposed to go through.

February 8, 2010

I am Evelyn Amony. Today I went to World Vision to meet some of the boys who had just returned from the Congo. At first they did not recognize me. I called them by name, but they still did not recognize me. I told them, "You may not recognize me, but I am Bakita's mother. When I went to the Congo during the peace talks I was very thin," and one of them said I looked very different now, that I looked like a young girl. I said, "I am leading a new life which is very different to my bush life. I no longer walk the way I used to. I no longer carry luggage that makes my head go bald the way I used to. I carry my child on my back when I want. When I do not want to carry it on my back, I don't, which means that here I am free. You will also be free like me. You will be free, and I will also be free. We shall all be free. Be strong and there will be a difference in your lives." This is what I told the kids who had just come back.

When I got home, Mark and Charles came for a visit. We talked about how I lived together with my sisters without a man in the house. I asked them to advise me on what to do, because people think that when you are renting a house on your own then you are a prostitute. Yet it is not true. We decided that it would be good to visit our family at home every six months so that people think we are good. Personally, I do not have a strong relationship with my father because I was very angry with him. When I was still at home I knew my father loved me, but I was secretly angry about my education. I think it was my father who facilitated my abduction, because on the day I was abducted I had been chased from school as my school fees weren't paid. It was when I was walking back that the LRA abducted me. Therefore I was very angry with my father, but I have forgiven him. I know that things can change.

February 12, 2010

I am Evelyn Amony. Today, I got up and prepared myself for work. There is nothing much I can talk about today. I walked to Bakita and Grace's school because the parents of pupils in Primary One and Two were required for a meeting. The meeting was good because we were able to get to know the teachers who teach our children. We also learned about what we can do so that we can work together with the teachers to ensure that learning is easier for our children. We were told to contribute 5,000 shillings a week per child in Primary One and Two so that they can begin to eat from school. I calculated and realized that each child will have to pay 60,000 shillings every term. In two terms the total will be 120,000 shillings. This is what we parents are supposed to pay whether our children are being sponsored or not. The parents were very sad, but even if you were sad you had to do it because you wanted your child to be educated. When it was time to go home, I left late and walked together with one of my former co-wives. She was going up to Lacor. I branched at the prison and went home. When I reached home, I went to the market, bought food, and went to cook. I cooked late, but I have a trick—I always tell my children to tell stories and chat when they have just bathed because I want them to take their time so that they do not sleep without eating. That is the trick I use with my children so that they do not sleep hungry. Thank you.

February 14, 2010

I am Evelyn Amony. This morning, I organized myself and went to prayers with my children. Kony's sister Lakot and his uncles came by.

Bakita made tea. We sat for some time waiting for my co-wives to come back from prayers. When they arrived, we told Kony's elders about what was bothering us, about the bad things happening to our children and that we wanted their clan to help support them. Then we said, "If you have a mad person in your family, you cannot allow him to run mad." You know, people say that Kony's children are mad.[5] We are worried about the future of our children, so for us it is important to go to their paternal clan and ask them for advice and support. We sat and spoke for some time and agreed that we should go to get to know the children's paternal home. One of Kony's uncles said he could not refuse any of Kony's children. In fact, he asked why we had not gone to visit him yet.

To be honest, most of the time the mothers of Kony's children say that they do not want to hear anything about Kony's home. They say they would rather live in poverty than in Kony's home. I did not tell the old man this, but instead I just said thank you for welcoming us to his home. The elder then said he knew me well from the time I had gone to their home for Nora's funeral and that he recognized me as a married woman in this family. He said, "If your husband was not in the wilderness, then you would be the first woman to be married in this home. You were the first woman to come to this home together with the children. You are a friendly person. You went to visit Mama Nora frequently. We acknowledge the problem."[6]

I began to talk: "We have come to look for you. We know that blood is thicker than water. Today we have a saying that when a dog bites a goat, the owner of the dog pays for it. We have given birth to Kony's children. If tomorrow one of our children makes a mistake and offends someone in this regime, where the issue of land and other things is very

5. People report that those who came back from the bush have "*cen,*" what Sverker Finnstrom describes as the ghostly vengeance of persons who "died in a bad way," such as through murder (*Living with Bad Surroundings*, 162). It is believed *cen* can manifest in the children of wrongdoers and that wrongdoers themselves can infest an entire family, resulting in misfortune and illness, including madness.

6. That Evelyn took leadership to visit the paternal clan on more than one occasion warranted her recognition as a first wife, one who had authority to speak and whose words would be respected in the paternal clan.

complicated, where shall we say is their home?[7] You are their family, but we do not have a good relationship with you. You do not accept that these are your children. Since we came back, we have waited for you to recognize them for a long time.[8] It is now six years for some of us. Personally it is five years that I have stayed here. No one has come up to say that he will give me help or will support his brother's wife or say that I am his brother's wife. It is so painful to us. We hear that Kony has a family, and we know that Kony was also born. He had a father. That is why we made up our mind to look for the home of our children's family. We want the right answer from you so that we know how to unite with you. Even if we were captured and children were born to us in the bush, these children have a clan. We will continue to raise this issue with you until we get the right answer from you. We thought that we should demonstrate on the streets, but where will that leave us? We decided that we needed to meet like this because we have tolerated the matter for too long, and it has become painful."

The elder then began to talk. He said openly that he did not know my co-wives. He said, "I know Bakita's mother because she was together with us in the past. When Kony's mother was sick, she was the one struggling with her. You had hidden yourselves." Then the elder said he wanted the names of *Ladit*'s children. They were read to him together with their mother's names, even those whose mothers were dead. They said there are so many children, and they had to look seriously at whether or not they could address the question of land. I wondered if they even knew how many children Kony had.

I then told them, "If you wanted to, you would have helped the children by now with financial support. That is fine. The reason why we said that blood is thicker than water is that the most important thing is

7. To safeguard the future of the children, one's link to the paternal clan is considered vital. A clan will vouch for a son or daughter and assume responsibility should the child do something wrong. Land is a sign of rootedness, connectedness, and belonging in Acholi, where farming and garden work are processes of building social relatedness and ties within the clan. Thus, Evelyn is asking the clan to recognize its children to safeguard their place in the clan and the community in the future.

8. Culturally, the paternal clan is responsible for the welfare of a child and must initiate a process of recognition and care for the child by visiting the maternal clan and paying *luk*, compensation to the mother's clan for the child. Failure to do so is an insult.

to build a relationship between us. We saw that you have no interest in our children at all. That is why we decided to meet with you. Your son gave birth to children with us. You might say that it was not your son's wish to give birth to children with us. We can also say that it was not our wish to have these children. Either way, you are the ones who need to decide whether you can take care of the children or not. This is what we came for. We want to find a way of getting relatives to recognize our children." The discussion ended only at nine o'clock in the evening. After that I went to relax with my friends in town and went to sleep at midnight. Today is a lover's day [Valentine's Day]. I do not know how to call it in English.

February 15, 2010

I am Evelyn Amony. At five o'clock, when I was going home from work, I passed by GUSCO. When I got there I found a lady I had once stayed with who was also Kony's wife. When I went to talk to her, she cried and I also cried because her hand was shot and her index finger was missing. Not only that, she had also lost a lot of weight. She told me, "Min Bakita, my sister. I am here. Please help me. No one [no relative] comes to help me wash my child's clothes despite the pain I am in. I wash clothes with one hand. I can use only one hand." She asked me, "Is my child there? Bring him to me."[9] I told her, "Your son is with your mother at your home. Your family has moved, and I do not know where they are now because they have gone to the village."

She asked me how she could find her child. I told her to ask GUSCO to arrange for her return to be announced on the radio. I felt sorry for her because when we went to the Congo she was very fat. Looking at her now, you would not think she is the same person. She told me people were badly off in the Congo; she said that there is hunger, and there are many battles. She said it is very painful to see how badly the children are doing and that Cecelia[10] has lost a lot of weight ever since

9. Her child was found and returned prior to her own escape and was now at her maternal home.

10. This is Cecelia, who returned with Evelyn to the LRA during the 2006–8 peace talks detailed in chapter 6.

Ladit left them. I thought about this so much; Cecelia told me she had to remain behind because of her son.

I leave all these people in God's hands. He brought my friend back today, and so He can also bring the rest back home. It is not yet too late. This is how I see it. It is painful to see the children who came back from the bush, how they appear. They say that was how we were when we came back, but when you see the state they are in you feel shocked. I was very sad. My friend asked me to bring Bakita and my other children to see her next time. I told her I would take them on Saturday.

February 19, 2010

I am Evelyn Amony. Today is a day for the children who died in the bush. We prayed for our friends who are still in the bush to come back like us. We marched through the streets in memory. A monument had been made for the children who died in the bush, those who are still alive in the bush, and those who got lost. For those who died, God should rest their souls in a good place. For those who were washed away by water, God should take care of their bones wherever they are.

I marched with the others because all of these things touched my life. First of all, my child Winnie was lost in the bush. Second, my brother is still in the bush up to now. There are also many people whom I know still in the bush. We marched in sorrow. We did not say anything. When we reached a place, the *boda boda* [motorcycle taxi] drivers asked us why we were marching in silence. They said, "Why don't you say something so that people know why you are marching?"

We did not say anything. We continued walking. We walked and reached the main market, and Madam Santa Okot [a politician] made a speech. She said, "These children are marching because of their friends who are lost. They are also marching so that something can be done so that their friends who are still in the bush can come back home like they did. They are mourning their friends who died from the bush, and they mourn how society stigmatizes them. Fingers are pointed at those who are returnees." We left and went to stand in front of a statue of people who had laid down their guns and turned to education instead. We stood there, and our photos were taken. From there I was told to speak on behalf of my friends.

I spoke together with one boy. I said, "We need to find a way to stop the war in northern Uganda. We need to make sure the corpses of no more children are consumed by wild animals.[11] In war young children are vulnerable. They are like small sticks for making fire. I am not happy because I have friends who are still in the bush and my child disappeared. I did not even see her dead body. We are sad. We would like to tell those people who say that we want to go back to the bush that life there was not easy.[12] Rain beats you. Bullets are aimed at you. Life in the bush was not easy. We abductees are not going back to the bush for a second time. Those who did not go to the bush think that we are different from them, but we are not." That is what I told them.

February 22, 2010

I am Evelyn Amony. As I was passing through town, I met some of my friends, including a young girl who was one of *Ladit*'s wives. I told them we had to make the time to sit and talk together as those who were abducted. There are things we can talk about only among ourselves. We were upset to hear some people say that those who have returned behave in a bad way.[13]

It is painful when you hear that children who came from the bush bully people or hear that they respond rudely when people talk to them. We asked each other, "How can we stop this?" We do not feel happy because we all went through the same problem of abduction. I asked them, "Why is it that a small group of people who do bad things ruins the name of the majority who do not? This is not good. It is not good to

---

11. An often-narrated fear is to die in the bush and not receive a proper burial, so that one's corpse is consumed by wild animals and never at rest.

12. Communities sometimes accuse those who have returned of having a better life in the bush than they did in the camps and say that they preferred to be there rather than return to the camps.

13. The women frequently refer to the ways their reputations are spoiled because of the actions of a few formerly abducted persons and because the community seemingly has come to expect those who have returned to act in a particular way that transgresses social norms and expectations. Thus, many women state they constantly regulate how they behave so as not to be accused of being "from the bush."

hear of such things." This is what I told them, and then I left and went back home.

When I got home, I spoke with my brothers and my sister for a long time. I wondered if my life as it is now would be like this until I got old? I asked my brothers, "I hear people say that when two or three women stay alone in a house, they are prostitutes. How do people look at us? Do they say that we are prostitutes or what?" Sara told me, "My sister, such things happen. The way I see it, you are living with us like a mother. People cannot call us prostitutes. In addition, people can clearly see that we do not lead the same lifestyle as those who rent houses for prostitution. We are living as if we were still at home. You are our mother. If our mother were alive, we would be living with her. You have taken over our mother's position because she is not around."

February 23, 2010

I am Evelyn Amony. Today I woke up in the morning and I boiled water. I bathed Grace. A lot of pus is flowing from her ears. She also had a high fever. I was cleaning her ears with a damp cloth. I tested her at the hospital, and she had malaria.

February 24, 2010

I am Evelyn Amony. Today I saw a girl who resembled Brenda, a girl who died from the bush. I trembled when I saw this girl, thinking she was Brenda. She said she was not the one. On my way back, I began to think of Brenda's mother. Her teeth are also white like Brenda's. This lady has photos of her daughter as a baby. I wondered how she kept those photos after all these years of war. Most people's photos and things were burned through the war. I thought the lady was very wise to have kept her daughter's photo all this time.

February 25, 2010

I am Evelyn Amony. Today I woke up early, boiled water, and then bathed Grace. I cleaned her ears and prepared her for school. She is vomiting a lot. She started vomiting in the night and up to now. I went to bathe and came back. I found she had vomited on herself. I changed her dress. I had only 2,500 shillings and I wanted to go to the hospital, but someone informed me that if I took her to World Vision they might be able to sponsor her treatment. I hurried, but the doctor was not there. As I was leaving, the woman at World Vision asked me if I was taking care of someone's child or if it was my child. I told her that it was my child. She asked me if I had also been abducted. I told her I was. She told me that I did not look like someone who came from the bush. She asked me how long I had spent in the bush and I told her that it was almost twelve years. She said, "Oh! God."

I then left. I crossed the road and got a *boda boda* and went to the hospital. We went inside and waited in the queue. The doctor was late. Grace vomited on a woman waiting next to us. I told the woman, "Remove your skirt and go with this one that I am wearing." She said, "I am also a mother like you, my child; do not worry." I told her to give me her skirt so that I could wash it. She refused and told me, "I am born again. This child is sick; otherwise she would not have vomited on me." I left the woman and went to sit on the queue. Grace kept on vomiting, and I thought she was going to be admitted. We stayed in the queue for some time until our medical results were read at three o'clock so that we were able to see the doctor.

What broke my heart is that a lady had an accident and she was brought to the hospital. When I see big wounds like that, I remember the bullet wounds that people used to get in the bush and the ones I nursed. I recalled and began to tremble. The wound was terrible. The wound resembled those of a man called Oketch who was bombed on the lips. This lady fell off a motorcycle and lost her teeth. Her mouth was swollen. When I saw her, I saw the picture of the other man called Oketch in my head. I wondered in my heart, saying, "Even at home people get such wounds!" I used to think that only guns caused such terrible wounds.

When we reached home, Grace said that I should fry eggs for her to eat. I had eggs in the house. I cooked them, and Grace ate very little. She kept on crying. She had no fever, but her vomit was yellow. When it was time for her to go to sleep, she slept.

March 8, 2010

I am Evelyn Amony. I would like to talk about our day, the Women's Day. I used to think that women did not have a day. Ever since I came back home I began to realize that women had a day. Since I knew that women had a day, I decided that today should be a good day for me. Unfortunately I am not feeling well. I have flu and cough. My chest is paining but I am trying my level best as a woman on our day. Today is our day to be a woman in various ways. It depends on how you as a woman you look at it. For me, Evelyn, I decided that today Women's Day has to be good to me to organize my house as a woman.

I looked for *ofuyu* [black soil] to smear my house. I smeared the kitchen very well. After smearing the kitchen, I began to smear my bedroom. I smeared it all neatly and then smeared it again with cow dung. The way I see on Women's Day I have to do things according to the Acholi *tekwaro* [culture, history]. People look at today in different ways. I hear some women say that today they will not cook or do anything but to me it is a day to do your work well. That is why today I made my house look good. After smearing the house I began to get my things. Today the eighth is good for me because I am organizing things in my home, the things that the children had not put in a proper place. I have scrubbed my saucepans so that you can see the reflection of your teeth. As an Acholi woman, my things have to be clean. I decided not to go anywhere on Women's Day and stay with my children like a good mother and spend time chatting with them. I am making my children feel better like a mother should, even if every day am sad. I decided to stay with my children today on Women's Day like a mother. I was with them the way my mother used to take care of us. To do this, I had to remove all the anger from my heart and I decided to stay well with my children.

At around three o'clock, one of my neighbors left in the morning without cooking. She was saying that today is Women's Day and we are free to do anything. She said her husband should be the one to cook. Her husband was annoyed. He did not even beat her. In most cases people think that if you beat your wife today you will be handled with the law. The way I see it, I find that the woman did something wrong.

This is because if you are a mother, you have to do things like cook. On such a day like Women's Day you have to do what you do best to show that you are a woman and you do not just pretend to be one.

You find that some women woke up early today to go to bars to have fun and do anything they think of. My advice to women is that today is Women's Day but when it is going to be celebrated in another year, I find that it is good for a woman to go together with her husband if she is thinking of going somewhere to have fun. Not only that, today is the day that you have to cook Acholi dishes. You can cook any traditional meal if there are things to use. This would show that we as women of Uganda are capable of doing certain things. There is nothing you are going to do today because there is no office you are going to go to [Women's Day is a national holiday in Uganda]. Therefore you have to do things according to the Acholi tradition that shows that you are a woman from Acholi. Cultures are different. I talk as an Acholi woman. If you are a Muganda, Nyankole, Lango, or other tribe, you have to do things as a mother the way Langis or Baganda do. That is what you are supposed to do, but do not do things that debase women. We women . . . are important in Uganda. . . .

We women are also important. [I began to] think of our sisters who died from the bush. Those who were lost in the bush. If God had helped them to come back home like I did, we would be celebrating Women's Day together. This is what I saw today. It has been a good day. Today I prayed for our colleagues who are still in the bush. It would be good if God also helped those who were not at home and are still in the bush so that they [could return] and also celebrate Women's Day how they want to.

Sometimes you feel that you should be dancing or drinking alcohol to show that today was Women's Day. My fellow women, girls and children who are still young and are just growing up to become mothers, you should show how you are a woman. Women have capacity! I know that these days we women also have rights the way I hear people say. Our day is even celebrated. This means that we also have a future because if you go to any office, you will find a woman. If you go to the bank you will find a woman. You will find her working. When you go to government jobs like in the UPDF, you will find a woman who has held a gun walking in the bush. . . . I know that these days we women are important and we also have rights. This is what I can talk about today. Do not let today make you become big headed to do things that you do not understand. Even if I did not go to celebrate, I did things that show that I am a woman [and] a real Acholi woman. If I was together with my husband, today I would have prepared for him the food that Acholi women make. Today is very important to me. It is Women's Day.

March 12, 2010

I am Evelyn Amony. This morning I told the kids to prepare themselves for school. Grace did not want to go to school. I washed her legs, and she went to sit behind the house. I thought she had gone to get dressed when I came and found her sitting behind the house. I got a stick and beat Grace. I asked her if she thinks going to school is not important. I told her to go to school. She told me, "Mum, my ears cannot hear anything." I told her, "If your ears do not hear, then your backside will."

March 13, 2010

I am Evelyn Amony. Today is a Saturday. Today I fetched water to wash the clothes before I realized I would never be able to catch up with all the clothes that needed to be washed. My brother then came and asked me to come and see his wife, who was sick. Her eyes were swollen almost shut. I prepared herbs for her to take. My brother asked me how I knew about herbs. I told him, "I know herbs because the father to my children used to show me how to prepare herbs. We used a lot of Acholi traditional herbs for medical purposes. When I came back here, I used to prepare them for people, but I became fearful of doing so because it reminded me of the past. There was a time when a lady said to me she was not surprised I knew how to prepare herbs because Kony is a strong witch doctor. After she said that, I never prepared another herb." I told him, "I am going to give it to you only because you are my brother."

March 20, 2010

I am Evelyn Amony. In the morning, I woke up and went to the well to fetch water. There were very many people at the well. We queued to wait for water. Bakita remained at home cooking. When we got the water, I washed the clothes. The nuns from St. Monika's School[14] sent a woman to assemble the mothers who had returned with children. We walked to St. Monika's School, and when I reached there I saw very many people had come with empty bags, baskets, and basins, assembling to receive something, yet we did not even know what it was they were going to distribute.

When the nuns saw people coming with empty bins, they asked me what was happening. They were not amused that people had arrived expectant like that. The goods the nuns were going to distribute were packed away and placed back inside the storeroom. No one was given anything. I was embarrassed with the way people ran to St. Monika's School with their empty baskets. As I was leaving, one of the nuns began to scold me for not following up with Grace at school. They asked me why I did not take care of her sick ears. I just kept quiet and listened to them.

I went upstairs and found Grace had put on trousers and a pink dress, and she was dancing *zigzag* [*larakaraka*, an Acholi style of dancing]. You should have seen my daughter; people laughed. No one knew she was my child. The whites took her photo. They laughed at her. Grace also amused me, because she thought she was doing the dance very well, yet she was not.

Later I went to a medical clinic, because I heard they were giving away free medicine. When we reached there, we were told there was no medicine left and were turned away. I later learned that people who went later on received medicine, and I felt so annoyed. I know that sometimes you get some things and other times you do not. But I am trying to get medicine for Grace's ears. At some point, some medicine might work and heal her sick ears. I felt heartbroken.

At around two o'clock in the morning, I woke up from a dream that I was together with Kony. In the dream, I touched his fingernails and asked, "You are the one?" He replied, "I am the one." I asked him, "How

14. Recall Evelyn did a year of training in tailoring at St. Monika's in a program designed for women who had returned with children.

did you come here?" He said, "You still sleep. I have come, and we are staying together. Can't you be happy?" I then woke up immediately.

March 28, 2010

I am Evelyn Amony. I woke up at three o'clock in the morning. I felt like I should dig the place and plant *tula* [a bitter vegetable that is like an eggplant]. When morning came, I borrowed a hoe and went to the garden to dig. I went to the market to buy *tula* seeds and planted them. I then went back home to prepare breakfast for the children and to wash clothes. I washed two blankets, but before I could finish my body began to shake and my eyes could no longer see. I asked myself what was happening to me. A neighbor thought it was because I had not eaten and brought me some bread and tea. After taking them, I felt better. I do not know what happened to me, but I felt better and continued washing the clothes. Maybe it was hunger.

March 29, 2010

I am Evelyn Amony. In the morning I got up and watered my *tula*. I prepared Grace and walked her to school. As I walked to work I began to think about an invitation I had received to go to a traditional marriage from the owner of the Sunset Hotel. I asked myself why I should go and witness a marriage because it will only make me worry. I get worried when I see someone get married. It only makes me sad. I begin to think that I will never be married.

I then walked to go back home, but as I was about to cross the road some students from Layibi College were fighting. They had just come from a football match. The police were trying to stop them. The police were running, and so were the students. I walked without knowing what was happening. The *boda boda* drivers told me, "You run. They cause havoc wherever they go." When the students reached the front of the Bank of Uganda, no vehicle could pass. They stood in the middle of the road. Even if a car hooted, they did not give way. They stood there for a long time, and then the policemen came. When the policemen came, they walked and went near Centenary Bank. They stood there. I was seeing them from the grounds near Grace's school. I stood and watched them go. The students had divided themselves into groups. I looked at them and concluded that there were behaving like the LRA did with the NRA.

Everyone in our area went to witness the traditional marriage today. They said the marriage was so nice. The woman is from a wealthy family, and the man is also from a family that is not badly off. What hurt me is that they said the woman had the highest bride wealth in her family because she had finished her studies. The woman was waving her hands, greeting people, and thanking her father. She said, "Thank you, Daddy," whenever anything was read out because it was her father who made sure she finished her studies. For you to get a good man, you have to have studied. This is what I see. In the evening, I could hear people dancing, and I realized the kids were there. I went to look for the kids, but when they saw me, they ran and hid.

April 1, 2010

I am Evelyn Amony. I woke up and prepared to go to the hospital to meet the doctor working on Grace's ears. I walked and went there. I waited at the hospital until 11:00 A.M., when a nurse told me that the doctor would not arrive until 2:00 P.M. When a nurse says such a thing, you just know that it is a flopped program, so I took Grace home. Pus was just flowing from her ears. I gave her drugs, and as soon as I was about to take off, a white woman who pays my adopted daughter's school fees came and wanted to take us to town to buy her new clothes. They were in a hurry as they were traveling to Kampala. We went to town and bought clothes and a pair of shoes, and we then took her back to school in their vehicle. On the way, I asked them to please drop me where I work, but they just left me at the school.

April 4, 2010

I am Evelyn Amony. Today is Easter. My co-wives came, and we talked about the past. They believe Winnie did not die but was taken by some-one and adopted. I have really looked for Winnie everywhere in Uganda, but I do not know where she is. I do not like to talk about things that are painful, so I told them to change the topic, as I did not want to talk about Winnie. We ate together to show love and cooperation, even though we sometimes had our differences. I think because of what we were talking about, I had a dream in the night that Winnie was with me and it was her father who brought her to me. So I really do not know. I think talking about her brought her to my dream. For as long as she is alive, I pray that whoever is keeping her should take good care of her; even if she is forced to live like a slave, God should protect her so that one day she comes back to me. I know a human being cannot just disappear forever. Look at me—I was abducted as a young girl and I grew up with a problematic life. God should have spared my child from the same problems I lived through.

April 8, 2010

I am Evelyn Amony. Today I met with a humanitarian organization, and they gave me a hoe and a five-kilogram bag of seeds for planting beans. At 10:00 A.M. we were supposed to go to St. Monika's School. When I reached there, the sister told me to wait for a white person who wants to help educate me on Grace's sick ears. I sat there and waited until 3:00 P.M., when the *munu* [white person] arrived and started teaching me how to clean Grace's ears. People think I do not know how to keep things clean. As I was leaving, the *munu* asked me if I knew how to sew clothes. I told her yes I do. She carried a bag with materials and asked me to sew bags for carrying mats. I was afraid at first, but I decided to do it. I then started cutting the clothes and sewed three bags. It was getting late by that time. She suggested that I spend the night in St. Monika's to sew at night since she was going away the following morning. I told her that I would have loved to help her but I cannot as I have a little baby at home, I cannot stay till late or even spend the night. She insisted I sew for her, as she would pay me 5,000 shillings per bag. I told her that it was not possible. Sister told me that if I was able to go and get my baby, I could come back and sew from there, but I still found it difficult. Even if they wanted me to help, they should have told me earlier, not at the last minute like that. So I told her that I would be going back home. Then the white woman told me that I should first wait for her. I really spent a long time waiting for her. Then she came and told me that she would be coming back in July, so I should continue making the bags. She said we could enter into a contract to make those bags and asked me how many I could make in one day. I told her that I could make seven or eight of them in a day from the way I saw it. But I told her that I have work that I do and I will not do that every day. Then she asked when I could make the bags and I told her that I could make them on Saturdays.

She said that she was going to the Congo and Rwanda before returning to Gulu. I told her it was okay; when she returns, we shall make the bags. She gave me 10,000 shillings for the two bags that I had already made. It is so easy to make those bags. All that time that I spent waiting for that *munu*, I could have sewn seven of those bags. This is what happened today.

As soon as I reached home, I learned that our neighbor's child had died. He was a young boy, and he just fell and died. I worried so much about his death, and it reminded me of the kind of death that happened in the bush. You might have just talked to your colleague minutes ago, and soon you might hear he has died. This boy only fell, and that led to his death. So this was something bad that happened today. It was so sad to see his sisters. Their young parents were in Anaka.

As we ate dinner, I watched Bakita. You know, Grace slapped Bakita and she just sat; she slapped her again. Then Bakita beat her, and Grace ran to me, crying, "Mum, I have been beaten!" I told her that it was good that Bakita beat her because she does not respect her sister. Grace said that Bakita is older and how could I allow her to beat her like that? Then she told me that she would not spend the night with me; she would go and sleep in the other room. So she went and spent the night with Bakita. She is such a stubborn child.

April 11, 2010

I am Evelyn Amony. I prepared to go to the market when something happened that made my mind go silent. I met a woman who was with us in the bush. Her name was Catherine; she was one of the senior commander's wives. When she returned, she stayed in GUSCO; they supported her studies in primary school, and when she passed Primary Four very well, the people at GUSCO were so impressed that they paid for her to continue studying. When she was in Primary Seven, she met a man. He lied to her and made her pregnant.[15]

I was shocked by the way she looked. She was carrying the baby, but it was so small, and she wore rags. At first I was not sure if it was even her, but I knew she had a scar on her body, so I looked for that and concluded that was Catherine. I called to her, "*Lamego* [mother], please come." She came and said, "This looks like Betty." When I responded that I was the one, she threw down the goods she had carried from the market. Tears rolled down my cheeks. I had already been to market, and I did not have any more money; if I had had any money, I would have given it to her.

I remember when Catherine was still in school we would visit her with the people who worked at GUSCO. At school she was doing very well. She was fat and looked youthful; you would have never known that she had ever even given birth to a child. But the woman I saw before me . . . it was as if she had just returned from the bush. Her veins were all out, yet she insisted that she was doing fine. I asked her, "How is your husband?" She said, "He is okay." I asked again, "Does he take good care of you?" She said, "Yes," yet if you see the condition she is in, carrying her baby on the back with a torn, stained bed sheet, you can tell she is not well. The baby she was carrying was even more different from the children she had earlier on. This baby's head is very big. Tears rolled down my cheeks; I really cried. It was so sad to see her. She also started crying.

Meeting her reminded me of the day we descended the mountain called Agoro. Her husband carried her child for her because you had to move slowly on your backside. Her husband really loved her. He carried the baby down the mountain. When I saw how he acted, I even wished I were his wife.

15. Women in the project often refer to the period of courtship before sexual relations with a man as "deception" or "lies" if they abandon them after the women fall pregnant; that is, they promise to marry or care for them, then abandon them.

April 19, 2010

I am Evelyn Amony. I woke up and went to the well and fetched water. After that, I came and bathed Grace and gave her medication with warm water as prescribed by the doctor. I plaited Grace's hair, cleaned her shoes, and sent my children off to school. After they left, I sat down and breastfed Cynthia until her babysitter arrived and they left. I swept the compound, bathed, and walked very fast to the office. I walked so fast to GUSCO because I had learned my friends from the bush had just returned and were there. I met my friend after so long, and we spoke. She told me that when she was arrested, she spent a very long time with the Congolese army, moving through the bush. She spent three months with those people. There were some government soldiers who moved with them, and as they were moving, they bumped into Kony himself and started firing at him. One boy who was Kony's escort was shot and his legs were broken as the rest escaped. She told me they found the bag of our friend Irene, but she was not sure if she had been shot or not, that she might have died or survived the attack. I grew very worried. I remember when I went to the Congo for the peace talks, Irene begged me to convince Kony to release her so that she could return with me to Uganda. I found it hard to do this for her because during the peace talks things were so tense, and I wanted him to release me to return home as well. So I feel so worried about her because she really wanted to return home, but she was afraid that if she tried to escape she might be killed.

April 27, 2010

I am Evelyn Amony. Today I woke up and washed clothes, Cynthia is sick, and we went to the clinic and then came back to find Grace crying terribly because her ears were paining badly. I wondered what kind of disease it was that makes her keep having pain like this. I gave her bread, and then I warmed food and we started eating together. Grace kept quiet and then said, "Mum, my ears are now cooling." I told her, "Grace, you sometimes tell me your ears are paining, yet you may just be hungry." She told me that sometimes she feels pain in her ears to the extent that her head also hurts. In the middle of the night, a neighbor woke me up.

I could not get back to sleep, and I was so angry at her. I kept thinking about different things that worry me, including Grace's ears. I worried a lot.

May 16, 2010

I am Evelyn Amony. In the morning, I woke up and started washing clothes but Cynthia was sick and she kept crying. As I tried to wash the clothes, she vomited and had diarrhea seriously. Each time I tried to give her medicine, she would vomit up the drugs. Each time I breastfed, she would vomit again. It took me a long time to finish the laundry.

Margaret came by and said we should go register to vote. I put Cynthia on my back and we walked to Gulu Public School where they took our photo and fingerprints for the voter card. You were expected to put all ten fingers on a certain thing and it would be scanned into a machine. I grew annoyed as the man registering us asked me to spell my name. I was pissed off, I told him that if he was literate, he should know how to write and yet here he was asking for me to spell my name. He asked me three times, "How do you write the name Evelyn?" I wondered what was wrong with this man? Didn't he know that I didn't know how to write? That I never studied at school? Why did he ask me such questions?

I decided to let the issue go, but then the very same man asked me questions like, "Are you married? What is your husband's name?" There were many people listening who knew me. One boy whom I stayed with in the bush whispered that they were just looking for the name. I worried he would say Kony's name and gave him a bad look. I did not like what was happening, nor did I want anyone to say Kony's name. It was as if he was accusing me. So I just made up a name for my husband: Justine Otukene. When Margaret finished registering we left.

July 16, 2010

I am Evelyn Amony. . . . [After work] I went to plait my hair. . . . After [the woman] had plaited twelve lines in my hair, I was called that I had a visitor at home. I went and found many people in my compound. I did not know what to do. I asked myself what had happened. I saw eleven white people and three black people. One of them was black but did not know Acholi. I do not know her tribe. She looked like a Muganda. There was a man called Kevin who said he was [a government official]. I have never seen him before.

They said I was supposed to tell them [the visitor] my name and the year I was abducted. . . . I told them that I was abducted in 1994. They asked me how many children I had come back with. I told them I had given birth to three children but one of them got lost during a war in Sudan. I told them when she got lost I was given a child to take care of from Gusco when I came back and I look at her like my child who got lost. They asked me how I was surviving. I told them I was surviving the way people in Gulu survive. I told them I was reluctant talking to white people because some whites come and take your picture and promise to build you a house or give you money but it does not happen and I felt it was useless talking to them. I told them talking to whites reminds us of what happened in our lives and it was bad.

They said they were different from other people. One of them was from Canada and another one was from another country. They said they had plans for young mothers of northern Uganda and were most interested in Gulu. They said they wanted to work with the young mothers and wanted to find something they could do to make them earn money. They asked me what they should do for me or what I wanted. I told them that what I wanted was a lot. I told them that first of all I wanted them to get for me land and build for me a house. I also told them secondly that I wanted my children to go to school. I also told them I wanted to be given something that can make me earn money. They asked me what I thought they would give me so that I would get money.

I told them I had tailoring skills but did not have a sewing machine. They asked me many questions and I told them that I was tired of talking and had reached a point where am fed up. I said, "You see I have come late because I am not interested." When I said that some whites use us to get money, their leader called me and gave me his email address. He said if I do not have an email address then I should open one. He said he wanted to communicate with me when he goes back to their country. I got the email address. . . . When they finished talking they went to the bus and brought clothes, pens, color markers, and gave them out to the children. They took Margaret's photo with the clothes. They said they were going to find a way of connecting with us. . . . That is what happened today. . . . Thank you. I wish you the best. God should give you blessings the world cannot give.

Epilogue

When I first returned, life was really difficult. In 2011, my life started changing. I worked at the Justice and Reconciliation Project [JRP] as a volunteer, and I started slowly forgetting about the past as I worked with new people. If they saw me lost in thoughts, they would come and speak to me, asking what the problem was. At JRP, we started the Women's Advocacy Network [WAN] to conduct advocacy for other women affected by the war. I was elected to be its chairperson.

WAN has nine groups of women in northern Uganda, who originate from different subcounties. The network operates only in Acholi sub-region, but one day we hope to work in West Nile, Teso, and Lango. WAN provides counseling and peer support. If you learn of the conditions some of the women are in, if you see how heartbroken they are, you have to talk to them. For instance, you see how heartbreak manifests in how a woman treats her children; she can take her anger out on them. If a woman is abusing her children, we try to get her to talk and lighten her heart. The woman might say, "Do you see this child? The father destroyed my future; he mistreated me and caused me so much pain, and I avenge this pain on his child." We tell them the child should not suffer for what happened to the woman at the hands of the father. Also, there are some mothers whose mothers have rejected their children, and they become so angry with their mothers. The mother's anger toward her child is sometimes greater than her anger toward those who took her to the bush. These are the kind of women we talk to; we try to put them at ease.

If you stayed with that person in the bush, you can counsel her better than her own sister; you can relate to what she went through. If you are to sit down with someone who also returned from the bush like you, you can recall the past together and even laugh about some of the things that happened. But if you are to narrate such stories to someone from here at home, it can become a source of tension between you. For instance, you might tell of your experiences to your sister, and when there is a quarrel, she uses those stories to hurt you. She might say to you in anger, "Who was raped in the bush?" It is difficult to live with those who did not go to the bush. We live well together for the most part, but there are limits.

When we started WAN, I got to know people in the communities and they got to know me [through community outreach and dialogues on justice and reconciliation]. Today, I can go and speak in any community without fear. The work we do in the community gives us consolation. They tell us not to cry, that they cried for us when we were abducted.

Today, people cannot differentiate between me and someone who has studied. If someone says something so hurtful, I now know how to handle them. I also know how to handle members of WAN; I know each and every one of the members and that when they do something hurtful, it is because of their experiences in the past. My leadership skills just keep increasing.

Today, I can speak to the leaders in the district, like the members of Parliament. In the past, when I went to their offices, it reminded me of the past. They referred to me as Kony's wife. I kept insisting I was speaking as a member of WAN, and eventually they stopped calling me Kony's wife. This makes my work much easier. I feel that if I continue doing this work, I might even be able to stand for a leadership position, for instance, to stand for office.

As members of WAN, we try to help each other when someone falls sick. We visit people in the hospital and contribute money, even if it is little, to support them. For instance, our friend's husband has been sick for more than four months in the hospital, and she has had to stay home alone to care for her children. We each contributed money and bought her sugar and soap. When we visited her, we realized she had the disease of these days [HIV] and is on medication [antiretroviral drugs, or ARVs], but she had become angry and stopped taking the drugs. She felt there was no one taking care of her [that she was alone in this world], and she had nothing in her house. Her neighbors wanted to help her, but she was bitter, and eventually they accused her of not wanting to work or help herself. When we went to visit her in her home, we found her in a terrible state; she was so weak she was unable to walk. We spoke to her and convinced her to go to the hospital for treatment. Later on, I began to raise money from the staff of the Gender Justice Unit [GJU] at JRP to bring to her. Everyone contributed money, and I brought it to her and her family. Another example was when a member of WAN and I got into an accident. So many members came to help us while we were in the hospital. Even when we had been discharged from the hospital, some group members came all the way from Atiak and Palaro to see us. It was then that I realized our unity is a strong unity. Some of our own relatives did not come to see us in the hospital, yet our group members came to see us. These are important things the group is doing.

We also help mothers of children born in the LRA [as a result of forced marriage] to trace the paternal clans of their children and help restore the relationship. In one case, the uncles to some of the children reached out to us, calling us and asking us if we could help to arrange a meeting with their nephews. We spoke to both families and arranged for the relatives to first meet in the office. At a later date, we arranged to bring the children to their paternal home in Pader so they could get to know where they are from. Two members of WAN went with the mother and children. When we arrived, we were warmly welcomed. You could see the uncle's family had really prepared to receive the visitors. Ever since that day, that family has become our friends; they often call me. Later on, they again took the children to visit their home in Pader. The grandfather announced his time for dying was near and that he had decided to distribute the land to his children. He ensured that the children were the first to be given land, because their father had died in the LRA. The grandfather also gave the children cattle and advised them to care for it well, as they will multiply.

Even my own children came and asked to be taken to their paternal home. It was then that I realized the issue of paternal identity is very important to the future of these children. So I met with my children's grandfather. I met with the brother of the grandfather of Kony. He advised me to take the children to their home in Odek, but I felt I could not go alone. I asked JRP to support this visit, to accompany me to Odek. The organization agreed. I also thought that perhaps a representative of the cultural leaders should also be there, and they too agreed. Another member of WAN and I were the ones to return to Odek with the team, to hear what they had to say about the future of our children. The clan members said they would like for the children to visit their home and that we should bring them. They asked us so many questions, for instance the number of children that Kony has. All of these questions surprised me, because I had already sent them the names of the children ahead of time. I am not sure if they suddenly became fearful thinking there were too many children for them to support. There was a day they came to the office to meet with GJU, but they did not speak to me. They stipulated the laws of their clan and stated that there was a day they would accept the children and that JRP should be witnesses, although pictures were forbidden. Actually they always refuse to let us take even a single photo at their place. They asked for our advice on how they might begin to get to know the children. I told them it would be impossible to go visit each one from door to door; Kony has many children. If they wanted to come to the office, we could talk and exchange privately; no one would know what was happening.

When we were in Odek, the grandfather asked me to sit and speak with the elders. He told me that what we were trying to do was good, that he had heard of me. He asked if I was interested in living in Odek. I listened to what he had to say before responding. He said that he was going to construct a home for my children and me in the homestead of Kony's mother, where she is buried. I waited for him and the elders to finish their talk and said, "Look here, I have no interest in coming to live here in Odek. In Acholi, a woman can be inherited by the brothers of her husband who has died, yet Kony is still alive! Second, you should know that I have only girls. Why don't you choose other women who are mothers to boys [land is inherited and passed down through the male child; the female child marries into her husband's family]. My girls are counted as human beings, that is true, but you should remember that they all leave home eventually."

The grandfather thought I could return to Odek and be the one to take care of all of Kony's children, since many of them like me and are used to me. The grandfather asked to speak to me privately behind the hut, away from others. He told me not embarrass him and to accept before the clan that I would live in the house he was going to construct for me. I told him there was absolutely no way. Later on, we met as the mothers of Kony's children here in town and discussed the issue. We agreed it was important that all the children know where their father's home is, especially the boys. If we don't do it now, the boys will definitely do it in the future. So we supported the idea that everyone continue to meet his relatives and get to know their home but not to live there.

In other cases, the paternal relatives of children refuse to acknowledge them. For instance, one mother wanted our help in locating and contacting the clan of her son. The woman's own family rejects the child, so we accepted to try to help her identify and meet with the child's father's clan. The children even are not going to school, so she thought maybe the children could go and live with the father's relatives. The relatives live in a village out of town, and so the group from that region went with the mother of the child to meet them. Yet, when the clan gathered, some of them stated they wanted nothing to do with the child. They accused the father of killing people in their village. They said to accept the child would not redress the past. We are still talking and meeting with them.

This year, WAN had an interest in widening our activities. JRP is supporting us. We want to ensure that at least every three months we do voluntary work to help other women. For instance, we visit women in prison and in the hospital to give them encouragement. We felt it was important to include the children in this program as well; for instance, we visit the children of women in prison or in the hospital.

You know, in our Uganda, if you want to do something, you also need support. We wanted to engage the women and children to gain their support so that one day if we plan a public march they will join us and we won't be alone. We are afraid of tear gas or being put in prison, but we know women in other parts of the world march.

Beyond this motivation, we did it for memory. Women and children suffered a lot in this war. Children were abducted and taken to the bush; many of them drowned, and others died of cholera. We felt it was important to remember them. It was also important to remember mothers whose children were abducted. Some soldiers arrested women and took them away, and up to now we do not know where they are. Because of these reasons, we felt it was important to engage with the women; even with limited resources we are able to do something. There is a saying that however little you have, if you use it well, God will still accept it.

We told the women we met that we were also once in prison, but a different kind of one. The most painful thing about the prison we were in was that we never saw any of our relatives. We encouraged them, that at least their situation was a little bit better, that their relatives and children could see them, unlike our own.

One thing we did was we began to clean public offices as a group. We felt that doing this, we could illustrate that we can do things on our own, that we are useful. Maybe the media would ask what we are doing and why and that would be a chance to tell them about WAN. We also thought it was a way to develop a relationship with the District Leader and that he would then become involved. When the District Leader speaks, people take what he has to say seriously. Thirty of us organized to clean his office. We collected all the trash in the compound of his office, and many people walking past would stop to ask us who we were. There was trash there that had collected over the years, and so few people would volunteer to clean a public space like that. This had a result. Some of the big people from the offices came to praise our work and invited us to start working in other public offices such as the High Court, which needs a lot of work. Some people started to say we should be paid for the work we had done, but we informed them we had not come to make money. This really contributed to advancing our cause: on our anniversary launch, the District Speaker came, and he praised our work. He said he had felt embarrassed, but at the same time it calmed his heart. He said he is a very busy person and rarely attends launches but felt that he had to do his utmost to attend ours.

In April 2014, WAN went to Kampala to present a resolution in Parliament. We wanted to make sure the world knew all the challenges that we faced and continue to face. The Speaker of Gulu district local government, Douglas Peter Okao, encouraged us. He said he would help us present it in Parliament. We felt that if we are to table the resolution in Parliament and if it is worked upon, it will heal the pain we have. Among the issues are the issues of our children born in captivity who have no identity. We also felt that the government should acknowledge what we went through and provide reparations. Even just presenting the resolution in Parliament was a big feeling of relief, and the start of my own healing [the full petition is available on justiceandreconciliation .com]. My hope is that after having presented the petition, many people will get to know about WAN and the challenges we continue to face.

On November 4, 2013, I received the Women for Peace Award. I was so happy on that day because I looked at myself as mere Evelyn who did not deserve that. The day I received the award, I was able to give a message that whether you were abducted or not, educated or not, you can still utilize the skills and knowledge that God has given you and achieve. God gave me the gift of making good speeches and courage to speak before people, and I believe this is what made me win the award. My strong attachment and commitment toward working together with the women made me win the award. If I have a flashback on how we started and then see where WAN is now and myself being honored, then I feel so great.

Abbreviations

GUSCO   Gulu Support the Children Organization
JRP   Justice and Reconciliation Project
LRA   Lord's Resistance Army
NRA   National Resistance Army
SPLA   Sudanese People's Liberation Front
UN   United Nations
UNLA   Ugandan National Liberation Army
UPDA   Ugandan People's Democratic Army
UPDF   Ugandan People's Defense Force
WAN   Women's Advocacy Network

Glossary of Names

Evelyn's Children

Bakita	Evelyn's first daughter, born 1997
Cynthia	Evelyn's fourth daughter, born 2009
Grace	Evelyn's third daughter, born 2005
Winnie	Evelyn's second daughter, born 2000, missing since 2003

LRA Commanders

Kenneth Banya	Brigade Commander (captured 2004)
Ocan Bunia	Brigade Commander (died 2010)
Acellam Caesar	Head of Intelligence (captured/surrendered 2013)
Fatima	First wife to Kony, Second Lieutenant (died 2003)
Omona	Field Second in Command, 1994–97 (died 1997)
Joseph Kony	Chairperson and General (at large)
Otti Lagony	Second in Command 1997–99 (died 1999)
John Lakati	Brigade Commander (died 2004)
Raska Lukwiya	Brigade Commander of Stockree and Army Commander (died 2006)
John Matata	Second in Command, 1999–2003 (died 2003)

Okot Odhiambo	Second in Command, 2007–15 (died 2015)
Dominic Ongwen	Brigade Commander (surrendered 2015, transferred to the International Criminal Court)
Nixman Oryang "Opuk"	Senior Level Commander (died 2009)
Vincent Otti	Second in Command, 2003–7 (died 2007)

Political Figures

Alice Auma (Lakwena)	Spirit medium who guided Joseph Kony; founder of the Holy Spirit Movement
Betty Bigombe	Former Minister of Pacification of the North; mediator in talks with the LRA, 1994 and 2004
Joaquim Chissano	Former president of Mozambique; UN special envoy to the conflict
Riek Machar	Vice President of South Sudan, mediator during peace talks
Yoweri Museveni	President of Uganda, 1986–
Milton Obote	President of Uganda, 1963–71 and 1980–85
Ruhakan Rugunda	Foreign Minister, leader of the government peace team at the Juba peace talks, 2006–8

TIMELINE
SITUATING EVELYN'S LIFE IN ITS
UGANDAN POLITICAL CONTEXT

1980   Milton Obote wins national elections after Uganda is
        liberated from the dictatorship of Idi Amin, who was respon-
        sible for up to 500,000 deaths.

1982   Evelyn is born November 25 in Pawiro Ato in Atiak sub-
        county, Gulu District, Uganda.

1985   Okello "Tito" Lutwa becomes president of Uganda after the
        UNLA take over power from Obote.

1986   In January the NRA defeats the UNLA and deposes
        President Okello. Yoweri Museveni is sworn in as the new
        president of Uganda. By March, the NRA occupies Acholi.
        The UNLA forms different rebel groups under the name
        Ugandan People's Democratic Army (UPDA). By August,
        Lakwena (Alice Auma) forms the Holy Spirit Movement,
        attracting civilians to her cause.

1987   In August, the Holy Spirit Movement launches an offensive
        against the NRA. By November, the Holy Spirit Movement
        is defeated and Auma flees into exile in Kenya. NRA launches
        Operation Sim Sim.

1988   Evelyn turns six years old and attends kindergarten, location
        unknown.
            Pece Peace Agreements are negotiated, providing for
        the return of UPDA soldiers. Some leaders demobilize and

are executed, others join the NRA, and still others become politicians. UPDA who do not come out reorganize into new armed groups, and some begin to follow Joseph Kony.

1989   Evelyn turns seven years old and attends Primary One in Parabongo, living with her maternal grandmother. Evelyn recalls sleeping and practicing *alup* [hiding in the bush] and often shifting houses to avoid soldiers. She and her grand-mother are locked in a hut, and it is set on fire by NRA soldiers, but they are rescued by an NRA commander.

1990   Evelyn turns eight years old and attends Primary Two in Parabongo.

The LRA establish their name under the leadership of Joseph Kony.

1993–94   Peace talks between the government of Uganda and LRA begin but fail in early 1993 following a government ultima-tum. The LRA establishes bases in southern Sudan with the assistance of Khartoum.

1994   Evelyn is abducted in August. Following several months of being forced to carry goods in Kilak, she walks in Kony's group to Sudan, where she receives military training. She becomes Kony's escort as well as a babysitter for his first wife, Fatima.

1995–96   Evelyn continues to act as an escort to Kony and a babysitter for Kony's first wife.

The LRA resumes large-scale attacks against civilians, including mass abductions of children. The Ugandan gov-ernment creates "protected villages," displacing hundreds of thousands of persons.

1997   In January, at the age of fourteen, Evelyn is forced to become Kony's eleventh wife. In September she gives birth to their first child. Evelyn moves between different LRA bases.

LRA continues its operations in Uganda, targeting civilians.

1999   Internal tensions within the LRA lead to a leadership challenge and Kony kills Otti Lagony, second in command.

2000   Evelyn gives birth to her second child and continues to live on different LRA bases.

2001   LRA is placed on the US Terrorist Watchlist.

2002   Evelyn and her two children begin a long journey with Kony's group through Sudan and the Imatong Mountains, trying to evade the UPDF and find safe haven.

    Uganda and Sudan restore diplomatic relations, and Sudan grants the Ugandan military permission to launch Operation Iron Fist against the LRA in South Sudan. LRA resumes campaign of terror against civilians, including abduction of up to five thousand children

2003–4   The war spreads to eastern Uganda. In northern Uganda, up to 1.7 million persons are internally displaced and forced into underserviced camps. The LRA continues its campaign against civilians.

2004   In midyear Evelyn's second daughter goes missing following a UPDF attack on the LRA. Evelyn departs from Kony's group and crosses the border into northern Uganda.

2005   In January Evelyn gives birth to her third daughter. Ten days later she is captured by the Ugandan military and spends eight months in a rehabilitation center.

    International Criminal Court issues arrest warrants for Kony and four top LRA commanders.

2006   Evelyn hopes to find her missing daughter when a former LRA officer informs her the child had been found in Kenya; the story was false. Evelyn is asked by the government of Uganda to become part of the Juba peace talks and she returns to the LRA in Garamba, where Kony was then based.

    LRA and government of Uganda enter into Juba peace talks brokered by Riek Machar, vice president of South Sudan.

2007   Evelyn travels between Gulu and Garamba as a peace delegate.

    Despite progress in the agreements, the peace talks start and stop. In October, Vincent Otti, second in command, is killed by Kony, casting serious doubt on the future of the talks.

2008   Evelyn returns to Gulu, where she begins working as a tailor for a charitable organization. She never speaks to Kony again.

After Kony fails to sign the final peace agreements, the Ugandan military leads Operation Iron Thunder against the LRA base in Garamba.

2009   Evelyn begins working under the organization JRP and recording daily diaries. She later forms the Women's Advocacy Network.

The LRA are pushed deeper into the Democratic Republic of Congo, Central African Republic, and South Sudan, resuming campaigns of violence and abduction of children.

2012   The Women's Advocacy Network is launched, and Evelyn is elected chairperson. The following year she wins the Women for Peace Award.

As of 2015, Joseph Kony remains at large despite the United States providing more than one hundred Special Operations forces to aid in his capture.

WOMEN IN AFRICA
AND THE DIASPORA

31901056651203

Printed in the United States
By Bookmasters